COMMON COR
MATH 8
WORKBOOK

prepaze

www.prepaze.com

Author: Ace Academic Publishing

Ace Academic Publishing is a leading supplemental educational workbook publisher for grades K-12. At Ace Academic Publishing, we realize the importance of imparting analytical and critical thinking skills during the early ages of childhood and hence our books include materials that require multiple levels of analysis and encourage the students to think outside the box.

The materials for our books are written by award winning teachers with several years of teaching experience. All our books are aligned with the state standards and are widely used by many schools throughout the country.

Prepaze is a sister company of Ace Academic Publishing. Intrigued by the unending possibilities of the internet and its role in education, Prepaze was created to spread the knowledge and learning across all corners of the world through an online platform. We equip ourselves with state-of-the-art technologies so that knowledge reaches the students through the quickest and the most effective channels.

For inquiries and bulk orders, contact Ace Academic Publishing at the following address:

Ace Academic Publishing
3736 Fallon Road #403
Dublin CA 94568

www.aceacademicpublishing.com

This book contains copyright protected material. The purchase of this material entitles the buyer to use this material for personal and classroom use only. Reproducing the content for commercial use is strictly prohibited. Contact us to learn about options to use it for an entire school district or other commercial use.

ISBN:978-1-949383-32-4

© Ace Academic Publishing, 2020

INTRODUCTION

About the Book
The contents of this book includes multiple chapters and units covering all the required Common Core Standards for this grade level. Similar to a standardized exam, you can find questions of all types, including multiple choice, fill-in-the-blank, true or false, matching and free response questions. These carefully written questions aim to help students reason abstractly and quantitatively using various models, strategies, and problem-solving techniques. The detailed answer explanations in the back of the book help the students understand the topics and gain confidence in solving similar problems.

For the Parents
This workbook includes practice questions and tests that cover all the required Common Core Standards for the grade level. The book is comprised of multiple tests for each topic so that your child can have an abundant amount of tests on the same topic. The workbook is divided into chapters and units so that you can choose the topics that you want your child needs to focus on. The detailed answer explanations in the back will teach your child the right methods to solve the problems for all types of questions, including the free-response questions. After completing the tests on all the chapters, your child can take any Common Core standardized exam with confidence and can excel in it.

For additional online practice, sign up for a free account at www.aceacademicprep.com.

For the Teachers
All questions and tests included in this workbook are based on the Common Core State Standards and includes a clear label of each standard name. You can assign your students tests on a particular unit in each chapter, and can also assign a chapter review test. The book also includes two final exams which you can use towards the end of the school year to review all the topics that were covered. This workbook will help your students overcome any deficiencies in their understanding of critical concepts and will also help you identify the specific topics that your students may require additional practice. These grade-appropriate, yet challenging, questions will help your students learn to strategically use appropriate tools and excel in Common Core standardized exams.

For additional online practice, sign up for a free account at www.aceacademicprep.com.

www.prepaze.com

Other books from Ace Academic Publishing

TABLE OF CONTENTS

The Number System ... 9
- UNDERSTANDING IRRATIONAL NUMBERS ... 13
- APPROXIMATION OF IRRATIONAL NUMBERS ... 18
- CHAPTER REVIEW ... 22
- EXTRA PRACTICE

Functions ... 31
- EVALUATE AND COMPARE FUNCTIONS ... 40
- UNDERSTANDING LINEAR AND NON – LINEAR FUNCTIONS ... 48
- USE FUNCTIONS TO MODEL RELATIONSHIPS ... 55
- CHAPTER REVIEW ... 61
- EXTRA PRACTICE

Expressions and Equations ... 69
- RADICAL AND INTEGER EXPONENTS ... 73
- PROPORTIONAL RELATIONSHIPS AND LINEAR EQUATIONS ... 81
- SOLVING LINEAR EQUATIONS ... 86
- CHAPTER REVIEW ... 92
- EXTRA PRACTICE

Geometry ... 101
- CONGRUENCE AND SIMILARITY ... 111
- PYTHAGOREAN THEOREM APPLICATION ... 116
- VOLUME OF 3 – DIMENSIONAL SHAPES ... 120
- CHAPTER REVIEW ... 128
- EXTRA PRACTICE

Statistics and Probability ... 137
- APPLICATION OF SCATTERPLOTS ... 147
- APPLICATION OF LINEAR MODELS ... 154
- APPLICATION OF BIVARIATE DATA ... 166
- CHAPTER REVIEW ... 173
- EXTRA PRACTICE

Comprehensive Assessment 1 ... 185

Comprehensive Assessment 2 ... 200

Answers and Explanations ... 215

THE NUMBER SYSTEM

UNDERSTANDING IRRATIONAL NUMBERS	9
APPROXIMATION OF IRRATIONAL NUMBERS	13
CHAPTER REVIEW	18
EXTRA PRACTICE	22

prepaze

www.prepaze.com

THE NUMBER SYSTEM

UNDERSTANDING IRRATIONAL NUMBERS

1. What type of number is $\sqrt{2}$?

   A. Whole Number
   B. Integer
   C. Rational Number
   D. Irrational Number

2. What type of number is π?

   A. Whole Number
   B. Integer
   C. Rational Number
   D. Irrational Number

3. What type of number is $\overline{3.12}$?

   A. Whole number
   B. Integer
   C. Rational Number
   D. Irrational Number

4. What type of number is $-0.\overline{15}$?

   A. Whole Number
   B. Integer
   C. Rational Number
   D. Irrational Number

5. What type of number is $\frac{2\sqrt{2}}{2}$?

   A. Whole Number
   B. Integer
   C. Rational Number
   D. Irrational Number

6. Which decimal is equivalent to $\frac{27}{33}$?

   A. 0.89
   B. $0.\overline{81}$
   C. 0.76
   D. $0.\overline{85}$

THE NUMBER SYSTEM

UNDERSTANDING IRRATIONAL NUMBERS

7. Which decimal is the equivalent of $\frac{19}{20}$?

   A. 0.95   B. $0.\overline{56}$ C. 0.59   D. $0.\overline{98}$

   (8.NS.A.1)

8. Which decimal is the equivalent of $\frac{103}{90}$?

   A. 1.32   B. 0.87   C. 1.1414   D. $1.\overline{45}$

   (8.NS.A.1)

9. Which decimal is equivalent to $\frac{7}{9}$?

   A. 0.77   B. 0.8   C. $0.\overline{12}$ D. 0.9

   (8.NS.A.1)

10. Which decimal is equivalent to $\frac{44}{88}$?

    A. 0.44   B. $0.\overline{46}$ C. 0.5   D. $0.\overline{9}$

    (8.NS.A.1)

11. Which decimal is the equivalent of $\frac{72}{99}$?

    A. 0.99   B. $0.\overline{96}$ C. 0.92   D. 0.7272

    (8.NS.A.1)

12. Which decimal is equivalent to $\frac{11}{15}$?

    A. 0.11   B. $0.\overline{51}$ C. $0.\overline{43}$ D. 0.7373

    (8.NS.A.1)

13. Which decimal is the equivalent of $\frac{11}{88}$?

    A. 0.125   B. $0.155\overline{5}$ C. 0.18   D. $0.\overline{88}$

    (8.NS.A.1)

THE NUMBER SYSTEM

14. Which decimal is equivalent to $\frac{46}{96}$?

    A. 0.4791666667   **B.** 0.4742268047

    C. 0.47916666666   **D.** $0.4\overline{4666666}$

(8.NS.A.1)

UNDERSTANDING IRRATIONAL NUMBERS

15. Which decimal is the equivalent of $\frac{2}{9}$?

    A. 0.52   **B.** 0.5622   **C.** $0.\overline{9}$ **D.** 0.22222

(8.NS.A.1)

16. Which decimal is equivalent to 1.444?

    A. $1\frac{5}{9}$ **B.** $\frac{15}{9}$ **C.** $\frac{15}{10}$ **D.** $1\frac{5}{10}$

(8.NS.A.1)

17. Which fraction is equivalent of 0.333?

    A. $\frac{3}{10}$ **B.** $\frac{1}{3}$ **C.** $\frac{33}{100}$

    D. The number cannot be written as a fraction.

(8.NS.A.1)

18. Which fraction represents the closest approximation of π?

    A. $\frac{3}{14}$ **B.** $3\frac{1}{4}$ **C.** $\frac{31}{14}$ **D.** $\frac{22}{7}$

(8.NS.A.1)

THE NUMBER SYSTEM

UNDERSTANDING IRRATIONAL NUMBERS

19. Which fraction is equivalent to 0.3737?

   A. $\frac{37}{99}$ B. $\frac{37}{100}$ C. $\frac{37}{10}$

   D. The number cannot be written as a fraction.

   8.NS.A.1

20. Which fraction is equivalent to 0.327327?

   A. $\frac{32}{100}$ B. $\frac{109}{333}$ C. $\frac{327}{1000}$

   D. The number cannot be written as a fraction.

   8.NS.A.1

UNIT 2: APPROXIMATION OF IRRATIONAL NUMBERS

NAME: .... DATE: 13

THE NUMBER SYSTEM

APPROXIMATION OF IRRATIONAL NUMBERS

1. Which radical has a value between 2 and 3?

   A. $\sqrt{5}$ B. $\sqrt{4}$ C. $\sqrt{9}$ D. $\sqrt{16}$

   8.NS.A.2

2. Which strategy could be a first step in determining the value of $\sqrt{8}$?

   A. Find the perfect squares $\sqrt{8}$ falls between.
   B. Multiply 8 and 8.
   C. Find the number that added twice gives you 8.
   D. Subtract 2 from 8 to determine the square.

   8.NS.A.2

3. Which number is greater than 7, but less than 8?

   A. $\sqrt{64}$ B. $\sqrt{121}$ C. $\sqrt{56}$ D. $\sqrt{49}$

   8.NS.A.2

4. Which two square roots can be used as a first estimate of $\sqrt{86}$?

   A. $\sqrt{9}$ and $\sqrt{81}$
   B. $\sqrt{81}$ and $\sqrt{100}$
   C. $\sqrt{8}$ and $\sqrt{9}$
   D. $\sqrt{64}$ and $\sqrt{81}$

   8.NS.A.2

5. Which expression has the greatest value?

   A. $x - \sqrt{76}$ when $x = 10$
   B. $x + \sqrt{62}$ when $x = 12$
   C. $x - \sqrt{66}$ when $x = 8$
   D. $x + \sqrt{79}$ when $x = 11$

   8.NS.A.2

6. Which value is closest to $\sqrt{96}$?

   A. 9.6 B. 9.7 C. 9.8 D. 9.9

   8.NS.A.2

THE NUMBER SYSTEM

APPROXIMATION OF IRRATIONAL NUMBERS

7. Which value is closest to $\sqrt{64}$?

　A. 5^2　　　**B.** 8^2　　　**C.** 9^2　　　**D.** 7^2

8.NS.A.2

8. Which of the following statements is true of a square root?

　A. A square root is always a rational number.

　B. A square root can be an irrational or rational number.

　C. A square root is always an irrational number.

　D. A square root is always an integer.

8.NS.A.2

9. Between which two points does $\sqrt{39}$ lie on this number line?

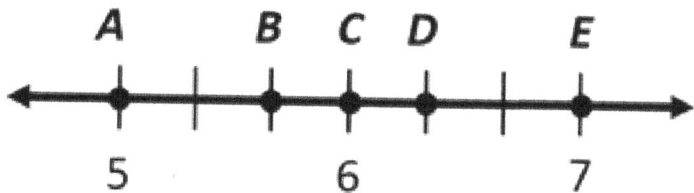

　A. Points B and C
　B. Points C and E
　C. Points C and D
　D. Points D and E

8.NS.A.2

10. Which irrational number has the smallest value?

　A. $\sqrt{17}$　　**B.** $\frac{7}{2}\pi$　　**C.** π　　**D.** $\sqrt{11}$

8.NS.A.2

THE NUMBER SYSTEM

11. Which point on this number line best represents √7?

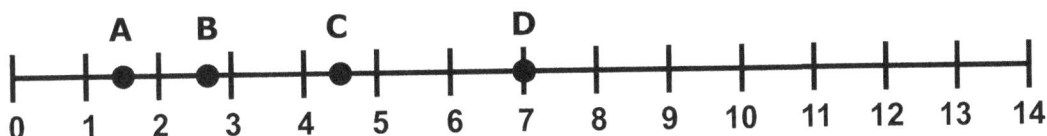

A. Point A B. Point B C. Point C D. Point D

12. Which point on this number line best represents √5?

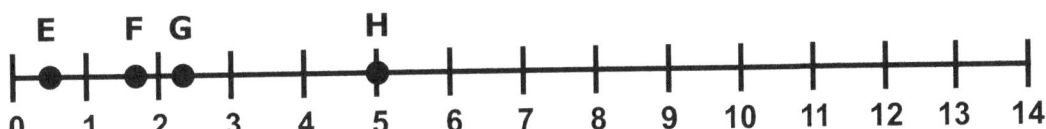

A. Point E B. Point F C. Point G D. Point H

13. Point A on the number line best represents which value?

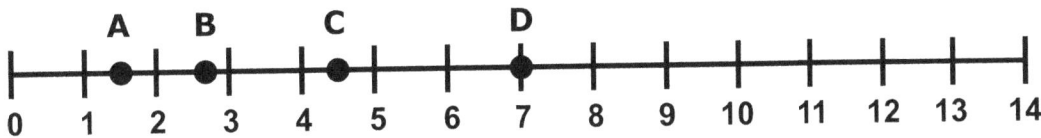

A. $\sqrt{2}$ B. $\sqrt{3/2}$ C. $\sqrt{9/2}$ D. $\sqrt{4}$

14. Point F on this number line best represents which value?

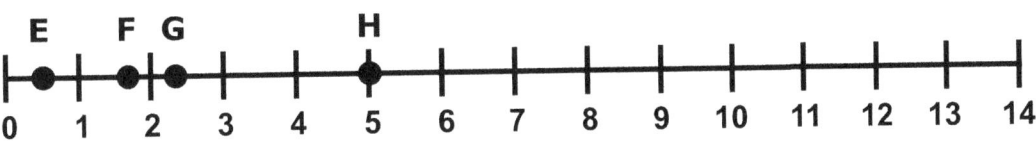

A. $\sqrt{6}$ B. $\sqrt{1}$ C. $\sqrt{2}$ D. $\sqrt{3}$

APPROXIMATION OF IRRATIONAL NUMBERS

THE NUMBER SYSTEM

APPROXIMATION OF IRRATIONAL NUMBERS

15. Which point on this number line best represents $\sqrt{32}$?

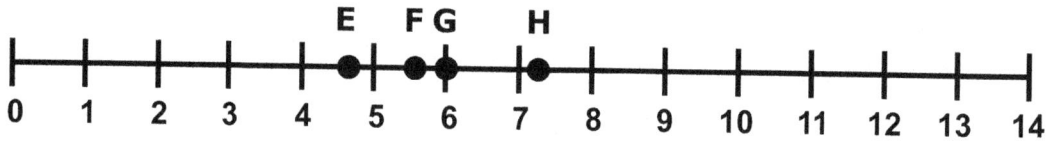

A. Point E **B.** Point F **C.** Point G **D.** Point H

16. Which point on this number line best represents $\sqrt{52}$?

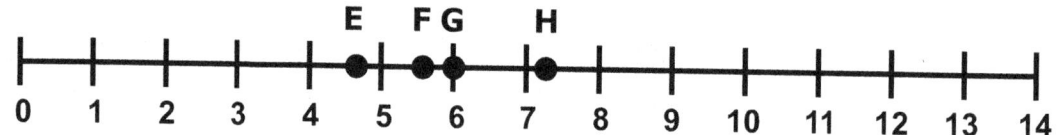

A. Point E **B.** Point F **C.** Point G **D.** Point H

17. Maria states that Point F represents the best approximation of $\sqrt{76}$.

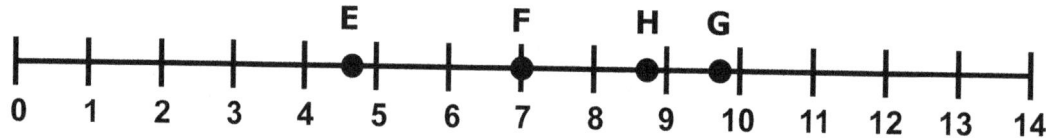

A. The square root of 76 is less than 10.

B. Point F represents a rational number.

C. The square root of 76 lies between 8 and 9 on a number line.

D. The value of Point F is less than 76.

THE NUMBER SYSTEM

APPROXIMATION OF IRRATIONAL NUMBERS

18. Jonathan states that Point G represents the best approximation of $\sqrt{96}$.

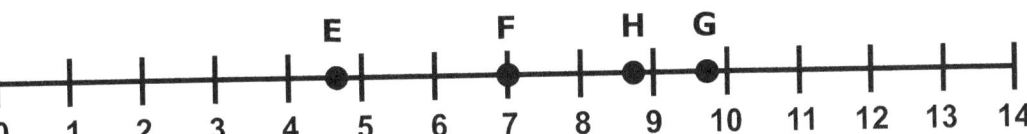

Which statement explains why he was correct?

A. Point G lies between 9 and 10.

B. The square root of 96 is a rational number.

C. Point G is a fractional value.

D. The square root of 96 is greater than 9.

(8.NS.A.2)

19. Which perfect square is most helpful in determining the placement of $\sqrt{23}$ on a number line?

A. $\sqrt{16}$ B. $\sqrt{25}$ C. $\sqrt{36}$ D. $\sqrt{49}$

(8.NS.A.2)

20. Which perfect square is most helpful in determining the placement of $\sqrt{45}$ on a number line?

A. $\sqrt{36}$ B. $\sqrt{100}$ C. $\sqrt{49}$ D. $\sqrt{64}$

(8.NS.A.2)

CHAPTER REVIEW

THE NUMBER SYSTEM

CHAPTER REVIEW

1. Which fraction is equivalent to $0.\overline{13}$?

   A. $\frac{13}{10}$ B. $\frac{13}{9}$ C. $\frac{13}{100}$ D. $\frac{13}{99}$

   8.NS.A.1

2. Which fraction is equivalent to $0.4\overline{5}$?

   A. $\frac{41}{90}$ B. $\frac{45}{99}$ C. $\frac{45}{100}$ D. $\frac{455,555}{1,000,000}$

   8.NS.A.1

3. Which rational expression is equivalent to $\sqrt{2}$?

   A. $\frac{2}{10}$ B. $\frac{2}{9}$ C. $\frac{14}{100}$

   D. The number cannot be written as a fraction.

   8.NS.A.1

4. Which number is equal to 2^2?

   A. 7   B. $\frac{223}{50}$ C. $\frac{446}{100}$

   D. The number cannot be written as a fraction.

   8.NS.A.1

5. Which fraction is equivalent to $0.1\overline{23}$?

   A. $\frac{123}{1000}$ B. $\frac{123}{999}$ C. $\frac{61}{495}$ D. $\frac{61}{95}$

   8.NS.A.1

6. Which fraction is equivalent to $0.\overline{1}$?

   A. $\frac{1}{9}$ B. $\frac{11}{100}$ C. $\frac{2}{9}$ D. $\frac{9}{1}$

   8.NS.A.1

THE NUMBER SYSTEM

7. Which fraction is equivalent to $0.25\overline{7}$?

   A. $\dfrac{257}{1000}$ B. $\dfrac{257}{999}$ C. $\dfrac{58}{225}$ D. $\dfrac{58}{100}$

   (8.NS.A.1)

8. Which fraction is equivalent to $0.\overline{97}$?

   A. $\dfrac{97}{100}$ B. $\dfrac{97}{99}$ C. $\dfrac{9}{10}$ D. $\dfrac{44}{45}$

   (8.NS.A.1)

9. Which number is equivalent to $\sqrt{25}$?

   A. $\dfrac{25}{100}$ B. $\dfrac{5}{2}$ C. 5 D. $\dfrac{1}{4}$

   (8.NS.A.1)

10. Which fraction is equivalent to $0.\overline{567}$?

   A. $\dfrac{567}{1000}$ B. $\dfrac{21}{37}$ C. $\dfrac{281}{495}$ D. $\dfrac{511}{900}$

   (8.NS.A.1)

11. Which list of numbers is in order from least to greatest?

   A. $\sqrt{67}, 8.4, 8.1, \sqrt{64}$ B. $\sqrt{64}, 8.1, 8.4, \sqrt{67}$
   C. $8.1, 8.4, \sqrt{64}, \sqrt{67}$ D. $\sqrt{64}, 8.1, \sqrt{67}, 8.4$

   (8.NS.A.2)

12. Which list of numbers is in order from least to greatest?

   A. $\dfrac{93}{10}, \dfrac{47}{5}, \sqrt{89}, \dfrac{19}{2}$ B. $\dfrac{19}{2}, \dfrac{47}{5}, \dfrac{93}{10}, \sqrt{89}$
   C. $\dfrac{93}{10}, \dfrac{47}{5}, \dfrac{19}{2}, \sqrt{89}$ D. $\sqrt{83}, \dfrac{47}{5}, \dfrac{19}{2}, \dfrac{93}{10}$

   (8.NS.A.2)

THE NUMBER SYSTEM

13. Which list of numbers is in order from greatest to least?

    A. $6.8, 6.7, \sqrt{45}$ **B.** $6.8, \sqrt{45}, 6.7$

    C. $\sqrt{45}, 6.8, 6.7$ **D.** $6.7, \sqrt{45}, 6.8$

14. Which list of numbers is in order from greatest to least?

    A. $1\frac{3}{4}, \sqrt{3}, 1.7$ **B.** $1.7, 1\frac{3}{4}, \sqrt{3}$

    C. $\sqrt{3}, 1\frac{3}{4}, 1.7$ **D.** $1\frac{3}{4}, 1.7, \sqrt{3}$

15. Which symbol can be used to compare these numbers?

$$3\frac{7}{8} \,\underline{}\, \sqrt{11}$$

    A. $=$ **B.** $<$ **C.** $>$ **D.** $\approx$

16. Which symbol can be used to compare these numbers?

$$4.761 \,\underline{}\, \sqrt{24}$$

    A. $=$ **B.** $<$ **C.** $>$ **D.** $\approx$

17. Which symbol can be used to compare these numbers?

$$\sqrt{21} \,\underline{}\, \sqrt{16}$$

    A. $=$ **B.** $<$ **C.** $>$ **D.** $\approx$

THE NUMBER SYSTEM

18. Olivia claims the $\sqrt{89}$ is greater than 9.34. Which statement explains why she correct?

A. The square root of 89 is approximately 9.43.
B. The square root of 89 is approximately 9.52.
C. The square root of 89 is approximately 9.76.
D. The square root of 89 is approximately 9.89.

8.NS.A.2

19. Which of these numbers is the greatest?

A. $\sqrt{41}$ B. 6.32   C. $\sqrt{40}$ D. 6.71

8.NS.A.2

20. Which of these numbers is the least?

A. 7.88   B. $\sqrt{62}$ C. 7.87   D. $\sqrt{65}$

8.NS.A.2

CHAPTER REVIEW

EXTRA PRACTICE

THE NUMBER SYSTEM

1. Which of these numbers has the greatest value?

   $$-1, -\sqrt{2}, -0.003, -\frac{1}{3}$$

   A. -1 **B.** $-\sqrt{2}$ **C.** -0.003 **D.** $-\frac{1}{3}$

2. Which set of equations can be used to determine x, the fractional value of $0.\overline{345}$?

   A. $x = 0.\overline{345}$ and $100x = 3.45\overline{345}$
   B. $x = 0.\overline{345}$ and $10x = 3.45\overline{345}$
   C. $x = 0.\overline{345}$ and $x = 3.45\overline{345}$
   D. $x = 0.\overline{345}$ and $1{,}000x = 345.\overline{345}$

3. Which set of equations can be used to determine x, the fractional value of $1.\overline{042}$?

   A. $x = 1.\overline{042}$ and $100x = 1{,}042.\overline{042}$
   B. $x = 1.\overline{042}$ and $1{,}000x = 1{,}042.\overline{042}$
   C. $x = 1.\overline{042}$ and $10x = 1.042\overline{042}$
   D. $x = 1.\overline{042}$ and $x = 104.2\overline{042}$

4. What is the decimal value of this fraction?

   $$\frac{7 \times 5^4}{2^4 \times 5^4}$$

THE NUMBER SYSTEM

5. What is the decimal value of this fraction?

$$\frac{1}{2^3 \times 5^3}$$

(8.NS.A.1)

6. The length of one side of a square is $3\frac{1}{5}$ inches. Write an expression to show the calculation of the area of the square using decimals.

(8.NS.A.1)

7. Bryce is constructing a large window in the living room of his new house. The window is to be square with an area of 31 square feet. Which type of number represents the length of one side of the window?

A. Rational **B.** Irrational **C.** Integer **D.** Natural

(8.NS.A.1)

8. A small portrait of Harriet Tubman is square with an area of 151 square centimeters. Exactly how long is each side of the portrait?

(8.NS.A.1)

9. The area of square ABCD is a rational number. Give an example of when the side length of the square is a rational number, and an example of when the side length of the square is an irrational number.

(8.NS.A.1)

THE NUMBER SYSTEM

10. Shelby states that $\frac{1}{3}$ is a rational number because it can be represented as 33.3%. Do you agree with Shelby? Explain your reasoning.

___

11. The variable Y is the square root of the value marked with X on the number line below.

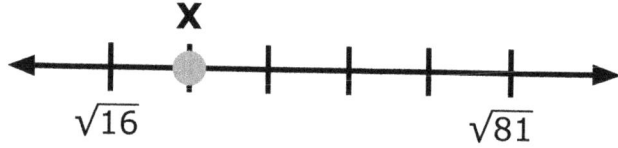

What is the value of Y?

___

12. The variable T is the square root of the value marked with S on the number line below.

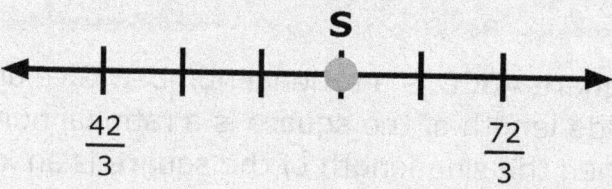

The variable T is between which two whole numbers?

___

THE NUMBER SYSTEM

13. Erica is playing a number game with her friends. She writes clues to describe one of these numbers:

$$50 \qquad 223 \qquad 250 \qquad 625$$

The clues are:
- The cubed root of this number falls between 6 and 7.
- The number is a composite number.
- One factor of the number is 125.

What number is Erica describing? Show your work.

(8.NS.A.2)

14. Aditya is playing a number game with his friends. He writes clues to describe one of these numbers:

$$\sqrt{5} \qquad \frac{1}{9} \qquad \sqrt[3]{64}$$

The clues are:
- The number is irrational.
- The number squared is equivalent to a prime number.
- The value of the number is between 2 and 3.

What number is Aditya describing. Show your work.

(8.NS.A.2)

THE NUMBER SYSTEM

EXTRA PRACTICE

15. Add 3 points to this number line to represent irrational numbers.

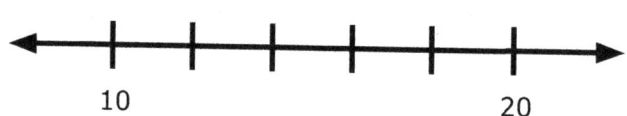

16. Add 3 points to this number line to represent irrational numbers.

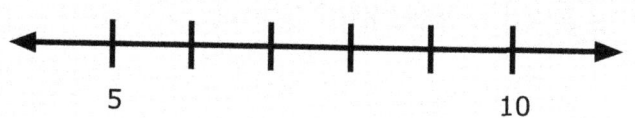

17. Jolene sees a drawing of a circle, with a diameter of 10 inches, and writes this expression to represent its area:

$$(4)(4)(5)$$

Do you agree with Justin? Explain why.

_____
_____
_____

18. Mishon draws a cone with a base area of 196π square centimeters and a height of 18 centimeters. What is the approximate area of the base of the cone, to the nearest whole square centimeters?

_____

THE NUMBER SYSTEM

19. Tara states that these expressions have the same value:

$$4\pi \qquad (2\sqrt{\pi})^2$$

Do you agree with Tara? Explain your reasoning.

_____

_____

_____

8.NS.A.2

20. Byron states that these expressions have the same value:

$$\pi \times \pi \qquad \sqrt{\pi} \times 2\pi$$

Do you agree with Byron? Explain your reasoning.

_____

_____

_____

8.NS.A.2

FUNCTIONS

EVALUATE AND COMPARE FUNCTIONS	**31**
UNDERSTANDING LINEAR AND NON – LINEAR FUNCTIONS	**40**
USE FUNCTIONS TO MODEL RELATIONSHIPS	**48**
CHAPTER REVIEW	**55**
EXTRA PRACTICE	**61**

www.prepaze.com

FUNCTIONS

1. Does the data in this table represent a function? Why or why not?

Time (seconds)	Height (meter)
0	7
2	10
4	5
6	0
7	0
8	3

   A. Yes, each input has exactly one output.
   B. Yes, there is an input and output value of 0.
   C. No, there is more than one input for each output.
   D. No, there is more than one output for each input.

   (8.F.A.1)

2. Does the data in this table represent a function? Why or why not?

Age (years)	Income (Thousands)
24	34
26	38
26	37
28	44
30	45

   A. Yes, the input values are less than the output values.
   B. Yes, each input has exactly one output.
   C. No, there is more than one input for each output.
   D. No, there is more than one output for a given input.

   (8.F.A.1)

EVALUATE AND COMPARE FUNCTIONS

FUNCTIONS

EVALUATE AND COMPARE FUNCTIONS

3. Do the values on this graph represent a function?

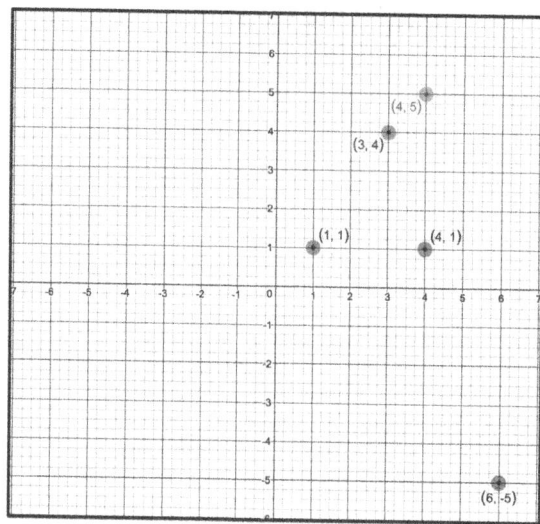

A. Yes, there is exactly one input for each output.

B. Yes, there is exactly one output for each input.

C. No, there is more than one input for each output.

D. No, there is more than one output for each input.

8.F.A.1

4. Do the values on this graph represent a function?

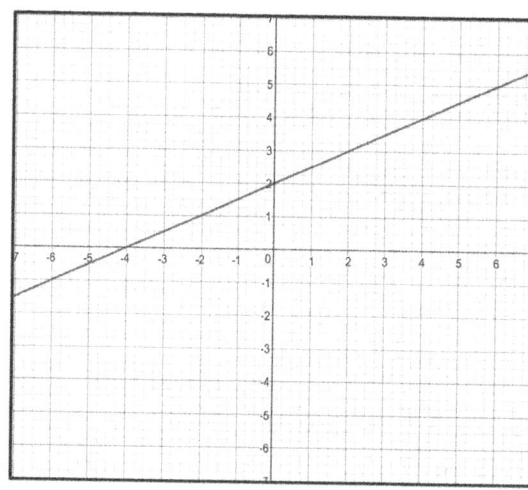

A. Yes, there is exactly one input for each output.

B. Yes, there is exactly one output for each input.

C. No, there is more than one input for each output.

D. No, there is more than one output for each input.

8.F.A.1

FUNCTIONS

5. What is the domain of the function $y = 3x + 4$?

    A. All real values of x.
    B. All real values of x such that $x \neq \frac{3}{4}$
    C. All real values of x such that $x \neq \frac{4}{3}$
    D. All real values of x such that $x > 0$.

8.F.A.1

6. What is the domain of the function $f(x) = \sqrt{2x - 5}$?

    A. All real values of x.
    B. All real values of x such that $x \geq \frac{5}{2}$
    C. All real values of x such that $x \leq \frac{5}{2}$
    D. All real values of x such that $x \geq 0$.

8.F.A.1

7. What is the domain of the function $f(x) = \frac{2x + 1}{3 - x}$?

    A. All real values of x.
    B. All real values of x such that $x \neq -\frac{1}{2}$.
    C. All real values of x such that $x \neq 3$.
    D. All real values of x such that $x \geq 3$.

8.F.A.1

8. What is the domain of the function $f(x) = \frac{x + 5}{4x - 2}$?

    A. All real values of x.
    B. All real values of x such that $x \neq -5$.
    C. All real values of x such that $x \leq \frac{1}{2}$.
    D. All real values of x such that $x \neq \frac{1}{2}$.

8.F.A.1

EVALUATE AND COMPARE FUNCTIONS

FUNCTIONS

EVALUATE AND COMPARE FUNCTIONS

9. Determine the range of the function in the graph.

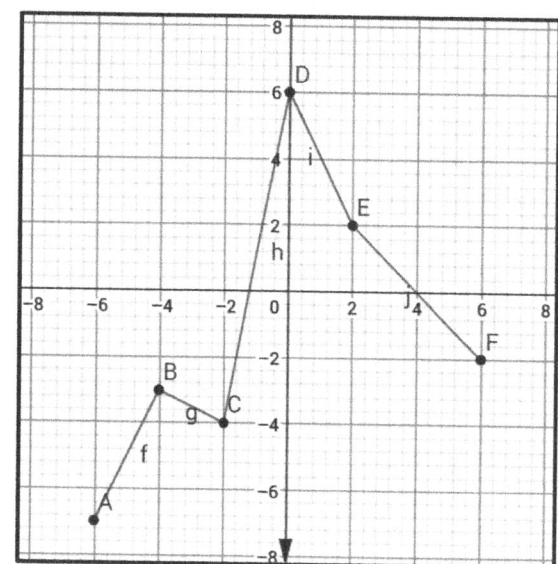

A. $-7 \leq y \leq 6$
B. $-6 \leq y \leq 5$
C. $-7 < y < 6$
D. $5 \leq y \leq -6$

10. Determine the domain of the function in the graph.

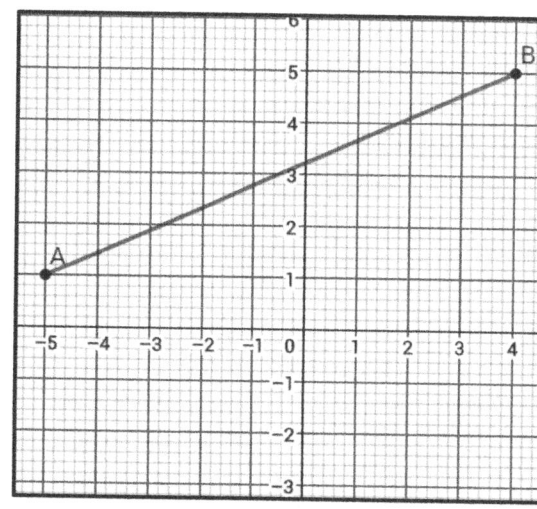

A. $4 \leq x \leq -7$
B. $-5 \leq x \leq 4$
C. $-5 < x < 4$
D. $6 \leq x \leq -5$

FUNCTIONS

EVALUATE AND COMPARE FUNCTIONS

11. Alicia and Ryan are trying to make some money as dog walkers on their street. Alicia charges $10 per walk for her services. Ryan charges $25 per day and guarantees three dog walks each day. If a person wants to hire a dog walker for three dog walks per day for three days, who offers the better deal?

    A. Alicia
    B. Ryan
    C. They are the same cost.
    D. There is not enough information to determine which is a better deal.

    (8.F.A.2)

12. Maria and Jacob are trying to make some money as dog walkers on their street. Maria charges $10 per walk for her services. Jacob charges $25 per day and guarantees three dog walks a day. If a person wants to hire a dog walker for two walks, who offers the better deal?

    A. Maria
    B. Jacob
    C. They are the same cost. There is not enough information to determine which is a better deal.
    D. There is not enough information to determine which is a better deal.

    (8.F.A.2)

13. The table below represents Function A.

x	y
2	8
4	9
6	10

    What is the rate of change of Function A?

    A. 2   B. 7   C. $\frac{1}{2}$ D. $\frac{7}{2}$

    (8.F.A.2)

FUNCTIONS

14. The table below represents Function A.

x	y
2	8
4	9
6	10

Function B can be represented by the equation, $y = 3x + 9$. Compare the rate of change for each function.

A. Function A has a smaller rate of change.

B. Function B has a smaller rate of change.

C. Both functions have an equal rate of change.

D. It is impossible to tell the rate of change of each function based on the information given.

15. Function C is represented by the graph below.

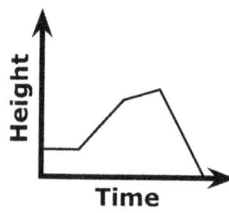

Which situation best represents the graph?

A. Rain falls and fills a river with more water.

B. A cold snap, snow falls and accumulates on the ground, then rapidly melts.

C. A water faucet is opened, and a barrel of water is gradually emptied.

D. A climber starts at the top of a mountain and descends in altitude.

FUNCTIONS

16. Leaves fall off a tree during a short windstorm. Which graph below represents the number of leaves on the tree?

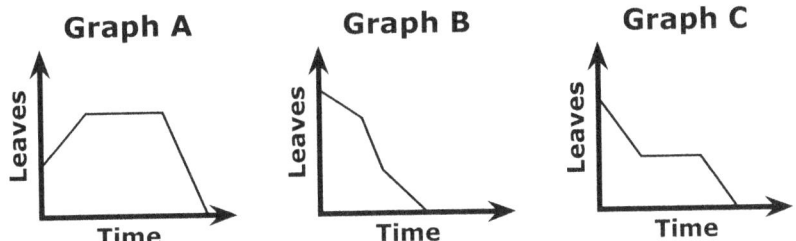

- **A.** Graph A
- **B.** Graph B
- **C.** Graph C
- **D.** None of these graphs represent the situation described.

17. Function G is represented in the table below.

x	y
−1	11
0	8
1	5

Function H is represented by the equation $y = \frac{1}{2}x + 7$. Compare the rate of change for each function.

- **A.** Both functions can be described as increasing.
- **B.** Both functions can be described as decreasing.
- **C.** Function G can be described as increasing and Function H can be described as decreasing.
- **D.** Function G can be described as decreasing and Function H can be described as increasing.

FUNCTIONS

EVALUATE AND COMPARE FUNCTIONS

18. Evan's mom is considering joining a movie club. The club requires members to pay a $25 yearly membership fee and charges $5 per movie purchased.

When she buys movies at the store, each movie costs $7.50. If she is considering purchasing 15 movies per year, which scenario is a better deal?

A. The movie club is a better deal.

B. Buying movies at the store is a better deal.

C. There is no difference between either option.

D. There is not enough information to determine which is a better deal.

(8.F.A.2)

19. Function F is represented by the equation $y = x^3$; Function G is represented by the equation $y = x^2$. How are these functions similar?

A. They have similar rate of change.

B. They are both steadily increasing.

C. They are both steadily decreasing.

D. They are not linear functions.

(8.F.A.2)

20. Which equation matches the graph below?

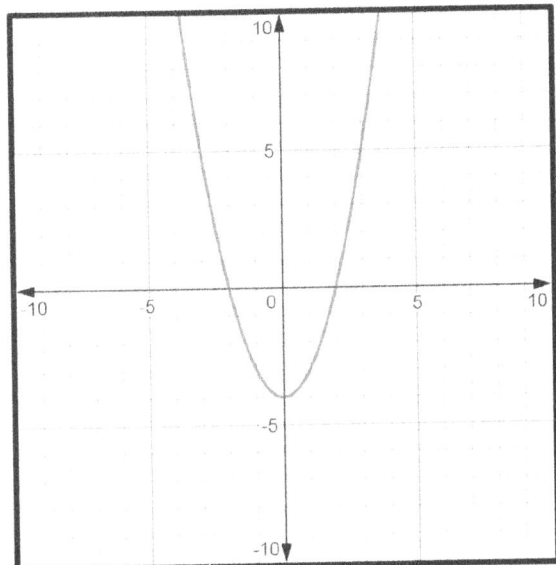

A. $y = x - 4$

B. $y = x^3 + 4$

C. $y = x^2 - 4$

D. $y = 4x^2$

FUNCTIONS

UNDERSTANDING LINEAR AND NON-LINEAR FUNCTIONS

1. For the function $y = \frac{1}{3}x + 6$, what does $\frac{1}{3}$ represent?

   A. The value of y when $x = 1$
   B. The place where the line intercepts the x-axis.
   C. The place where the line intercepts the y-axis.
   D. The rate of change of the line.

   (8.F.A.3)

2. For the function, $y = \frac{1}{3}x + 6$, what does the 6 represent?

   A. The value of y when $x = 1$.
   B. The place where the line intercepts the x-axis.
   C. The place where the line intercepts the y-axis.
   D. The rate of change of the line.

   (8.F.A.3)

3. Which statement describes the orientation of this line?

   $$y = -2x - 7$$

   A. The line shows a decrease from left to right.
   B. The line shows an increase from left to right.
   C. The line is a horizontal line.
   D. The line shows a vertical line.

   (8.F.A.3)

4. What is the slope-intercept form of this equation?

   $$3y + 6x = 18$$

   A. $y = 6x + 18$
   B. $y = -2x + 6$
   C. $3y = 18 - 6x$
   D. $x = 3 - \frac{1}{2}y$

   (8.F.A.3)

FUNCTIONS

5. What information can be drawn about this function: $y = -\frac{3}{4}x - 12$?

   A. The graph has an increasing slope of $\frac{3}{4}$.

   B. The graph intersects the y-axis at 12.

   C. The graph has a decreasing slope of 12.

   D. The graph intersects the y-axis at -12.

6. Does the figure below show the graph of a linear function?

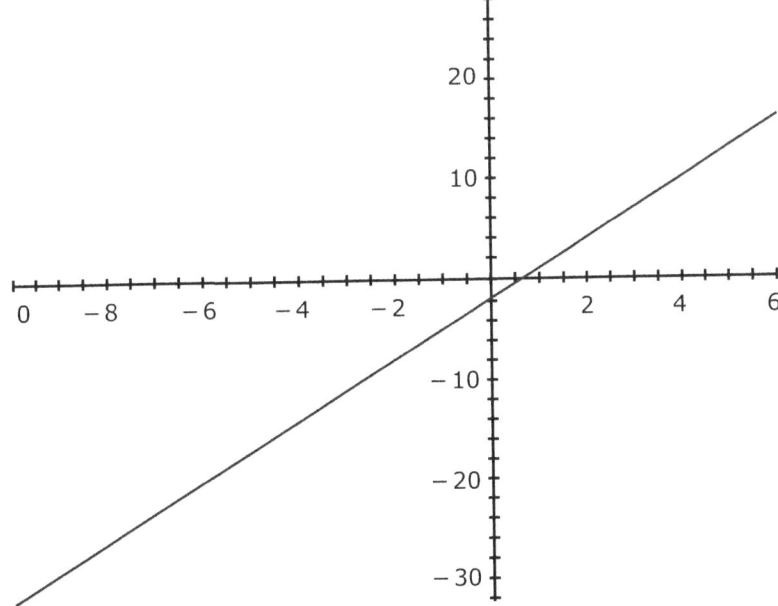

   A. No, because it starts at 0 and ends at 6.

   B. No, because it is a straight line.

   C. Yes, because it starts at 0 and ends at 6.

   D. Yes, because the graph is a straight line.

FUNCTIONS

7. Does the figure below show the graph of a linear function?

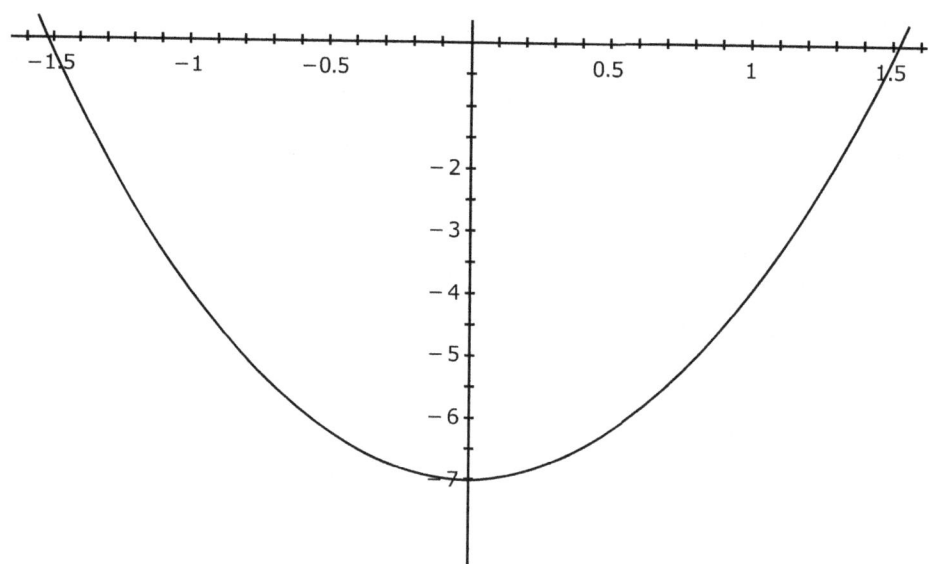

- **A.** No, because the graph intersects the y-axis at −7.
- **B.** Yes, because the graph is that of a curve.
- **C.** No, because the graph is that of a curve.
- **D.** Yes, because the graph intersects the y-axis at −7.

8. Is this function linear?

$$y = -\frac{1}{6}x - 12$$

- **A.** Yes, because it involves multiples of 6.
- **B.** Yes, it would be graphed as a line.
- **C.** No, because it contains negative values.
- **D.** No, because it would be graphed as a curve.

FUNCTIONS

9. How can the function $y = x^2 + 5$ be described?

   A. It is a nonlinear function because it involves an exponential form of x.

   B. is a linear function that intersects the x-axis at (5, 0).

   C. is a nonlinear function because it is a positive function.

   D. is a linear function that intersects the y-axis at (0, 5).

   8.F.A.3

10. Which factor makes a function linear?

   A. The function contains a slope.

   B. The function intersects the y-axis at some point on the graph.

   C. The function is a line when graphed.

   D. The function is made of points that cannot be connected.

   8.F.A.3

11. How can the relationship represented in the table below best be described?

x	y
−5	3
0	1
5	3

   A. This is not a function because each x value has multiple y values.

   B. This is not a linear function because when plotted because the points do not form a line.

   C. This is a linear function because when plotted because the points form a line.

   D. This is not a function because the plots cannot be connected.

   8.F.A.3

UNDERSTANDING LINEAR AND NON-LINEAR FUNCTIONS

FUNCTIONS

12. Which function represents a line?

- **A.** $y = |x^2 + 2|$
- **B.** $y = x^2 + 2$
- **C.** $x^2 + y^2 = 12$
- **D.** $y = \frac{1}{2}x - 11$

13. How can you describe the graph below?

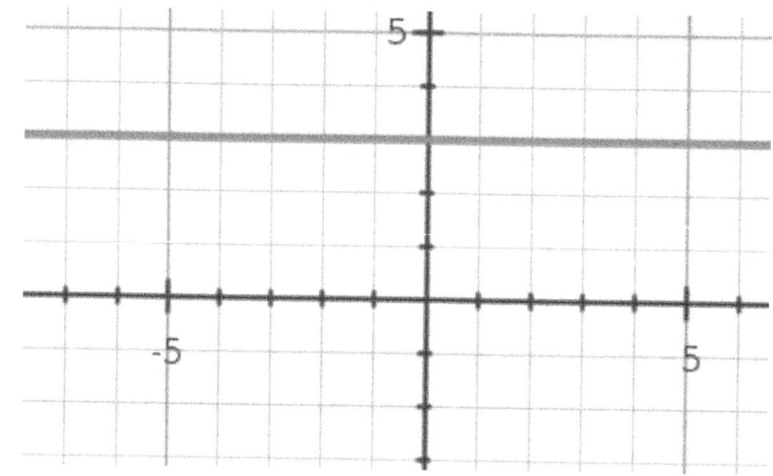

- **A.** This graph is a nonlinear function because it is a vertical line with no rate of change.
- **B.** This graph is not a function because there is no rate of change.
- **C.** This graph is a linear function because its slope changes depending on the point.
- **D.** This graph is a horizontal linear function because it is a line with no rate of change.

FUNCTIONS

14. Generally, what conclusions can you draw about horizontal lines on a graph?

   A. They are linear functions because they are horizontal lines.

   B. They are nonlinear functions because they have a changing slope.

   C. They are not functions because horizontal lines have no determined slope.

   D. They are not functions because they have a changing slope.

15. Generally, what conclusions can you draw about vertical lines on a graph?

   A. They are linear functions because they are lines.

   B. They are nonlinear functions because they have a changing slope.

   C. They are not functions because they have no determined slope.

   D. They are not functions because they have a changing slope.

16. How does the vertical line test relate to functions?

   A. Any line which a vertical line is a function.

   B. Any line which intersects a vertical line is a function.

   C. Any vertical line drawn through a function should only touch the function once.

   D. Any vertical line drawn through a function should touch the function multiple times.

FUNCTIONS

17. What does the following image represent?

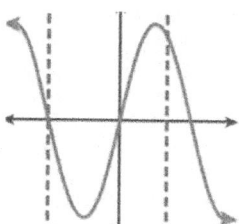

- **A.** The dotted line is a function, which passes the vertical line test.
- **B.** The graph is a function, which passes the vertical line test.
- **C.** The dotted line is not a function because it fails the horizontal line test.
- **D.** The graph is not a function because it fails the horizontal line test.

(8.F.A.3)

18. What does the following image represent?

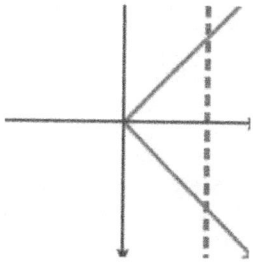

- **A.** The dotted line is a function because it fails the vertical line test.
- **B.** The graph is not a function because it fails the vertical line test.
- **C.** The dotted line is not a function because it fails the horizontal line test.
- **D.** The graph is not a function because it fails the horizontal line test.

(8.F.A.3)

FUNCTIONS

19. Is the relation shown as points below a function?

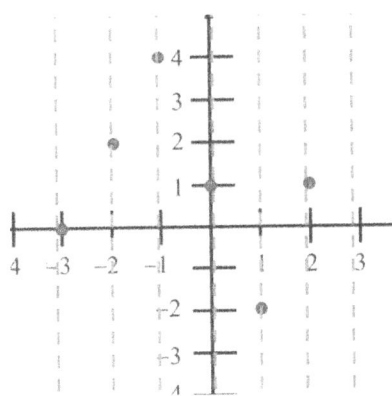

A. No, because it is not a connected line.

B. No, because it is not a straight line.

C. Yes, it contains many straight lines.

D. Yes, because it passes the vertical line test.

8.F.A.3

20. Which equation graphs as the line shown on this graph?

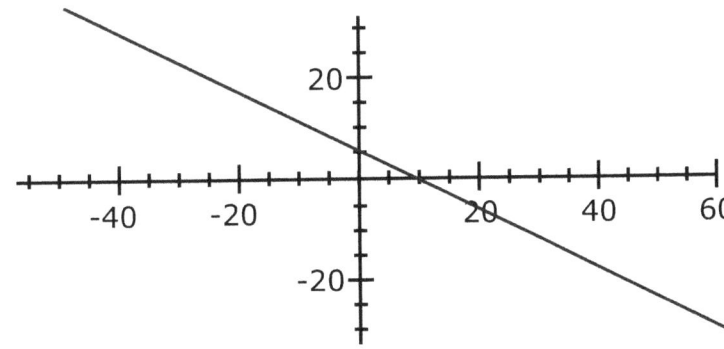

A. $y = 2x + 4$

B. $y = -2x + 4$

C. $y = x^2 - 4$

D. $y = \frac{1}{2}x - 4$

8.F.A.3

UNIT 3: USE FUNCTIONS TO MODEL RELATIONSHIPS

FUNCTIONS

USE FUNCTIONS TO MODEL RELATIONSHIPS

1. What does a function represent?

   A. A function is a relation where each input relates to exactly one output.

   B. A function is a relation where each output is given by the graph.

   C. A function is a relation that shows a relationship between an infinite number of points on a graph.

   D. A function is a relation that represents a relationship as a straight line.

   (8.F.B.4)

2. Given three points, how can you tell if their relationship can be constructed as a function?

   A. The function is a relationship of the average of their x-values.

   B. The function is a relationship of the average of their y-values.

   C. The function can be constructed by connecting points after they are graphed.

   D. The function can be constructed by squaring the x-values.

   (8.F.B.4)

3. Given a function in algebraic terms, how can you construct the function in table form?

   A. Use the numbers in the function to fill out the table.

   B. Substitute various values for x and calculate the y-values based on the given equation.

   C. Substitute various values for x and random values for the y-values.

   D. Use random values for y and calculate the x value based on the function.

   (8.F.B.4)

FUNCTIONS

USE FUNCTIONS TO MODEL RELATIONSHIPS

4. Given a function in table form, how can you construct the function in algebraic terms?

   A. Plot the values on the coordinate plane and calculate the function based on the graph.

   B. Use the numbers in the table to write the function based on the formula $y = mx + b$.

   C. Pick random values for x and y and write a formula using those values.

   D. Use the numbers in the table to calculate more values for x and y.

   (8.F.B.4)

5. Given the function in a narrative, how can you construct the function in algebraic form?

   A. Use whatever numbers are included in the narrative as x and y values.

   B. Analyze the situation to determine how the numbers in the narrative relate the x-values to the y-values.

   C. Use all the numbers as x values and calculate the value of y.

   D. Analyze the narrative and use the numbers as the slope and y-intercept of the function.

   (8.F.B.4)

6. Given the function rule, what is the first step in graphing the function?

   A. Choose a few values for y and calculate the corresponding x-values.

   B. Choose a few values for x and calculate the corresponding y-values.

   C. Test the function with the vertical line test.

   D. Connect the points mentioned in the actual rule.

   (8.F.B.4)

FUNCTIONS

USE FUNCTIONS TO MODEL RELATIONSHIPS

7. After you construct a table using the function rule, what is the next step in graphing the function?

    A. Test the function with the vertical line test.
    B. Calculate more values for y, using additional x coordinates.
    C. Choose many points on the line and check them against the function rule given.
    D. Plot the points in the table that you created using the rule.

    (8.F.B.4)

8. How many ordered pairs from a graph are needed to create a table of values from a function?

    A. One
    B. Two
    C. Three
    D. Enough so you can determine the pattern of the function.

    (8.F.B.4)

9. Given a narrative of a linear function, what do you need to identify before you write the equation?

    A. Dependent and independent variable.
    B. The slope and y-intercept.
    C. The dependent variable and slope.
    D. The independent variable and y-intercept.

    (8.F.B.4)

FUNCTIONS

10. Which algebraic function is represented in this table?

x	−1	0	1
y	5	6	7

A. $f(x) = x - 6$ **B.** $f(x) = \frac{x}{6}$ **C.** $f(x) = x + 6$ **D.** $f(x) = 6x$

8.F.B.4

11. Which type of function describes the graph below?

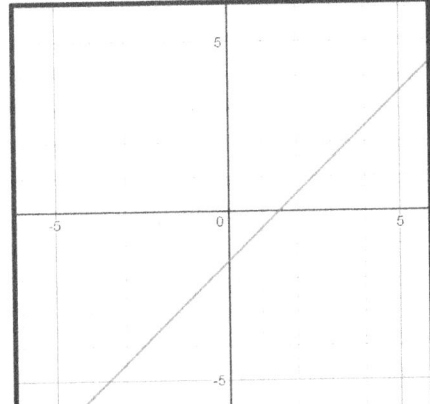

A. Increasing linear function

B. Decreasing linear function

C. Increasing nonlinear function

D. Decreasing nonlinear function

8.F.B.5

12. Which type of function describes the graph below?

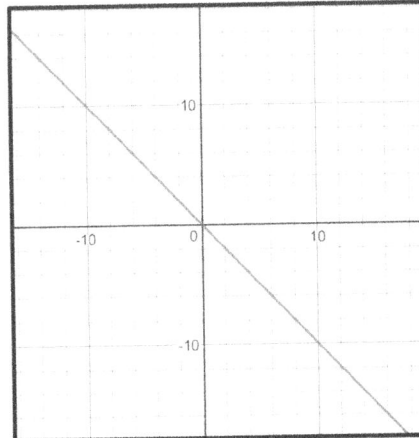

A. Increasing linear function

B. Decreasing linear function

C. Increasing nonlinear function

D. Decreasing nonlinear function

8.F.B.5

USE FUNCTIONS TO MODEL RELATIONSHIPS

FUNCTIONS

13. Which function contains increasing values?

  A. $y = -2x - 7$

  B. $y = -\frac{8}{9}x + 12$

  C. $y = \frac{2}{3}x - 9$

  D. $-y = 3x - 8$

14. Which function contains decreasing values?

  A. $y = \frac{4}{5}x + 7$

  B. $-y = -\frac{1}{2}x - 13$

  C. $y = \frac{7}{8}x + 14$

  D. $y = -\frac{2}{3}x - 6$

15. Morgan stated the function below is an increasing function. Was she correct?

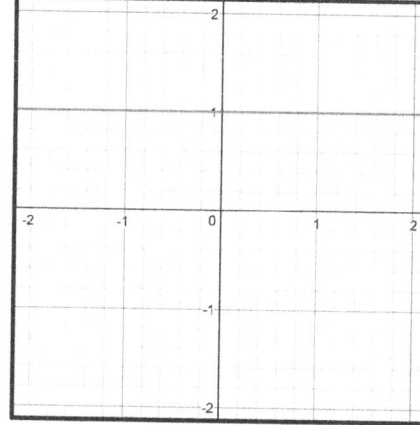

  A. Yes, this line is a function and its y values increase as its x values increase.

  B. Yes, this line is a function and its x values increase as its y values increase.

  C. No, while this line shows increasing x values, it is not a function.

  D. No, this line is a horizontal function, so it cannot be defined as increasing.

FUNCTIONS

16. Which response describes this function?

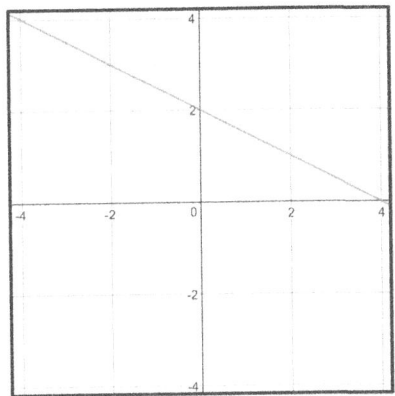

A. This function decreases in value.

B. This function increases in value.

C. This function is nonlinear.

D. This line is not a function.

(8.F.B.5)

17. Which function is decreasing?

A. $y = \frac{1}{3}x + 6$ B. $y = 3x + 6$ C. $y = -3x + 6$ D. $y = \frac{1}{3}x$

(8.F.B.5)

18. Which function is increasing?

A. $y = -\frac{1}{3}x + 6$ B. $y = \frac{1}{3}x + 6$ C. $y = -3x$ D. $y = -3x + 6$

(8.F.B.5)

19. Sidney stated the function below is a decreasing function. Was she correct?

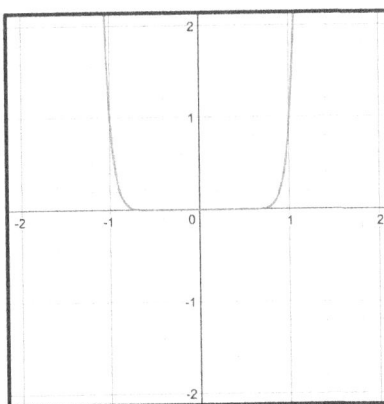

A. Yes, this graph shows a decrease in y values as x increases.

B. No, this graph is a nonlinear function and does not only increase or decrease.

C. Yes, this graph shows a decrease in x values as y increases.

D. No, this graph shows an increase in y values as x increases.

(8.F.B.5)

FUNCTIONS

20. Evan stated the function below is a decreasing function. Was he correct?

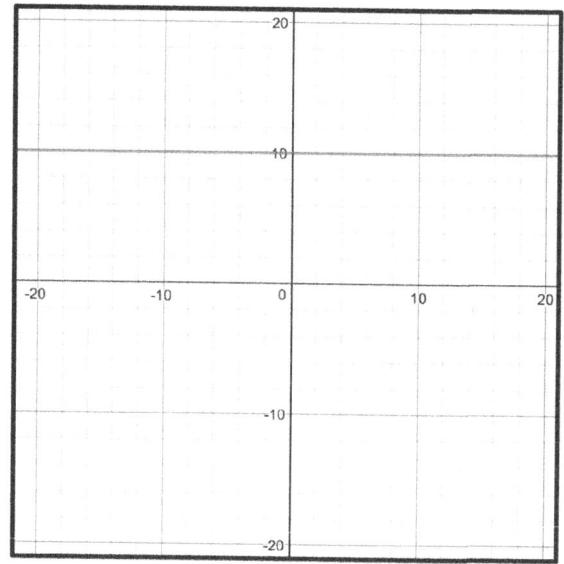

- **A.** No, this line is horizontal line and is neither increasing nor decreasing.
- **B.** No, this line is increasing, as x increases so does y.
- **C.** Yes, this line is decreasing, as x increases, y decreases.
- **D.** Yes, this line is decreasing because the y value remains constant.

(8.F.B.5)

FUNCTIONS

1. Determine the range of the function in the graph.

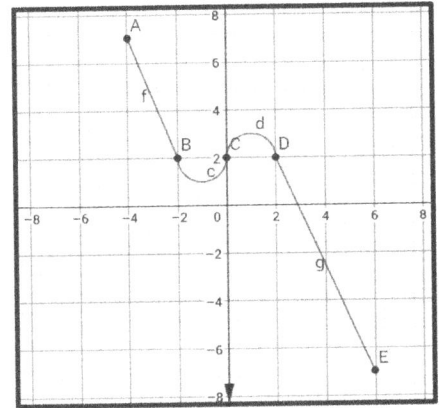

- **A.** $-7 \leq y \leq 7$
- **B.** $-5 \leq y \leq 5$
- **C.** $-7 < y < 7$
- **D.** $-5 \leq y \leq 7$

8.F.A.1

2. Determine the domain of the function in the graph.

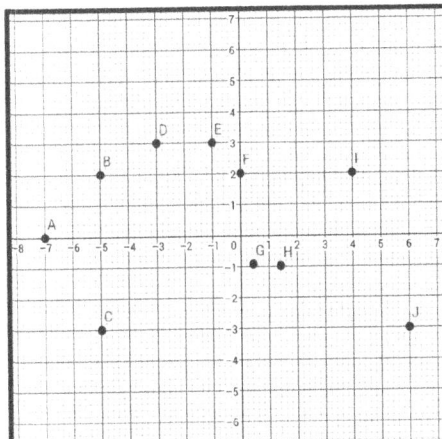

- **A.** $-7 \leq x \leq 6$
- **B.** $-3 \leq x \leq 3$
- **C.** $-7 \leq y \leq 6$
- **D.** $-3 \leq y \leq 3$

8.F.A.1

3. Evaluate the function $y = 3x + 1$ when $x = -3$.

- **A.** 10
- **B.** -8
- **C.** $-\frac{4}{3}$
- **D.** -9

8.F.A.1

4. What is the value of y in this function when $x = -2$?

$$y = \frac{x - 4}{2 - x}$$

- **A.** 1
- **B.** $-\frac{1}{2}$
- **C.** 2
- **D.** $-\frac{3}{2}$

8.F.A.1

FUNCTIONS

5. Oranges are sold at $1.27 per pound. Which table shows the relationship between the number of pounds x and the cost y?

A.
x	1	2	3
y	5	10	15

B.
x	1.27	2.54	3.81
y	1.27	2.54	3.81

C.
x	1	2	3
y	1.27	2.54	3.81

D.
x	1.27	2.54	3.81
y	1	2	3

8.F.A.2

6. Which table is a correct representation of the graph?

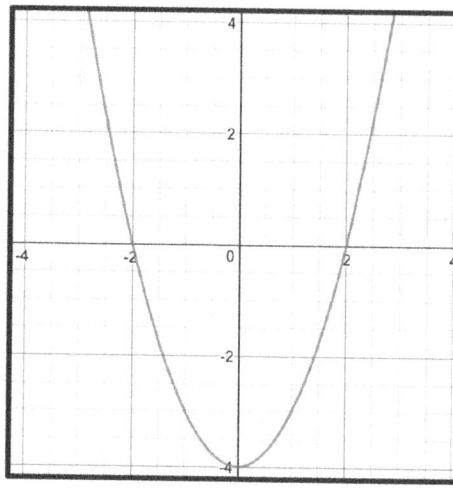

A.
x	−2	0	2
y	4	0	4

B.
x	−2	0	2
y	0	−4	0

C.
x	0	−4	0
y	−2	0	2

D.
x	1	2	3
y	1	4	9

8.F.A.2

FUNCTIONS

7. Which statement could represent information in the graph?

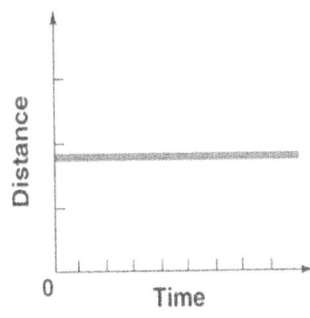

A. A car is stopped at a stop light for a set amount of time.

B. A car accelerates after stopping at a stop sign.

C. A car decelerates as it approaches a stop sign.

D. A car leaves its location at a constant speed.

(8.F.A.2)

8. Function A is defined as $y = \frac{2}{3}x - 6$ and Function B is defined as $y = -\frac{2}{3}x - 6$. How are these functions different?

A. Function A has a decreasing slope and function B has an increasing slope.

B. Function A intercepts y at $\frac{2}{3}$ and Function B intercepts y at $-\frac{2}{3}$.

C. Function B intercepts y at -6 and Function A intercepts y at 6.

D. Function B has a decreasing slope and function A has an increasing slope.

(8.F.A.2)

9. Jamal said when given the equation $y = 3x + 2$, the 3 represents the rate of change for this function. Was Jamal correct?

A. Yes, he was correct.

B. No, he was incorrect.

C. There is not enough information to determine whether he was correct.

D. He was neither correct or incorrect, there is another way to look at this problem.

(8.F.A.3)

FUNCTIONS

CHAPTER REVIEW

10. Which value in this expression represents the *y*-intercept?

$$y = 4x + 3$$

A. 3 **B.** 4 **C.** *x* **D.** *y*

(8.F.A.3)

11. Laura says this relation is not a function.

$$y = |x+2|$$

She believes it will not pass the vertical line test if represented on a graph. Is Laura correct?

A. Yes, she was correct.
B. No, she was incorrect.
C. There is not enough information to determine whether she was correct.
D. She was neither correct or incorrect, there is another way to look at this problem.

(8.F.A.3)

12. Which equation represents a linear function?

A. $y = 4x^2$ **B.** $x = 3$ **C.** $y = |x + 3|$ **D.** $y = 3x + 5$

(8.F.A.3)

13. What does the negative slope of a linear function represent?

A. A curved line.
B. An increase in *y*-values as the *x*-values increase.
C. A decrease in *y*-values as the *x*-values increase.
D. A horizontal line.

(8.F.A.4)

FUNCTIONS

14. What is the difference between the slope of Function A and the slope of Function B?

$$\text{Function A: } y = 4x$$
$$\text{Function B: } y = \frac{1}{4}x$$

A. Function B will be a steeper line.
B. Function A will be a steeper line.
C. Function B is non-linear.
D. Function A will be a horizontal line.

8.F.A.4

15. What is the *y*-intercept of this function?

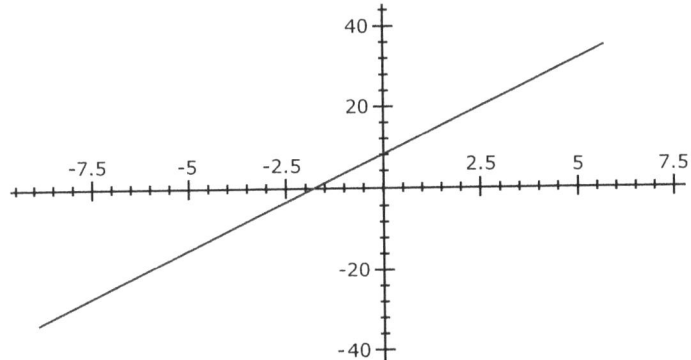

A. $(0, -2.5)$
B. $(0, -2)$
C. $(0, 10)$
D. $(0, -10)$

8.F.B.4

16. What is the *y*-intercept of this function?

$$y = 3x - 9$$

A. $(-1, 12)$ B. $(0, -9)$ C. $(1, -6)$ D. $(3, 0)$

8.F.B.4

17. Which function shows a nonlinear relationship?

A. $y = \frac{1}{3}x$ B. $y = x^3$ C. $y = 3x$ D. $y = \frac{1}{3}x + 3$

8.F.B.5

FUNCTIONS

18. How would you describe the relationship shown in this table?

x	y
1	1
2	4
3	9

A. Linear increasing
B. Nonlinear increasing
C. Nonlinear decreasing
D. Constant

19. Which strategy can you use to determine whether this function is linear?

$$y = |x - 3|$$

A. Create a table with enough points to see the pattern of the graph.
B. Create a table with three points and graph your results.
C. Create a table with 1, 0, −1 for x and graph your results.
D. You cannot determine whether the function is linear with the information given.

20. Which equation was used to create this graph?

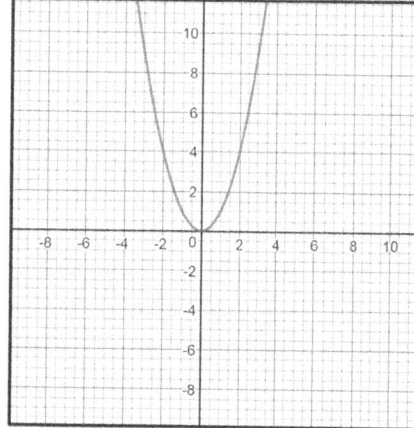

A. $y = 2x$
B. $y = 2x + 2$
C. $y = x^2$
D. $y = |x - 2|$

EXTRA PRACTICE

FUNCTIONS

1. Evaluate the function $g(x) = -\dfrac{2x-1}{3x+2}$ at $x=3$.

   A. 5   **B.** $-\dfrac{5}{11}$ **C.** $\dfrac{5}{8}$ **D.** Undefined

   (8.F.A.1)

2. Given the function $h(x) = \sqrt{4-x}$, evaluate h(5).

   A. 1   **B.** 0   **C.** Undefined   **D.** 5

   (8.F.A.1)

3. Which statement shows why $(-2, -1)$ is a solution for this function?

   $$y = 2x + 3$$

   A. $-2 = 3(1) + 2$ **B.** $1 = 2(-2) + 3$
   C. $-2 = 2(-1) + 3$ **D.** $-1 = 2(-2) + 3$

   (8.F.A.1)

4. What is the value of y when $x = 2$?

   $$y = -2x + 7$$

   A. 3   **B.** 11   **C.** -3 **D.** 5

   (8.F.A.1)

5. Which situation can be used to describe information provided in this equation?

   $$y = 0.3x$$

   A. The amount of medicine y a dog receives can be determined by multiplying 0.3 by the dog's weight in pounds x.
   B. A dog's height in 6 months y can be determined by adding 0.3 cm to the dog's current height in cm x.
   C. A dog's weight y can be determined by dividing the dog's current weight x by $\dfrac{1}{3}$.
   D. The number of miles a dog walks y can be determined by multiplying the number of steps the dog takes x by 3.

   (8.F.A.2)

EXTRA PRACTICE

FUNCTIONS

6. Jose has two car washes by his house.

- Car Wash A charges $0.75 per minute.
- Car Wash B charges $1.50 for three minutes and an additional 1.50 per minute.

Jose can wash his car in 8 minutes. Which car wash should he choose?

A. Car Wash 1

B. Car Wash 2

C. Car Wash 1 and Car Wash 2 cost the same.

D. There is not enough information to determine which is a better deal.

(8.F.A.2)

7. A family rents a moving truck for $29.99 per day d. The deposit on the truck is $149. Which equation can be used to determine y the total amount of money spent on the moving truck?

A. $y = (29.99 + d)149$

B. $y = 149d + 29.99$

C. $y = 29.99d + 149$

D. $y = 149 - 29.99d$

(8.F.A.2)

8. Which function has the same rate of change as Function A?

Function A: $y = \frac{1}{3}x + 6$?

A. $9x + 3y = 54$

B. $9x = -3y - 54$

C. $-54 - 3x = 9y$

D. $9y - 3x = 54$

(8.F.A.2)

FUNCTIONS

9. Which equation represents a linear relation but is not a function?

   A. $y = 4x^2$ B. $x = 3$ C. $y = |x + 3|$ D. $y = x^3 + 5$

10. Which equation represents a nonlinear function?

    A. $y = (x + 3)^2$ B. $y = x + 3$ C. $y = 3$ D. $y = 3x$

11. What characteristic of a graph can be determined from the vertical line test?

    A. The vertical line test determines whether the points create a line.

    B. The vertical line test determines whether the points create a nonlinear function.

    C. The vertical line test determines whether the points represent a function.

    D. The vertical line test determines how many points are on the y-axis.

12. Why is it helpful to write a linear function in slope – intercept form before graphing?

    A. It helps you determine whether a line is a function.

    B. It allows you to quickly determine the y-intercept and the rate of change.

    C. It is the only way you can get the points on a line.

    D. It helps you determine whether a function is linear.

FUNCTIONS

13. A DVD club offers a membership y with an annual fee of $29.99 and charges $14 per each DVD d. Which algebraic function represents this situation?

A. $y = 29.99 + d$ **B.** $y = 14d$

C. $y = 14 + 29.99d$ **D.** $y = 29.99 + 14d$

14. What is the rate of change of this function?

x	y
1	5
2	10
3	15

A. $\frac{1}{5}$ **B.** 5   **C.** 10   **D.** 2

15. What is the rate of change of this function?

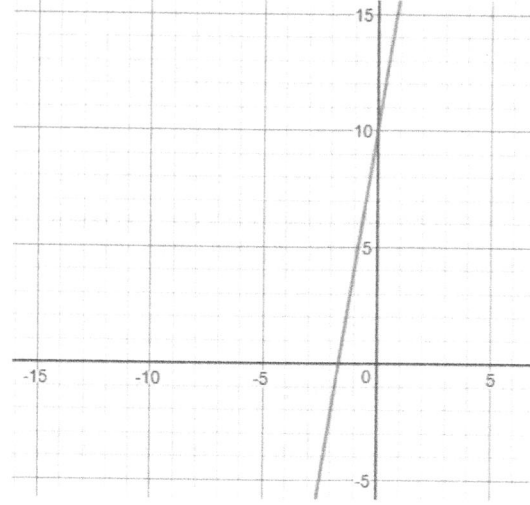

A. 6   **B.** -6 **C.** $\frac{1}{6}$ **D.** $-\frac{1}{6}$

FUNCTIONS

16. What is the rate of change of this function?
$$y = -7x + 13$$

A. -7 **B.** $\frac{1}{7}$ **C.** $-\frac{1}{7}$ **D.** 7

17. Which strategy could you use to graph this function?
$$4y + 3x = 12$$

A. Identify whether the function is linear or nonlinear.
B. Rewrite the equation in standard-form.
C. Use the vertical line test.
D. Rewrite the equation in slope-intercept form.

18. Sarah graphs this function.
$$y = x^2 + 8$$

Which response correctly describes the graph of the function?

A. The slope of the graph is 8.
B. The graph is constantly decreasing.
C. The graph is constantly increasing.
D. The y-intercept of the graph is 8.

19. Emily created a graph to represent the equation $y = 3x + 3$. Which response best describes the characteristics of this graph?

A. The graph is increasing.
B. The graph is decreasing.
C. The slope is greater than the y-intercept.
D. The slope is less than the y-intercept.

FUNCTIONS

20. Travis's teacher marked his graph below as partially incorrect. The function he was given was $f(x) = -2x - 2$. What did Travis do wrong?

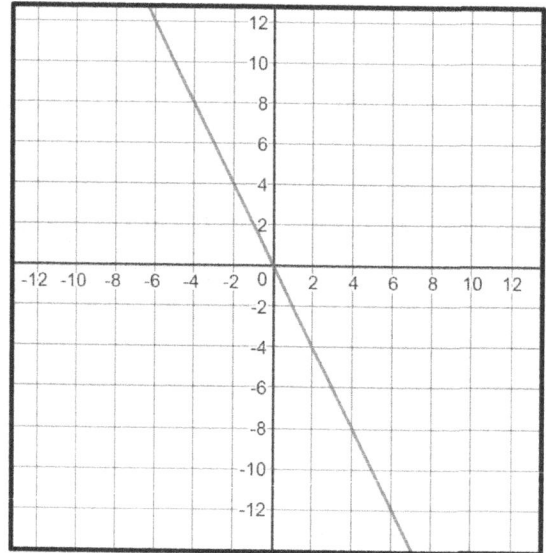

A. The y-intercept is in the wrong place.
B. The function is decreasing when it should be increasing.
C. The function is increasing when it should be decreasing.
D. The function should be non-linear.

8.F.B.5

EXPRESSIONS AND EQUATIONS

RADICAL AND INTEGER EXPONENTS	69
PROPORTIONAL RELATIONSHIPS AND LINEAR EQUATIONS	73
SOLVING LINEAR EQUATIONS	81
CHAPTER REVIEW	86
EXTRA PRACTICE	92

prepaze

www.prepaze.com

EXPRESSIONS AND EQUATIONS

RADICAL AND INTEGER EXPONENTS

1. Which of the following *y*-values makes the equation true?

    $$4^2 \times y = 4^8$$

    A. 4^4 B. 4^6 C. 2^6 D. 4^{10}

    (8.EE.A.1)

2. The dimensions of a rectangular field are 3^4 yards by 3^7 yards. What is the the area of the field?

    A. 3^{11} square yards   B. 3^{28} square yards
    C. 3^3 square yards   D. 9^{11} square yards

    (8.EE.A.1)

3. If *x* can be any integer, what must be true about the value of 2^x?

    A. It can be a positive or negative value
    B. It can be any positive value, including zero
    C. It can be any positive value
    D. It must be a whole number

    (8.EE.A.1)

4. The expression $3^3 \times 2^5$ is equivalent to which of the following?

    A. 256   B. 563   C. 6   D. 561   E. 864

    (8.EE.A.1)

5. What is the value of the expression x^6 when $x = -2$?

    A. 72   B. 64   C. 56   D. -64

    (8.EE.A.1)

6. Which of the following is an irrational number?

    A. $\sqrt{36}$ B. $\sqrt{16}$ C. $\sqrt{20}$ D. 8

    (8.EE.A.2)

EXPRESSIONS AND EQUATIONS

RADICAL AND INTEGER EXPONENTS

7. Which of the following values is the largest?

   A. $-\sqrt{81}$ B. 9.2   C. $\sqrt{81}$ D. $\sqrt{49}$

   (8.EE.A.2)

8. Which of the following is a rational number?

   A. $\sqrt{49}$ B. $\sqrt{38}$ C. $\sqrt{8}$ D. $\sqrt{27}$

   (8.EE.A.2)

9. Solve the equation:

$$x^2 = 36$$

   A. ±36   B. 6   C. −6   D. ±6

   (8.EE.A.2)

10. The area of a square is found using the equation A = s^2, where s is the length of one side. Russell knows the area of a square to be 64 square feet. What is the length one side of the square?

   A. 64   B. 32   C. 16   D. 8

   (8.EE.A.2)

11. How should 786,000,000 be expressed in scientific notation?

   A. 7.86×10^8 B. 78.6×10^8
   C. 7.86×10^{-8} D. 0.786×10^{-8}

   (8.EE.A.3)

12. How should 0.000000582 be expressed in scientific notation?

   A. 58.2×10^7 B. 5.82×10^{-7} C. 5.82×10^8 D. 58.2×10^8

   (8.EE.A.3)

EXPRESSIONS AND EQUATIONS

13. Jamiyah rewrote the 41,070,000,000 in scientific notation as 4.17×10^{10}. What mistake did she make?

  A. There are only 8 zeroes in the original number.

  B. The first-factor, 4.17, is too small to represent the original number.

  C. She did not include the zero in the hundred million place in the first factor.

  D. The second factor should not be expressed as 10^{10}.

  (8.EE.A.3)

14. Which number is 5 times larger than 80,000?

  A. 8×10^7 **B.** 8×10^9 **C.** 8×10^5 **D.** 4×10^8

  (8.EE.A.3)

15. Mackenzie wrote 0.000000000000345 as 3.45×10^{13}. What mistake did she make?

  A. The exponent should be negative.

  B. The exponent should be larger.

  C. The first-factor should be negative.

  D. The first-factor is incorrect.

  (8.EE.A.3)

16. When multiplying 4^2 and 4^9, what happens to the exponents in the product?

  A. They are added.
  B. They are multiplied.
  C. They are subtracted.
  D. They are divided.

  (8.EE.A.4)

EXPRESSIONS AND EQUATIONS

RADICAL AND INTEGER EXPONENTS

17. When dividing 4^{12} by 4^7, what happens to the exponents in the quotient?

   A. They are added.
   B. They are multiplied.
   C. They are subtracted.
   D. They are divided.

   8.EE.A.4

18. What is 0.0000014 expressed in scientific notation?

   A. 1.4×10^{-5}
   B. 1.4×10^{-6}
   C. 1.04×10^{-6}
   D. 0.14×10^{-6}

   8.EE.A.4

19. Which expression is equivalent to $4.3 \times 0.1 \times 0.1 \times 0.1$?

   A. 4.3×10^{3}
   B. 0.43×10^{3}
   C. 0.43×10^{-3}
   D. 4.3×10^{-3}

   8.EE.A.4

20. Which expression is equivalent to $5.5 \times 10 \times 10 \times 10 \times 10$?

   A. 5.5×10^{3}
   B. 5.5×10^{2}
   C. 5.5×100^{4}
   D. 5.5×10^{4}

   8.EE.A.4

UNIT 2: PROPORTIONAL RELATIONSHIPS AND LINEAR EQUATIONS

EXPRESSIONS AND EQUATIONS

1. Given the equation of a graph $y = kx$, what does k represent?

   A. k is the y–intercept value.
   B. k is the x–intercept value.
   C. k is the slope of the line.
   D. k is the solution of the line.

   (8.EE.B.5)

2. When a line is in form, $y = kx$, what value does the k have?

   A. k is a constant number.
   B. k increases as x increases.
   C. k decreases as y decreases.
   D. k increases as x decreases.

   (8.EE.B.5)

3. In the form $y = kx$, what is the proper way to refer to k?

   A. k is the constant of variation.
   B. k is the unit rate.
   C. k is the slope of the line.
   D. All these definitions correctly refer to k.

   (8.EE.B.5)

4. When a line has the form $y = kx$, where does the line intersect the y–axis?

   A. At the b value of the equation
   B. At the origin
   C. At the value of $\frac{y}{x}$
   D. At the value of k

   (8.EE.B.5)

PROPORTIONAL RELATIONSHIPS AND LINEAR EQUATIONS

EXPRESSIONS AND EQUATIONS

PROPORTIONAL RELATIONSHIPS AND LINEAR EQUATIONS

5. When a line has the form $y = kx$, where does the line intersect the x-axis?

   A. At the b value of the equation. **B.** At the origin.

   C. At the value of $\frac{y}{x}$ **D.** At the value of k

   8.EE.B.5

6. Given the equation, $y = 5x$, what is the slope?

   A. 5 **B.** $5x$ **C.** $5y$ **D.** y

   8.EE.B.5

7. Given the equation $y = \frac{1}{3}x$, what is the constant of variation?

   A. 3 **B.** $\frac{3}{y}$ **C.** $\frac{y}{3}$ **D.** $\frac{1}{3}$

   8.EE.B.5

8. Given the values in this table, what is the unit rate?

x	1	2	3
y	10	20	30

   A. 1 **B.** 5 **C.** 10 **D.** 15

   8.EE.B.5

9. What is the slope of the line represented by this table of values?

x	1	2	3
y	$\frac{1}{3}$	$\frac{1}{3}$	1

   A. 3 **B.** $\frac{1}{3}$ **C.** 1 **D.** 2

   8.EE.B.5

NAME: .... DATE: ....

EXPRESSIONS AND EQUATIONS

10. What is the constant of variation of the following graph?

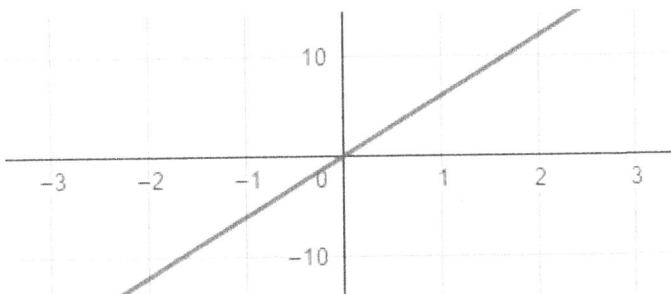

A. 6 **B.** $\frac{1}{6}$ **C.** $\frac{1}{3}$ **D.** 3

8.EE.B.5

11. Which proportion can be used to determine the slope of this line?

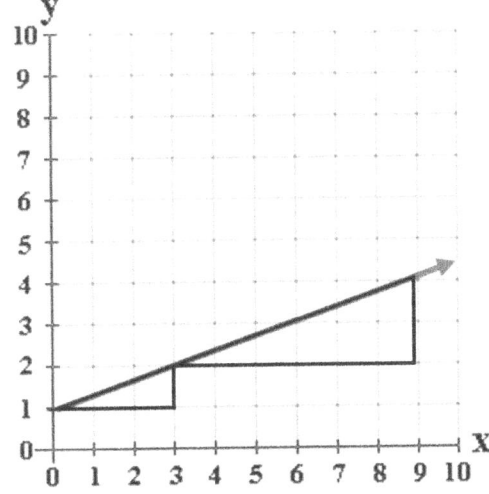

A. $\frac{3}{1} = \frac{2}{6}$ **B.** $\frac{2}{1} = \frac{4}{2}$ **C.** $\frac{1}{3} = \frac{2}{6}$ **D.** $\frac{3}{0} = \frac{9}{3}$

8.EE.B.6

PROPORTIONAL RELATIONSHIPS AND LINEAR EQUATIONS

EXPRESSIONS AND EQUATIONS

12. Which proportion can be used to determine the slope of this line?

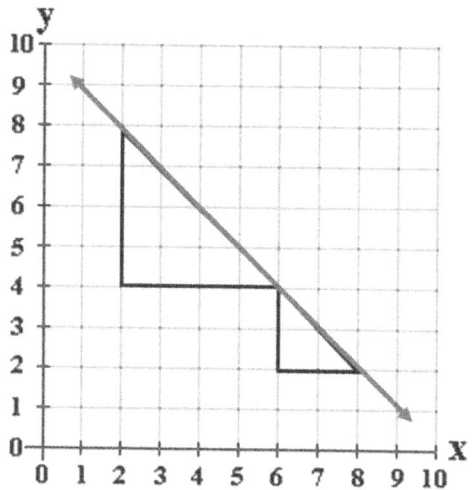

A. $-\frac{2}{6} = -\frac{6}{8}$ B. $-\frac{4}{4} = -\frac{2}{2}$ C. $-\frac{4}{8} = -\frac{2}{4}$ D. $-\frac{8}{6} = -\frac{6}{8}$

8.EE.B.6

13. Which two sets of ordered pairs could be used to find the slope of this line using similar triangles?

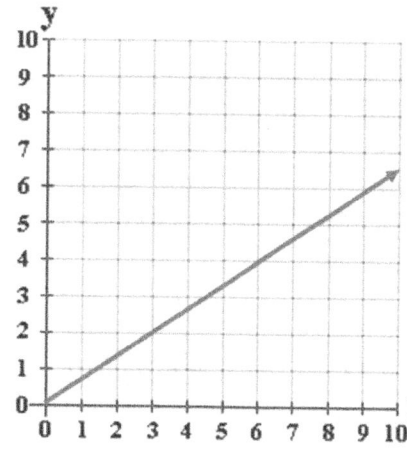

A. {(0,0), (3,3)} and {(6,4), (9,6)}

B. {(2,3), (4,6)} and {(4,6), (6,9)}

C. {(6,4), (3,2)} and {(0,0), (10,6)}

D. {(0,0), (3,2)} and {(3,2), (9,6)}

8.EE.B.6

EXPRESSIONS AND EQUATIONS

14. Which two sets of ordered pairs could be used to find the slope of this line using similar triangles?

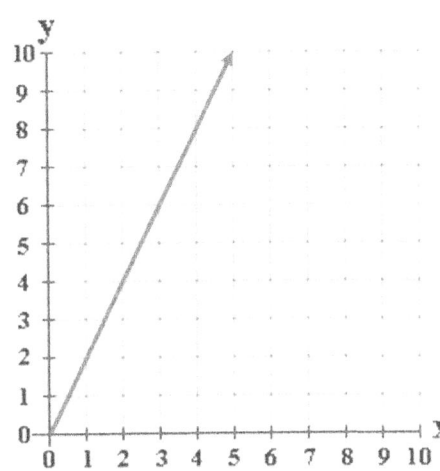

A. {(0,0), (2,4)} and {(0,0), (4,8)}

B. {(0,4), (2,0)} and {(2,0), (4,8)}

C. {(1,2), (3,4)} and {(0,0), (4,8)}

D. {(0,0), (2,4)} and {(1,2), (8,4)}

8.EE.B.6

15. Which two sets of ordered pairs could be used to find the slope of this line using similar triangles?

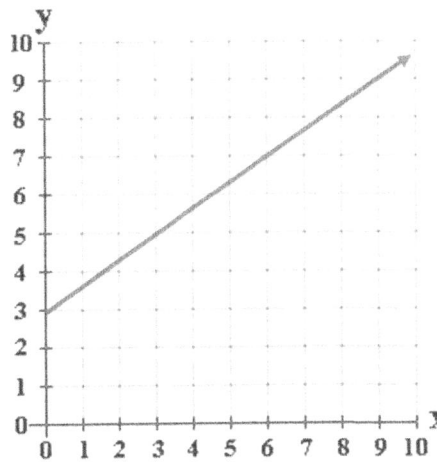

A. {(0,3), (1,3)} and {(3,5), (4,6)}

B. {(0,3), (3,5)} and {(3,5), (9,9)}

C. {(3,5), (6,7)} and {(9,9), (10,10)}

D. {(3,0), (5,3)} and {(7,6), (9,9)}

8.EE.B.6

EXPRESSIONS AND EQUATIONS

16. Which equation represents the line shown on this graph?

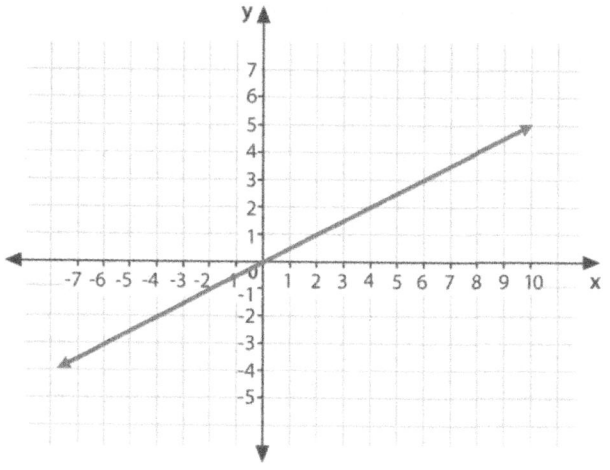

A. $y = x - 2$ **B.** $y = x + 2$ **C.** $y = 2x$ **D.** $y = \frac{1}{2}x$

8.EE.B.6

17. Which equation represents the line shown on this graph?

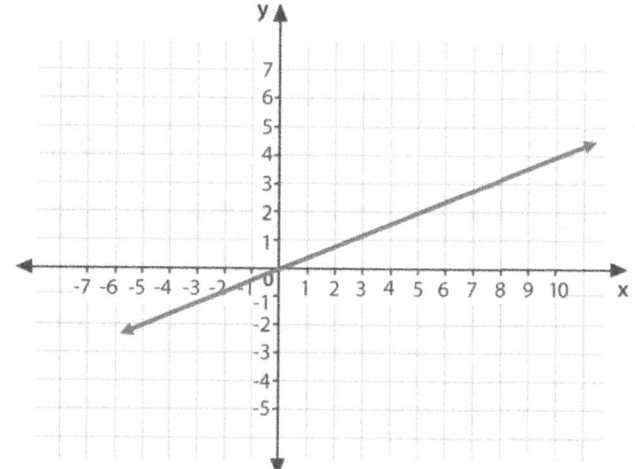

A. $y = \frac{2}{5}x$ **B.** $y = \frac{5}{2}x$ **C.** $y = -\frac{2}{5}x$ **D.** $y = -\frac{5}{2}x$

8.EE.B.6

EXPRESSIONS AND EQUATIONS

18. Write an equation to represent the line shown on this graph.

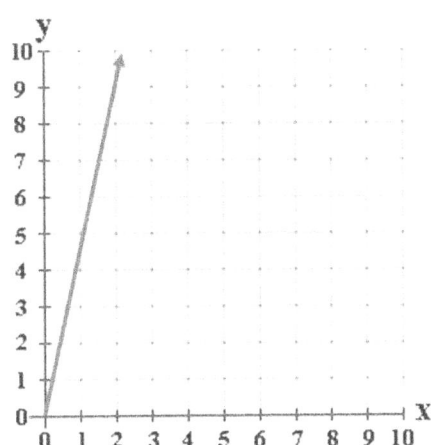

8.EE.B.6

19. Write an equation to represent the line shown on this graph.

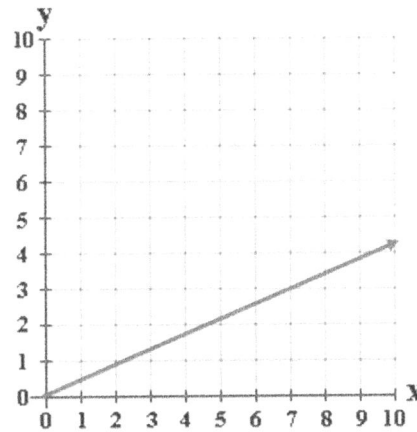

8.EE.B.6

EXPRESSIONS AND EQUATIONS

20. Which equation represents the line shown on this graph?

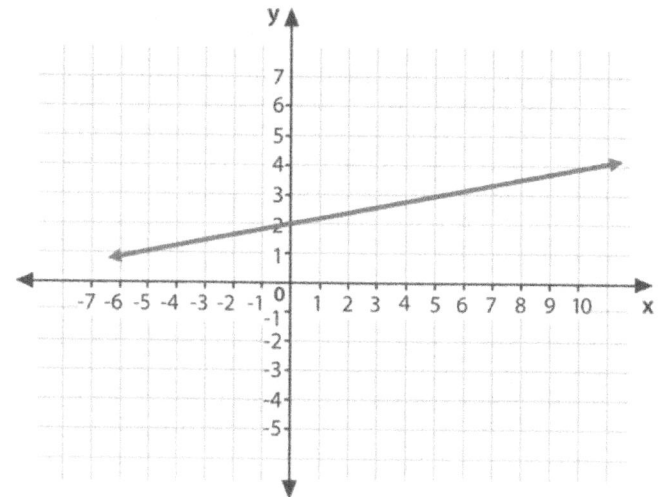

A. $y = 5x + 2$ **B.** $y = \frac{1}{5}x + 2$ **C.** $y = 2x + \frac{1}{5}$ **D.** $y = 2x + 5$

(8.EE.B.6)

UNIT 3:   SOLVING LINEAR EQUATIONS

EXPRESSIONS AND EQUATIONS

SOLVING LINEAR EQUATIONS

1. When given an equation, what is the best way to solve for a variable?

   A. Solve for the variable by using inverse operations.
   B. Solve for the variable by using order of operations.
   C. Start with 1 and plug in numbers until the equation is true.
   D. Start with −1 and plug in numbers until the equation is true.

   (8.EE.C.7)

2. When solving an equation, what rule must you keep in mind?

   A. Only manipulate the numbers and variables on the right of the equal sign.
   B. Only manipulate the numbers and variables on the left of the equal sign.
   C. Whatever is simplified within each expression must be undone.
   D. The same operation must be performed on each side of equation.

   (8.EE.C.7)

3. Solve $n + 7 = 17$, for n.

   A. $n = 17$ B. $n = 7$ C. $n = 10$ D. $n = 24$

   (8.EE.C.7)

4. What is the inverse operation of addition?

   A. Addition   B. Subtraction   C. Multiplication   D. Division

   (8.EE.C.7)

5. When given an equation with multiple operations without parentheses, which operations should be completed first?

   A. Multiplication and Division   B. Addition and Subtraction
   C. Multiplication and Addition   D. Subtraction and Division

   (8.EE.C.7)

EXPRESSIONS AND EQUATIONS

SOLVING LINEAR EQUATIONS

6. Solve for t. $2t + 8 = -4$

    A. $t = -8$ **B.** $t = 6$ **C.** $t = -6$ **D.** $t = 2$

(8.EE.C.7)

7. To simplify solving an equation, without parentheses, what is the first step you should take before solving for x?

    A. Make the equation more complicated by adding variables.

    B. Simplify using order of operations.

    C. Combine unlike terms (coefficients with variables).

    D. Combine like terms (both numbers and variables).

(8.EE.C.7)

8. Solve for y. $\dfrac{5y + 2}{2} = 11$

    A. $y = 4$ **B.** $y = -4$ **C.** $y = 3$ **D.** $y = -2$

(8.EE.C.7)

9. Solve for a.

$$-9 - 2a = 4a + 9$$

    A. $-3 = a$ **B.** $3 = a$ **C.** $-2 = a$ **D.** $2 = a$

(8.EE.C.7)

10. Solve for m.

$$10m + 4(m - 3) = 16$$

    A. $m = -2$ **B.** $m = 2$ **C.** $m = -4$ **D.** $m = 4$

(8.EE.C.7)

EXPRESSIONS AND EQUATIONS

SOLVING LINEAR EQUATIONS

11. When presented with an equation containing two variables, what do you need to solve for the variables?

    A. Nothing, you can solve it as is.

    B. Another equation with the same two variables.

    C. You cannot solve an equation with two variables.

    D. Only a computer can solve these equations.

(8.EE.C.8)

12. When graphing a system of two equations, what is important about the point where the graphs intersect?

    A. It is where one equation begins and another ends.

    B. It is where both equations are false.

    C. It is the solution to both equations.

    D. It is where one equation is true, and the other false.

(8.EE.C.8)

13. Which number of solutions is impossible for a system of equations?

    A. Two solutions   **B.** One solution

    C. Infinite solutions   **D.** No solutions

(8.EE.C.8)

14. Which response describes how the solution to a system of equations can be expressed?

    A. Another line.   **B.** A new equation.

    C. A set of other equations.   **D.** An ordered pair.

(8.EE.C.8)

EXPRESSIONS AND EQUATIONS

SOLVING LINEAR EQUATIONS

15. Wrenn and Lisa are reading the same book. Wrenn is on page 14 and reads 2 pages every night. Lisa is on page 6 and reads 3 pages every night. The variable y represents the number of pages to read, and the variable x is the number of nights.

Which system can be used to determine the total number of pages they read?

  A. $y = 3x + 16$; $x = 2y + 14$
  B. $y = 3x + 14$; $y = 2x + 6$
  C. $y = 2x + 14$; $y = 3x + 6$
  D. $x = 3y + 14$; $y = 2x + 6$

8.EE.C.8

16. When looking at a linear system of equations, what is the significance of graphed lines being parallel?

  A. A system of parallel lines has one solution.
  B. A system of parallel lines has no solution.
  C. A system of parallel lines has infinite solutions.
  D. A system of parallel lines cannot be solved.

8.EE.C.8

17. When a system of two linear equations is graphed, what does it mean when the two lines share many points?

  A. The system has one solution.
  B. The system has no solution.
  C. The system has infinite solutions.
  D. The system cannot be solved.

8.EE.C.8

EXPRESSIONS AND EQUATIONS

18. What is the solution to this system of equations?

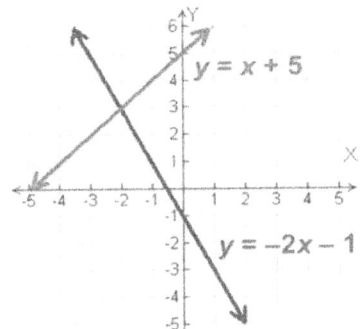

A. $(-2, 3)$
B. $(2, -3)$
C. $(-2, -3)$
D. $(2, 3)$

19. What is the first step when solving a system of equations by substitution?

A. Graph the first equation.
B. Graph the second equation.
C. Substitute 1 for the x variables.
D. Solve for one of the variables in one or both of the equations equation.

20. Jonathan is deciding between two cell phone plans. Plan A has a $25 signup fee and a monthly cost of $20. Plan B has a $40 signup fee and costs $18 per month. Which equations represent the two cell phone plans?

A. Plan A = $20m + 25$ and Plan B = $18m + 40$
B. Plan A = $18m + 40$ and Plan B = $20m + 25$
C. Plan A = $20m + 40$ and Plan B = $18m + 25$
D. Plan A = $25m + 40$ and Plan B = $20m + 18m$

CHAPTER REVIEW

EXPRESSIONS AND EQUATIONS

CHAPTER REVIEW

1. If the value of x and y are integers, which expression is equivalent to Expression A?

   Expression A: $a^x \cdot a^y$

   A. $2a^{xy}$ B. a^{x+y} C. a^{xy} D. a^{x-y}

   (8.EE.A.1)

2. Simplify the expression:

   $$\frac{24x^{10}}{4x^3}$$

   A. $6x^{13}$ B. $6x^8$
   C. $6x^7$ D. $\frac{6}{x^7}$

   (8.EE.A.1)

3. What is the value of this expression:

   $$\frac{-18a^{-1}}{3a^5}$$

   A. $\frac{-6}{a^6}$ B. $6a^6$
   C. $-6a^6$ D. $\frac{6}{a^6}$

   (8.EE.A.1)

4. Find the value of $\sqrt[3]{64}$.

   A. 4 B. 8 C. 16 D. 32

   (8.EE.A.2)

5. Which of the following is an irrational number?

   A. $\sqrt[3]{125}$ B. $\sqrt[3]{27}$ C. $\sqrt[3]{16}$ D. $\sqrt[3]{64}$

   (8.EE.A.2)

6. The volume of a cube can be found using the formula $V = s^3$, where s is the length of a side of the cube. If the volume of a cube is 125 cubic inches, what is the length of one of the sides of the cube?

   A. 125 B. 25 C. 5 D. 75

   (8.EE.A.2)

EXPRESSIONS AND EQUATIONS

7. Earth's orbit around the Sun represents 1 astronomical unit or 92,956,050 miles. How can this number be expressed in scientific notation?

    A. 9.295605×10^7 **B.** 9.29×10^7
    C. 9.29456×10^7 **D.** 9.2945605×10^{-7}

(8.EE.A.3)

8. The average human cell has a mass of 0.000000000001. What is this number rewritten as scientific notation?

    A. 10×10^{-12} **B.** 1×10^{-12} **C.** 10×10^{12} **D.** 1×10^{12}

(8.EE.A.3)

9. Which strategy represents a possible first step for converting this number to scientific notation?

$$5{,}237{,}000$$

    A. Divide the number by 10^3
    B. Divide the number by 10^5
    C. Divide the number by 10^{-6}
    D. Divide the number by 10^6

(8.EE.A.3)

10. The population of Georgia in 1950 was 3.451×10^6. The population in 2016 was estimated to be 1.03×10^7. How much has the population of Georgia changed from 1950 to 2016?

    A. The population is about 3 times larger.
    B. The population is about $\frac{1}{3}$ times smaller.
    C. More information is needed.
    D. The population is about 10 times larger.

(8.EE.A.4)

CHAPTER REVIEW

EXPRESSIONS AND EQUATIONS

11. The population of New Jersey in 2016 was estimated to be 8.94×10^6. The population of New York in 2016 was estimated to be 1.975×10^7. What is the total population of both states?

A. 2.869×10^6
B. 2.869×10^7
C. 10.915×10^{13}
D. 10.915×10^6

(8.EE.A.4)

12. If Washington is granted 10 seats in the House of Representatives and the estimated population per seat is 7.17×10^5, what is the total estimated population of Washington?

A. 7.17×10^7
B. 7.17×10^5
C. 7.17×10^6
D. 71.7×10^7

(8.EE.A.4)

13. What is the unit rate of the following graph?

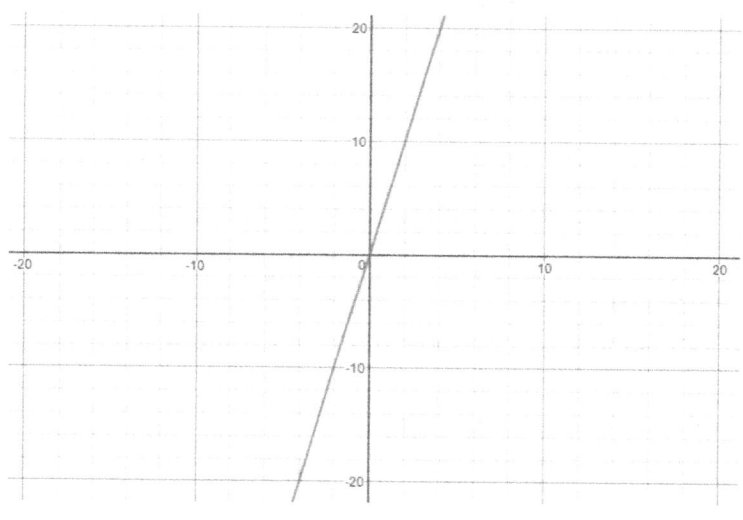

A. 5   **B.** 10   **C.** 20   **D.** 1

(8.EE.B.5)

EXPRESSIONS AND EQUATIONS

14. Which equation contains a larger slope than the function shown in the table?

x	1	2	3
y	3	6	9

A. $y = 2x$ **B.** $y = \frac{2}{3}x$ **C.** $y = x$ **D.** $y = 4x$

8.EE.B.5

15. Dina plans to use 2 similar triangles to determine the slope of this line.

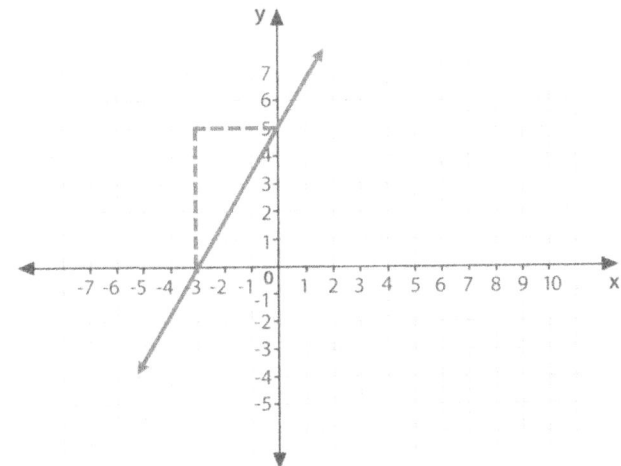

If the first ordered pair in the second triangle is (3,10), what could the second ordered pair be?

A. $(5, -3)$

B. $(-6, -5)$

C. $(5, 6)$

D. $(-5, 0)$

8.EE.B.6

EXPRESSIONS AND EQUATIONS

CHAPTER REVIEW

16. Which equation represents the line shown on this graph?

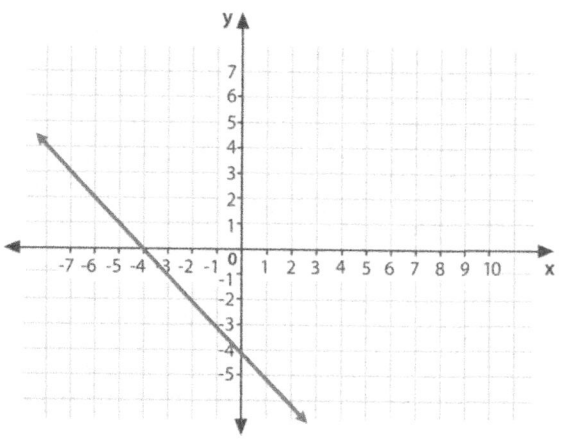

A. $y = -x - 4$ B. $y = -x$ C. $y = -x + 4$ D. $y = x - 4$

(8.EE.B.6)

17. If given the equation, $\frac{3}{4} + \frac{y}{8} = 6$, which is the equivalent simplified equation?

A. $5 + y = 42$ B. $6 + 8y = 48$ C. $6 + y = 48$ D. $24 + 4y = 14$

(8.EE.C.7)

18. If given the equation, $1.5 = 1.2y - 5.7$, which is the equivalent simplified equation?

A. $1.5 = 1.2y - 57$
B. $15 = 1.2y - 5.7$
C. $1.5 = 12y - 57$
D. $15 = 12y - 57$

(8.EE.C.7)

19. Alice has $9, and Elias has $18. Alice is saving $4 per week, and Ellen is saving $1 per week. After how many weeks will Alex and Ellen have the same amount of money?

A. 3   B. 2   C. 1   D. 4

(8.EE.C.8)

EXPRESSIONS AND EQUATIONS

20. Terrence and Ellen start a lawn mowing business and purchase the mowers and equipment for $1,750. They charge $25 for each lawn and use $1.75 worth of gas for each job. How many lawns must Terrence and Ellen mow before breaking even?

A. 64 **B.** 65 **C.** 66 **D.** 67

8.EE.C.8

EXPRESSIONS AND EQUATIONS

1. The volume of a box can be found by using the formula $V = lwh$. The length of a box is x^2, the width of the box is $2x$ and the height of the box is $6x$. Which expression models the volume of the box?

   A. $12x^3$ B. $12x^4$ C. $12x^2$ D. $8x^4$

   (8.EE.A.1)

2. The area of a circle is found with the formula $A = \pi r^2$, where r is the radius. Suppose the radius of a circle is y^4, which of the following expressions models the area of the circle?

   A. πy^8 B. πy^4 C. πy^6 D. πy^2

   (8.EE.A.1)

3. Simplify the expression $(2x^5 y^{-2})(3xy^3)^2$.

   A. $6x^7 y^4$ B. $18x^7 y^4$ C. $\dfrac{18x^7}{y^4}$ D. $18x^6 y^7$

   (8.EE.A.1)

4. Betsy takes the square root of a number n and then divides the result by 2 and obtains a positive even integer. Which of the following could be the value of n?

   A. 81 B. 25 C. 36 D. 16

   (8.EE.A.2)

5. Louis finds the cube root of a number x and then doubles the result to get 10. Which of the following is equal to x?

   A. 125 B. 64 C. 27 D. 8

   (8.EE.A.2)

EXPRESSIONS AND EQUATIONS

6. The area of a square is calculated using the formula $A = s^2$, where *s* is the length of a side of the square. Mary would like to create a square with an area of 144 square inches. What should the length of one side of the square be?

A. 10 inches   **B.** 11 inches   **C.** 12 inches   **D.** 15 inches

(8.EE.A.2)

7. When the decimal is moved to the right to convert a number to scientific notation, what value should the second-factor exponent be?

A. Positive   **B.** Negative   **C.** 10   **D.** 0

(8.EE.A.3)

8. How do you determine if the second-factor exponent is positive or negative?

    A. Exponents are always negative.
    B. Exponents are always positive.
    C. Very large numbers have positive exponents and very small numbers have negative exponents.
    D. Very large numbers have negative exponents and very large numbers have positive exponents.

(8.EE.A.3)

9. The temperature of the Sun is 15,600,000 (degrees Kelvin) at its core. How would you express this number in scientific notation?

A. 1.56×10^5 **B.** 1.65×10^5 **C.** 1.56×10^{-7} **D.** 1.56×10^7

(8.EE.A.3)

www.prepaze.com

EXPRESSIONS AND EQUATIONS

10. The state of Illinois has a population of around 1.2852×10^7 and each representative in the House of Representatives represents around 7.14×10^5 residents. How many representatives in the House of Representatives are from Illinois?

  A. 2   **B.** 10^2 **C.** 18   **D.** 6

(8.EE.A.4)

11. The least populous state in 2016 is Wyoming with a population of 5.85×10^5. The population of the most populous state California is around 39,580,000. What is the population of the two states combined?

  A. 401.65×10^7
  B. 1.992×10^5
  C. 4.0165×10^6
  D. 4.0165×10^7

(8.EE.A.4)

12. In 1950, Hawaii was not a state, but it had a population of 491,000. In 2016, the estimated population of Hawaii was 1.428×10^6. How much did the population change over the 66 years?

  A. The population increased to about 3 times the 1950 population.
  B. The population decreased to about 3 times the 1950 population.
  C. The population increased to about 6 times the 1950 population.
  D. The population decreased to about 6 times the 1950 population.

(8.EE.A.4)

EXPRESSIONS AND EQUATIONS

13. Use the following coordinate plane to graph the relationship, $y = 12x$.

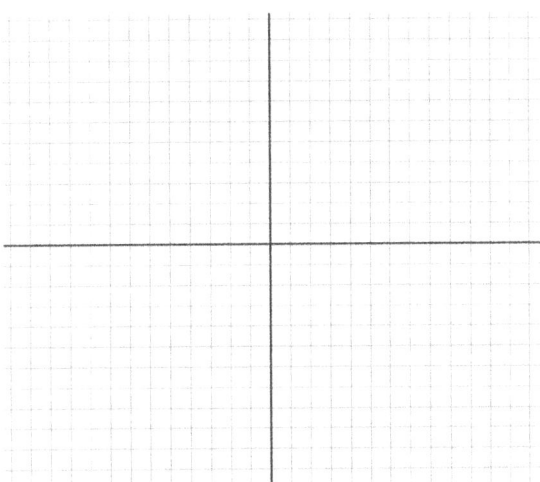

14. Use the following coordinate plane to graph the relationship, $y = 3.5x$.

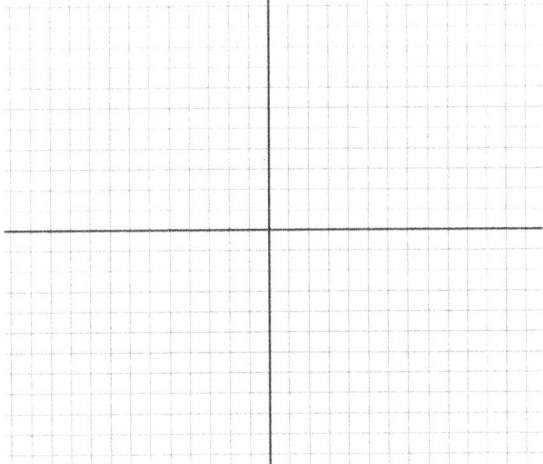

EXPRESSIONS AND EQUATIONS

15. Can you use similar triangles to determine the slope of this line? Explain your reasoning.

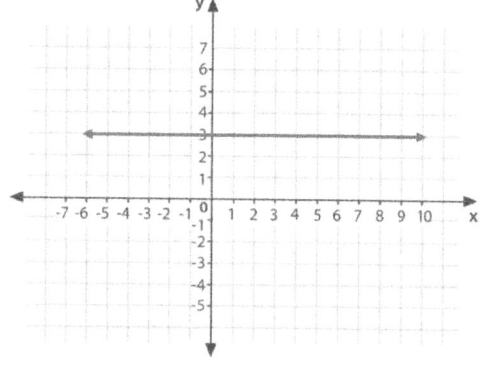

(8.EE.B.6)

16. Write an equation to represent the line shown on this graph.

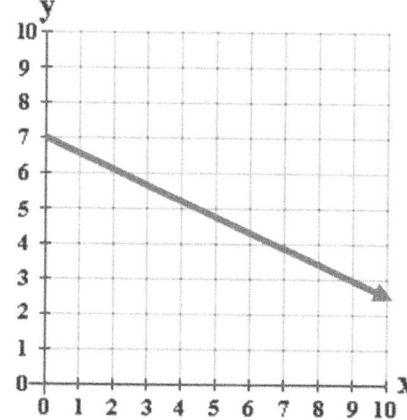

(8.EE.B.6)

EXPRESSIONS AND EQUATIONS

17. The equation $9.95 + 0.75s = c$ gives the cost c in dollars that a website charges for downloading songs. The variable s stands for the number of songs downloaded. Find the cost of downloading 36 songs.

_____

(8.EE.C.7)

18. Marissa and Manuel are going to the movies. They each bought a medium popcorn, and a large soft drink. Marissa had a $10 gift certificate to put toward the cost, and Manuel paid the rest, which came to $42.00. A movie ticket costs $12, and a medium popcorn costs $7.50. What was the cost for a soft drink?

_____

(8.EE.C.7)

19. The yearbook club is having a bake sale to raise money. Large cupcakes are sold for $1.25 each and small cupcakes are sold for $0.75 each. If 105 cupcakes were sold for a total amount of $109.75, how many large cupcakes did the yearbook club sell?

_____

(8.EE.C.8)

20. A farm raises cows and sheep. There are a total of 270 cows and sheep on the farm. There are twice as many sheep as cows. How many cows are on the farm?

_____

(8.EE.C.8)

GEOMETRY

CONGRUENCE AND SIMILARITY	**101**
PYTHAGOREAN THEOREM APPLICATION	**111**
VOLUME OF 3 – DIMENSIONAL SHAPES	**116**
CHAPTER REVIEW	**120**
EXTRA PRACTICE	**128**

prepaze

www.prepaze.com

GEOMETRY

1. Harry describes the transformation that transforms Figure A to Figure B as shown on this graph.

   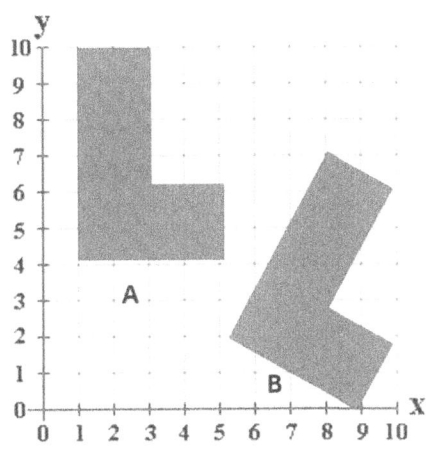

   Which description matches the transformation?

   A. Figure A is reflected twice.
   B. Figure A is reflected and rotated.
   C. Figure A is translated and rotated.
   D. Figure A is rotated 45 degrees.

   (8.G.A.1)

2. Hermione describes the transformation that transforms Figure A to Figure B as shown on this graph.

   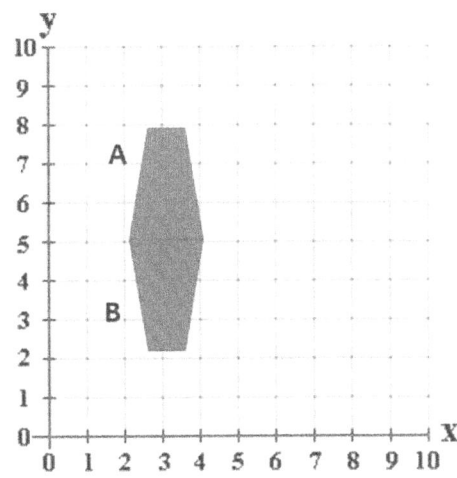

   Which description matches the transformation?

   A. Figure A is translated along the y – axis in the negative direction to create Figure B.
   B. Figure A is reflected across the line $y = 5$ to create Figure B.
   C. Figure A is translated across the line $x = 5$ to create Figure B.
   D. Figure A is rotated about one vertex to create Figure B.

   (8.G.A.1)

GEOMETRY

3. The ordered pairs $(-7, 3)$, $(-4, 3)$, $(-7, 6)$ and $(-4, 6)$ represent the vertices of Square A.

A new square is created by reflecting Square D across the x–axis.

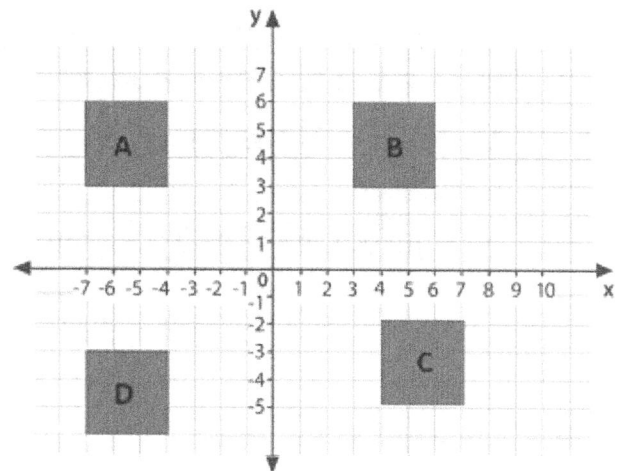

Which square is the reflection of Square A?

_____

(8.G.A.1)

4. The ordered pairs $(-2, -2)$, $(-7, -2)$, $(-2, -4)$ and $(-7, -4)$ represent the vertices of a rectangle.

A new rectangle is created by reflecting the first rectangle across the y–axis and translating it 8 units up.

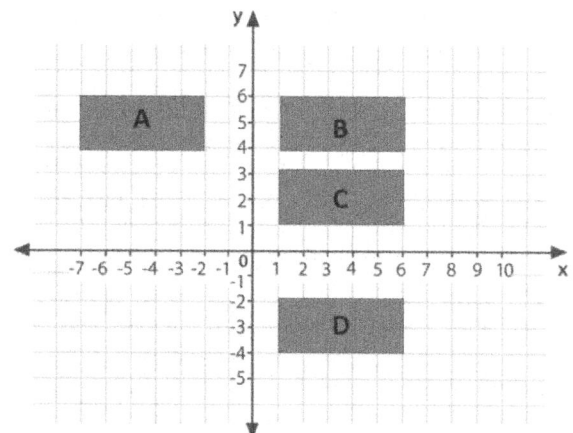

Which rectangle is is the new rectangle?

_____

(8.G.A.1)

NAME: _____ DATE: _____ 103

GEOMETRY

5. Triangles J and K are shown on the graph.

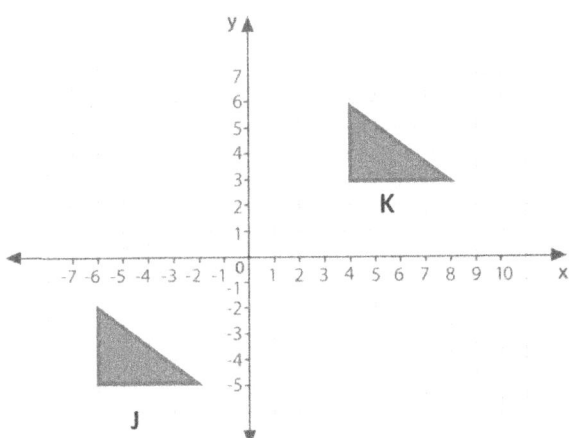

Which sequence is used to transform Triangle J to Triangle K?

A. Translate Triangle J up 8 units and to the right 10 units.

B. Translate Triangle J up 3 units and to the right 8 units.

C. Translate Triangle J down 8 units and to the left 10 units.

D. Translate Triangle J down 5 units and to the right 6 units.

(8.G.A.2)

6. Which sequence is used to transform Quadrilateral RSTV to Quadrilateral WXYZ?

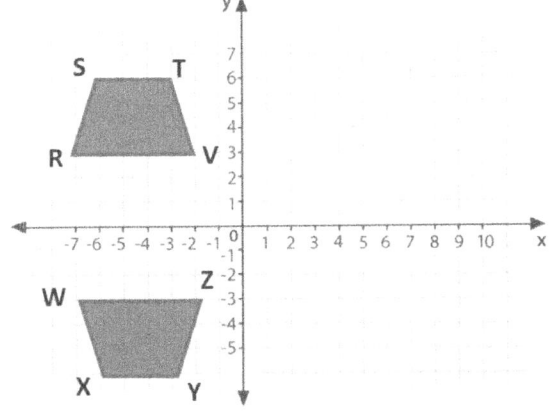

A. Quadrilateral RSTV is rotated about the origin.

B. Quadrilateral RSTV is reflected across the x-axis.

C. Quadrilateral RSTV is translated across the x-axis.

D. Quadrilateral RSTV is reflected across the y-axis.

(8.G.A.2)

CONGRUENCE AND SIMILARITY

www.prepaze.com   prepaze

GEOMETRY

7. Triangle ABC is shown on this graph.

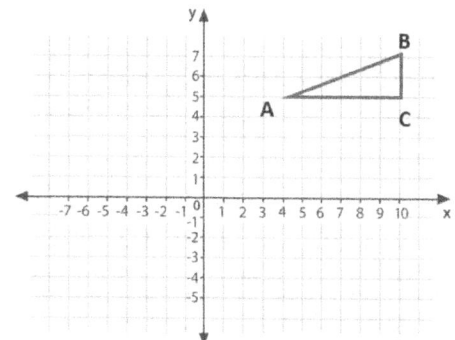

Triangle A'B'C' is created by rotating Triangle ABC 180 degrees about the origin and then translating it 1 unit down.

What are the coordinates of Triangle A'B'C'?

_____

8.G.A.2

8. Quadrilateral ABCD is shown on this graph.

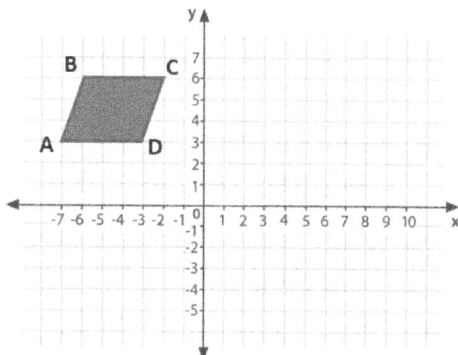

Quadrilateral A'B'C'D' is created by reflecting Quadrilateral ABCD across the y-axis and then reflecting it across the x-axis.

What are the coordinates of Quadrilateral A'B'C'D'?

_____

8.G.A.2

GEOMETRY

9. The point W (0, −6) is translated 2 units right. What are the coordinates of the resulting point W'?

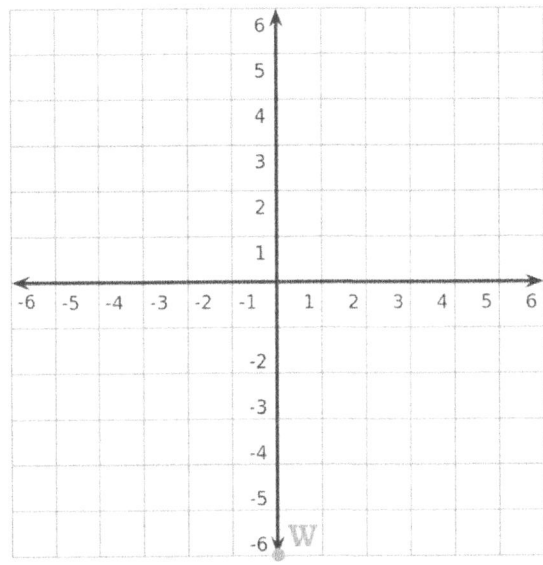

A. (−2, −6)

B. (2, −6)

C. (−2, −6)

D. (2, 6)

10. The point T (−3, 0) is translated 4 units right. What are the coordinates of the resulting point T'?

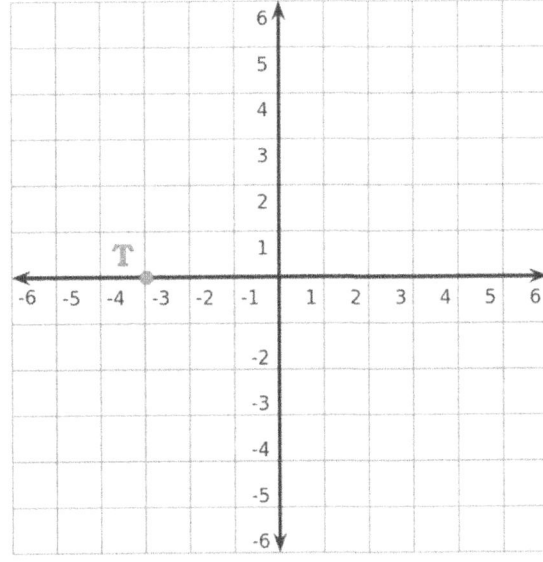

A. (1, 0)

B. (0, 1)

C. (2, 1)

D. (1, 2)

GEOMETRY

11. Point Q (−1, −5) is translated 1 unit up. What are the coordinates of the resulting point, Q'?

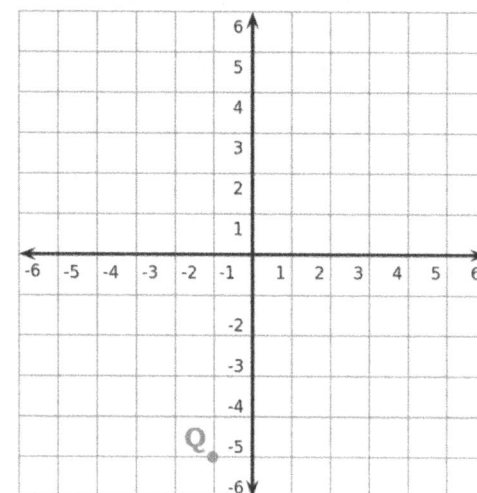

A. (−2, −1)

B. (−1, −4)

C. (2, −4)

D. (−1, −6)

12. Point S(−2, 0) is translated 1 unit right. What are the coordinates of the resulting point S'?

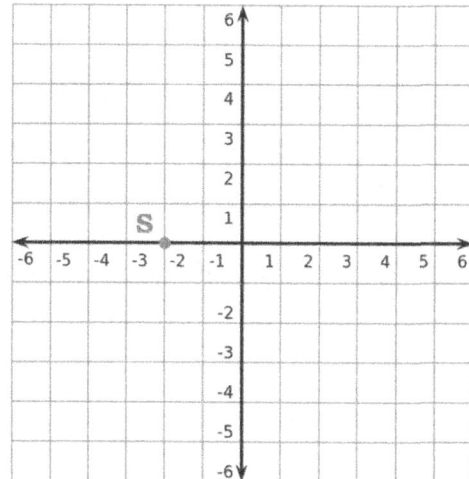

GEOMETRY

13. Triangle ABC is shown on the graph below.

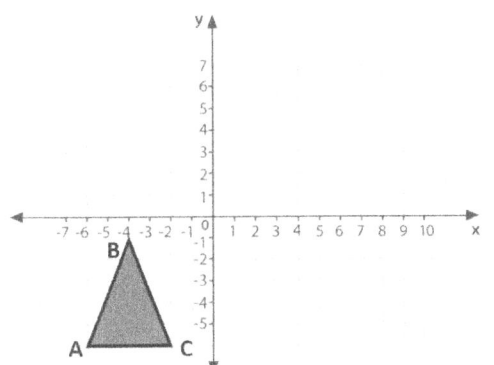

Triangle A'B'C' is created by dilating Triangle ABC by a scale factor of 2 about the origin and translating the shape up 3 units.

What are the coordinates of Triangle A'B'C'?

A. $(-12, 12), (-8, 12), (-4, 12)$
B. $(-6, -6), (-4, -1), (-2, -6)$
C. $(-12, -12), (-8, -12), (-4, -12)$
D. $(-12, -9), (-8, 1), (-4, -9)$

8.G.A.4

14. Triangle DEF is shown on the graph below.

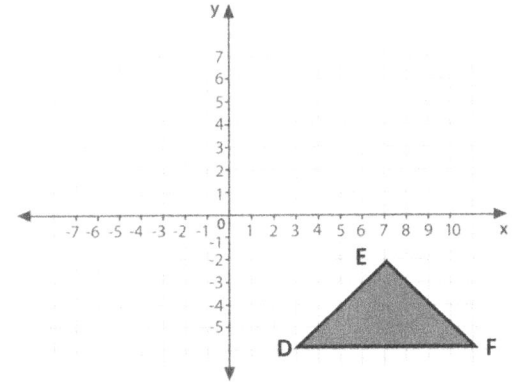

Triangle D'E'F' is created by dilating Triangle DEF by a scale factor of 3 about the origin and reflecting the shape across the y-axis.

What are the coordinates of Triangle MNO?

A. $(3, -6), (7, -2), (11, -6)$
B. $(-9, -18), (-21, -6), (-33, -18)$
C. $(9, -18), (21, -6), (33, -18)$
D. $(6, -3), (10, 1), (14, -3)$

8.G.A.4

CONGRUENCE AND SIMILARITY

GEOMETRY

15. Quadrilateral ABCD is shown on the graph.

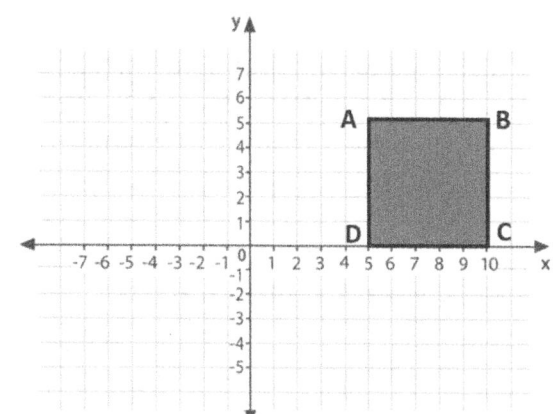

Quadrilateral A'B'C'D' is created by dilating Quadrilateral ABCD by a scale factor of $\frac{1}{5}$ about the origin.

What are the coordinates of Quadrilateral A'B'C'D'?

A. (1, 5), (2, 10), (2, 10), (5, 0) B. (5, 1), (2, 5), (2, −5), (1, −5)
C. (1, 1), (2, 1), (2, 0), (1, 0) D. (5, 5), (10, 5), (10, 0), (5, 0)

(8.G.A.4)

16. Trapezoid JKLM is shown on the graph.

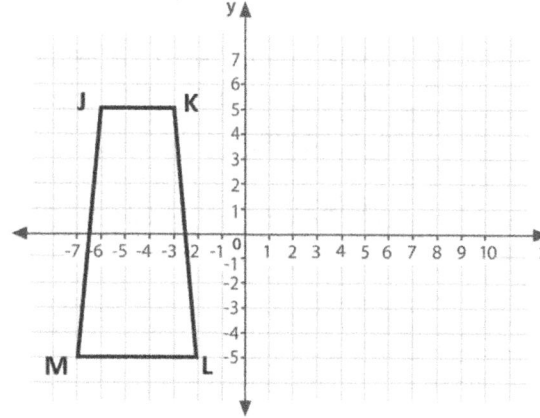

Trapezoid J'K'L'M' is created by dilating Trapezoid JKLM by a scale factor of 2 about the origin.

What are the coordinates of Trapezoid J'K'L'M'?

(8.G.A.4)

GEOMETRY

17. Evelyn uses this drawing to prove the triangle sum theorem.

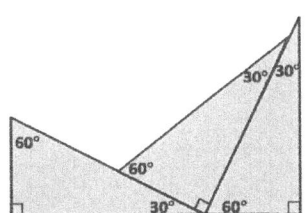

What conclusions can be made from her drawing?

- **A.** A right triangle will always have 30, 60, and 90 degree angles.
- **B.** The interior angles of a triangle have a sum of 180 degrees.
- **C.** A right angle is a complementary angle.
- **D.** The exterior angles of a triangle have a sum of 360 degrees.

(8.G.A.5)

18. Lines $\overline{AC}$ || $\overline{DE}$. Which statement can be justified by the diagram?

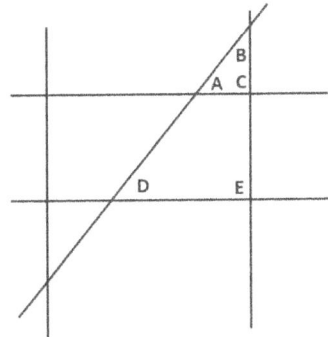

- **A.** Angle B is congruent to Angle D because Triangle ABC is an equilateral triangle.
- **B.** Angle A is congruent to Angle D because Triangle ABC is similar to Triangle DBE.
- **C.** Angle A is congruent to Angle B because Triangle ABC is similar to Triangle DBE.
- **D.** Angle A is congruent to Angle C because they are adjacent angles.

(8.G.A.5)

GEOMETRY

19. The parallel lines in this diagram are cut by a transversal. What is the measure of Angle B?

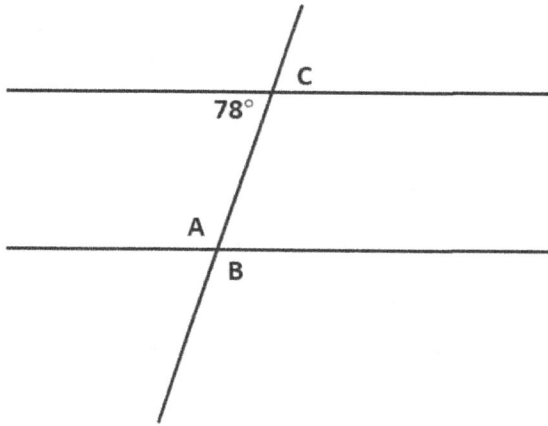

20. Lines l and m are parallel. Angle 6 has a measure of 89 degrees. What are the measures of Angles 3 and 5?

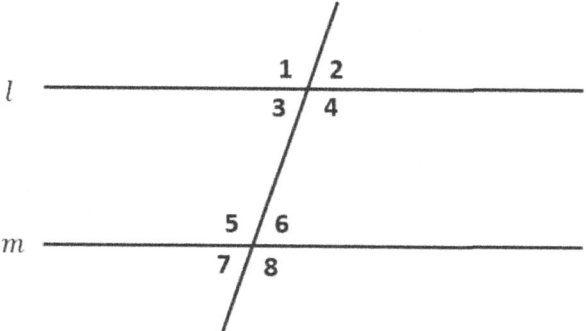

UNIT 2: PYTHAGOREAN THEOREM APPLICATION

GEOMETRY

PYTHAGOREAN THEOREM APPLICATION

1. If the lengths of the legs of a right triangle are 8 centimeters and 9 centimeters, what is the length of a hypotenuse?

   A. $\sqrt{145}$ cm   **B.** $7\sqrt{3}$ cm   **C.** $4\sqrt{5}$ cm   **D.** 12 cm

   (8.G.B.6)

2. If the lengths of the legs of a right triangle are 11 centimeters and 13 centimeters, what is the length of a hypotenuse?

   A. $10\sqrt{2}$ cm   **B.** 17 cm   **C.** $\sqrt{290}$ cm   **D.** 18 cm

   (8.G.B.6)

3. If the lengths of the legs of a right triangle are 14 centimeters and 16 centimeters, what is the length of a hypotenuse?

   A. $\sqrt{113}$ cm   **B.** $2\sqrt{113}$ cm   **C.** 20 cm   **D.** 21 cm

   (8.G.B.6)

4. If the lengths of the legs of a right triangle are 8 centimeters and 15 centimeters, what is the length of a hypotenuse?

   A. $12\sqrt{2}$ cm   **B.** 17 cm   **C.** 15 cm   **D.** 16 cm

   (8.G.B.6)

5. **True or False:** A triangle with side lengths of 5 kilometers, 12 kilometers, and 13 kilometers is a right triangle.

   A. True   **B.** False

   (8.G.B.6)

6. **True or False:** A triangle with side lengths of 3 meters, 4 meters, and 5 meters is a right triangle.

   A. True   **B.** False

   (8.G.B.6)

GEOMETRY

PYTHAGOREAN THEOREM APPLICATION

7. **True or False:** A triangle with side lengths of 3 meters, 6 meters, and 7 meters is a right triangle.

   A. True

   B. False

8. In a right triangle, the length of the hypotenuse is 17 mm and the length of one leg is 8 mm. What is the length of the other leg?

   A. 10 mm
   B. 15 mm
   C. 20 mm
   D. 5 mm

9. In a right triangle, the hypotenuse is 15 yds and length of one leg is 9 yds. What is the length of the other leg?

   A. 12 yds
   B. 15 yds
   C. 17 yds
   D. 13 yds

10. In a right triangle, the hypotenuse is 20 km and the other leg is 12 km. What is the length of the other leg?

    A. 15 km
    B. 14 km
    C. 17 km
    D. 16 km

11. In a right triangle, the hypotenuse is 13 in and the other leg is 12 in. What is the length of the other leg?

    A. 17 in
    B. 13 in
    C. 5 in
    D. 6 in

GEOMETRY

12. What is the length of the hypotenuse of the triangle below?

13. What is the length of the hypotenuse in the triangle below?

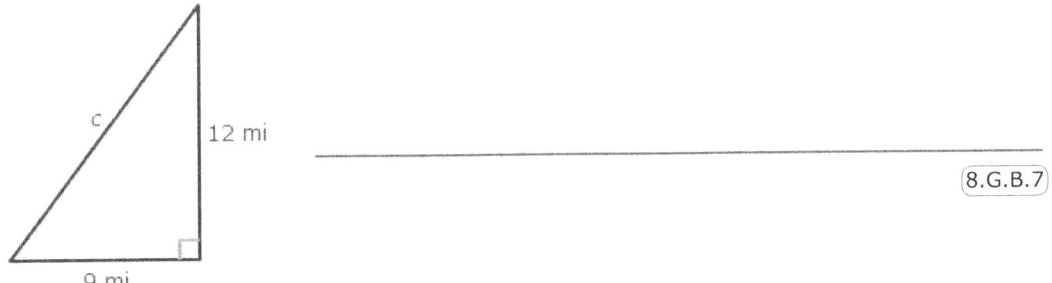

14. What is the length of the hypotenuse in the triangle below?

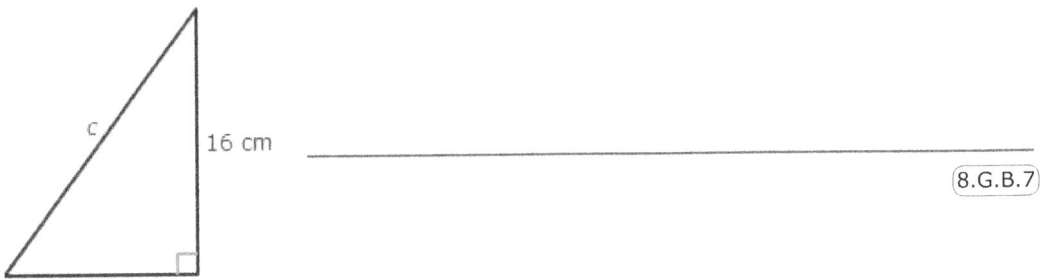

GEOMETRY

PYTHAGOREAN THEOREM APPLICATION

15. What is the approximate distance between Point B and Point C?

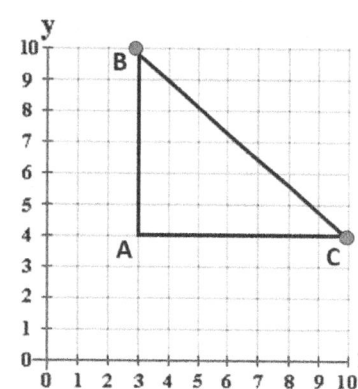

A. 11.1 units

B. 9.2 units

C. 8.9 units

D. 9.8 units

16. What is the approximate distance between Point B and Point C?

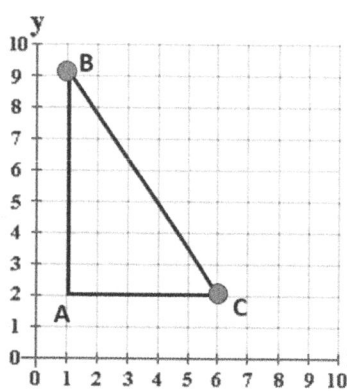

A. 7.2 units

B. 6.3 units

C. 8.6 units

D. 6.9 units

17. What is the approximate distance between Point B and Point C?

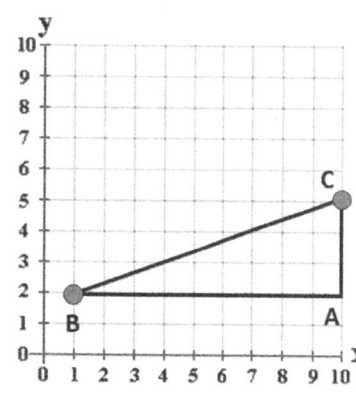

A. 8.7 units

B. 9.5 units

C. 9.0 units

D. 8.4 units

GEOMETRY

18. What is the approximate distance between the points (2, 4) and (7, 10)?

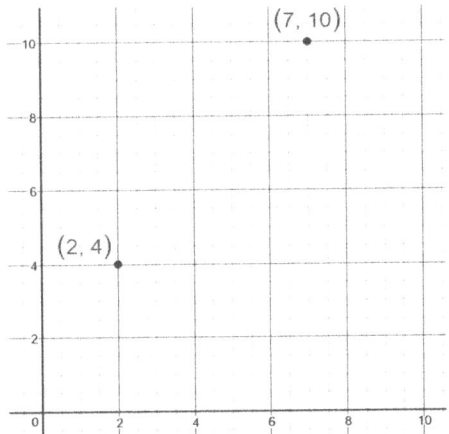

A. 7.8 units

B. 6.4 units

C. 8.0 units

D. 10.2 units

PYTHAGOREAN THEOREM APPLICATION

(8.G.B.8)

19. What is the distance between the 2 points (1, 10) and (1, 2) without using a graph?

_____

(8.G.B.8)

20. What is the distance between the 2 points (4, 4) and (4, 10) without using a graph?

_____

(8.G.B.8)

UNIT 3: VOLUME OF 3-DIMENSIONAL SHAPES

GEOMETRY

VOLUME OF 3-DIMENSIONAL SHAPES

1. What is the formula for the volume of a cylinder?

   A. $\frac{1}{2}bh$ B. $\pi r^2 h$ C. $\frac{1}{3}\pi r^2 h$ D. lw

   (8.G.C.9)

2. What is the formula for the volume of a cone?

   A. $\frac{1}{2}bh$ B. $\pi r^2 h$ C. $\frac{1}{3}\pi r^2 h$ D. lw

   (8.G.C.9)

3. What is the formula for the volume of a sphere?

   A. lw B. $\frac{4}{3}\pi r^3$ C. s^2 D. $\pi r^2 h$

   (8.G.C.9)

4. What is the approximate volume of a cone with a radius of 7 m and a height of 10 m? Use $\pi = 3.14$.

   A. $512.87 \, m^3$ B. $654.32 \, m^3$ C. $435.24 \, m^3$ D. $603.48 \, m^3$

   (8.G.C.9)

5. What is the approximate volume of a sphere with a radius of 3 ft?

   A. $65.32 \, ft^3$ B. $113.1 \, ft^3$ C. $84.5 \, ft^3$ D. $93.56 \, ft^3$

   (8.G.C.9)

6. What is the approximate volume of a cone with a radius of 5 yds and a height of 20 yds?

   A. $523.6 \, yd^3$ B. $453.2 \, yd^3$ C. $463.2 \, yd^3$ D. $582.5 \, yd^3$

   (8.G.C.9)

GEOMETRY

7. What is the approximate volume of a cylinder whose radius is 10 ft and the height is 7 ft? Use π = 3.14.

    A. 3961 ft^2 **B.** 2632 ft^2 **C.** 4233 ft^2 **D.** 2198 ft^2

(8.G.C.9)

8. What is the approximate volume of a cylinder whose radius is 6 ft and the height is 5 ft? Use π=3.14.

    A. 368.2 ft^3 **B.** 453.2 ft^3 **C.** 565.2 ft^3 **D.** 428.2 ft^3

(8.G.C.9)

9. What is the approximate volume of a cylinder whose radius is 9 m and the height is 7 m? Use π=3.14.

    A. 1768 m^3 **B.** 1532 m^3 **C.** 1780.4 m^3 **D.** 1283 m^3

(8.G.C.9)

10. Your parent's car has 6 cylinders in the engine. What is the approximate volume, to the nearest cubic cm, of a one of those cylinders if the height is 6 cm and the radius is 4 cm? Use π=3.14.

    _____ cm^3

(8.G.C.9)

11. Kristen wants to know how much ice cream she can place in her ice cream cone. Her cone has a height of 12 cm and a radius of 5 cm How much ice cream can it hold if the cone if filled level with the top? Use π=3.14.

    _____ cm^3

(8.G.C.9)

12. Caroline puts candy in some cones her friends made. What is the approximate volume, to the nearest whole number, of the candy one cone holds if the diameter of the cone is 20 cm and the height is 20 cm? Use π = 3.14.

    _____ cm^3

(8.G.C.9)

VOLUME OF 3-DIMENSIONAL SHAPES

GEOMETRY

VOLUME OF 3-DIMENSIONAL SHAPES

13. A group of parents in a Booster Club are decorating a float for the cheerleaders to ride on in the annual winter holiday parade. They want each of the cheerleaders to hold cylinders full of glitter to throw out on the crowd. How much glitter, to the nearest whole cubic unit, can each cylinder hold if each cylinder has a radius of 3 cm and a height of 7 cm?

_____ cm^3

(8.G.C.9)

14. Jameson found a large pine cone in Yellowstone National Park while on vacation with his family. The diameter of the pine cone (shaped like a cone) is 6 inches with a height of 9 inches? What is the approximate volume, to the nearest cubic inch, of the cone?

_____ in^3

(8.G.C.9)

15. While Lauryn was on a field trip with her class, she saw an unusual sphere filled with a blue liquid. What is the approximate volume, to the nearest tenth of a cubic yard, of the sphere if it has a radius of 10 yds? Use $\pi=3.14$.

_____ yds^3

(8.G.C.9)

16. A group of guys from the school's varsity basketball team volunteered some time at a local youth center. They brought a large round, lightweight ball to play some push ball games. What is the approximate volume, to the nearest tenth of a cubic foot, of the ball they will be playing with if the diameter is 5 ft?

_____ ft^3

(8.G.C.9)

GEOMETRY

17. What is the approximate volume, rounded to the nearest whole cubic meter, of a cone if the radius is 11.9 m and the height is 19.9 m? Use $\pi=3.14$.

_____ m^3

(8.G.C.9)

18. What is the approximate volume, to the nearest whole cubic meter, of a cone if the radius is 9.6m and the height is 14.1m? Use $\pi=3.14$.

_____ m^3

(8.G.C.9)

19. True or False: The approximate volume of a cylinder that has a radius of 10 m and a height of 8 m is 2512 m^3.

A. True   **B.** False

(8.G.C.9)

20. True or False: The approximate volume of a cylinder whose radius is 9 yd and height is 10 yd is 2500 yd^3.

A. True   **B.** False

(8.G.C.9)

VOLUME OF 3-DIMENSIONAL SHAPES

CHAPTER REVIEW

GEOMETRY

1. Ron describes the transformation that takes Figure A to Figure B as shown on this graph.

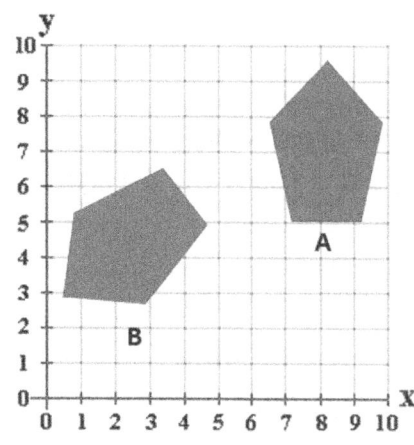

   Which description matches the transformation?

   A. Figure A is reflected across the x-axis and translated along the y-axis.
   B. Figure A is reflected across the line y = 5 and translated along the y-axis.
   C. Figure A is rotated clockwise and translated along the y-axis.
   D. Figure A is rotated counterclockwise and translated 2 units to the right.

   (8.G.A.1)

2. **True or False:** One transformation was used to create Image B from Image A.

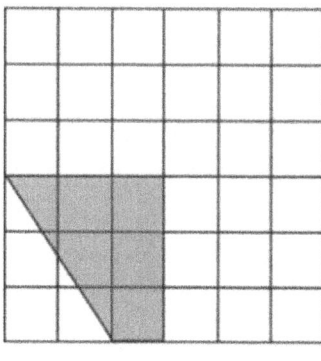

Image A

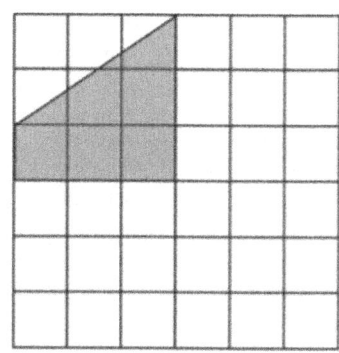

Image B

   A. True
   B. False

   (8.G.A.1)

GEOMETRY

3. **True or False:** If Point S (1, 0) is translated 2 units up, then the coordinates of the resulting coordinates of Point S' are (2, 2).

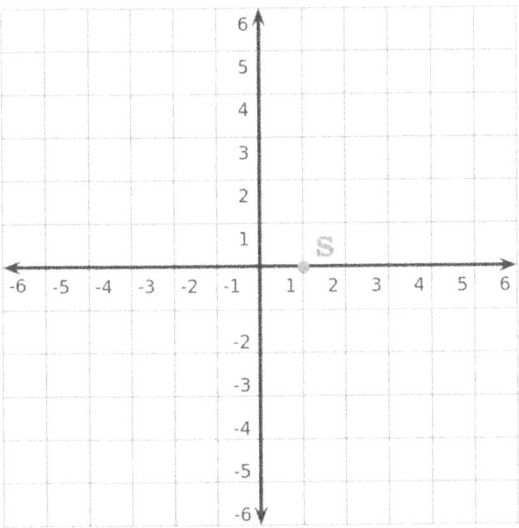

A. True

B. False

(8.G.A.1)

4. Quadrilateral MNOP is congruent to Quadrilateral YVWX. What is the length of line segment YV?

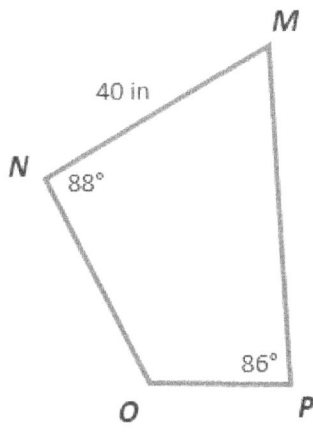

A. 25 inches **B.** 30 inches **C.** 40 inches **D.** 22 inches

(8.G.A.2)

GEOMETRY

5. These shapes are congruent. What is the length of $\overline{DB}$?

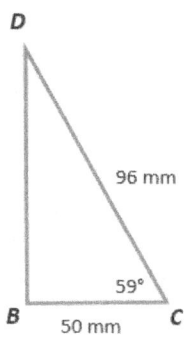 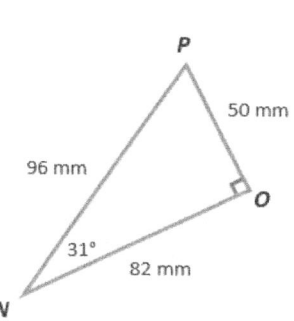

A. 83 mm
B. 82 mm
C. 84 mm
D. 50 mm

(8.G.A.2)

6. Squares ABCD and JKLM are shown on the graph.

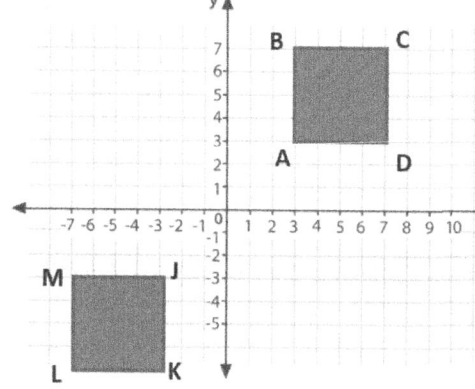

Which sequence of transformations of Square ABCD shows that it is congruent to Square JKLM?

A. A reflection across the y – axis and then a reflection across the x – axis.

B. A rotation by 180 degrees about the origin, and reflection across the x – axis.

C. A rotation by 90 degrees about the origin, and reflection across the y – axis.

D. A rotation by 180 degrees about the origin, and reflection across the y – axis.

(8.G.A.2)

GEOMETRY

7. Point L $(-4, -4)$ is translated 6 units right. What are the coordinates of the resulting Point L'?

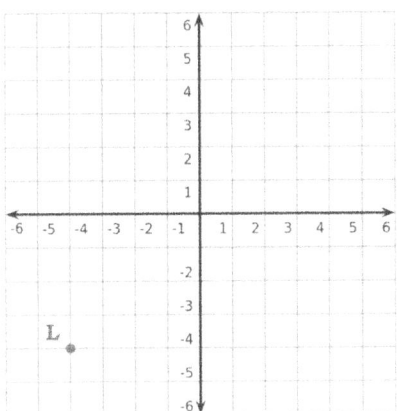

(8.G.A.3)

8. Point P $(6, -4)$ is translated 4 units up. What are the coordinates of the resulting Point P'?

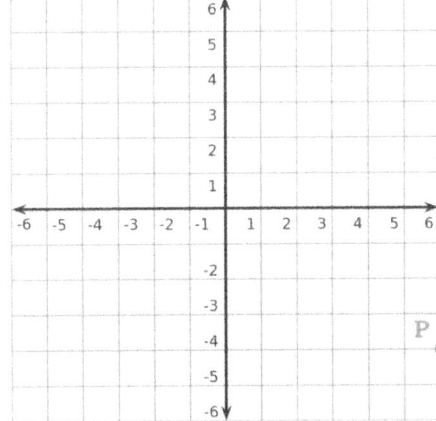

(8.G.A.3)

GEOMETRY

9. True or False: These shapes are not similar.

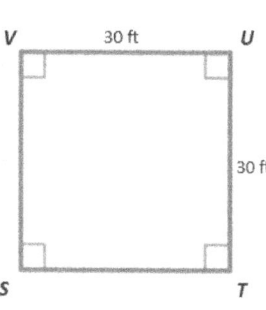
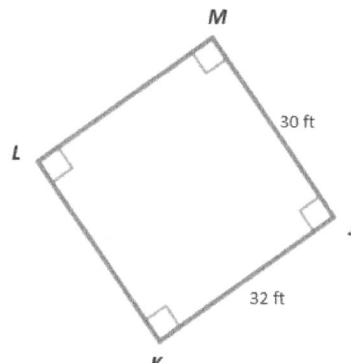

A. True

B. False

8.G.A.4

10. Triangle ABC is dilated by a scale factor of $\frac{3}{2}$ to create Triangle A'B'C'. How would you compare the side lengths of Triangle ABC to Triangle A'B'C'?

_____

_____

_____

8.G.A.4

11. Moremi rearranges the angles of a triangle so the angles connect to form a straight angle. Which set of angles could be the three angles?

A. 56°, 74°, 60°

B. 100°, 154°, 6°

C. 60°, 90°, 50°

D. 42°, 108°, 30°

8.G.A.5

GEOMETRY

12. If the measure of angle EGF is 300, what is the measure of the angle AGB?

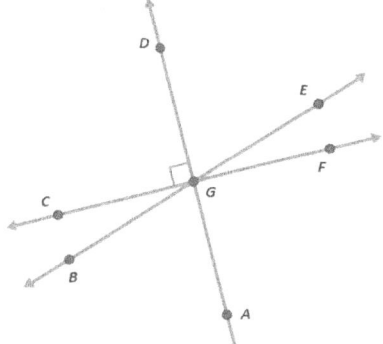

A. 30°
B. 60°
C. 180°
D. 90°

13. If the lengths of the legs of a right triangle are 9 centimeters and 12 centimeters, what is the length of the hypotenuse?

A. 14 cm   B. $15\sqrt{2}$ cm   C. 15 cm   D. $14\sqrt{3}$ cm

14. If the lengths of the legs of a right triangle are 6 centimeters and 15 centimeters, what is the length of the hypotenuse?

A. 16 cm   B. 17 cm   C. $6\sqrt{15}$ cm   D. $3\sqrt{29}$ cm

15. What is the perimeter of a right triangle when the lengths of its legs are 16 m and 12 m?

_____ m

16. What is the perimeter of a right triangle when the lengths of its legs are 3 yd and 4 yd?

_____ yd

GEOMETRY

17. What is the approximate distance between the Point A and Point B?

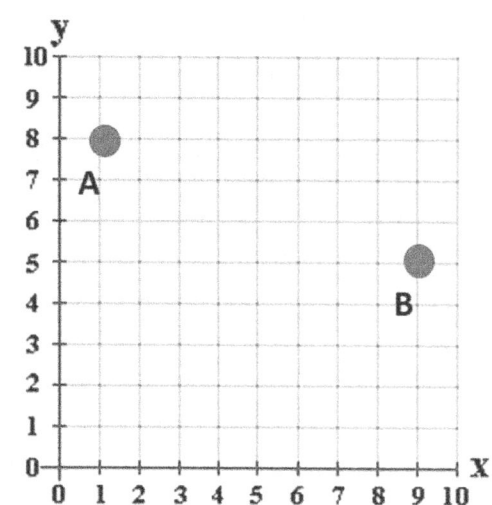

A. 8.0 units

B. 9.2 units

C. 8.2 units

D. 8.5 units

18. What is the approximate distance between Point A and Point B?

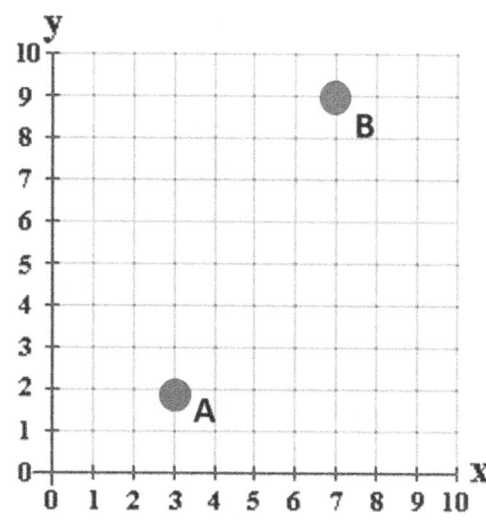

A. 7.9 units

B. 7.5 units

C. 8.6 units

D. 8.1 units

NAME: _____ DATE: _____ 127

GEOMETRY

19. True or False: The approximate volume of a cylinder with a radius of 5 mm and a height of 7 mm is 549.5 mm^3.

   A. True   **B.** False

   8.G.C.9

20. True or False: The approximate volume of a cone with a radius of 4 mm and a height of 11 mm is 46 mm^3.

   A. True   **B.** False

   8.G.C.9

CHAPTER REVIEW

EXTRA PRACTICE

GEOMETRY

1. 180° is how much of a full turn?

   A. Half   B. Third   C. Fourth   D. All

   (8.G.A.1)

2. If the number of degrees an image is rotated is negative, how do you rotate the image?

   A. Counterclockwise   B. Along the y-axis

   C. Along the x-axis   D. Clockwise

   (8.G.A.1)

3. How should a point be transformed across the y-axis for the x-coordinate to change signs?

   A. Rotated   B. Reflected   C. Translated   D. Transcribed

   (8.G.A.1)

4. Complete the congruence statement: QSTR ≅ _____

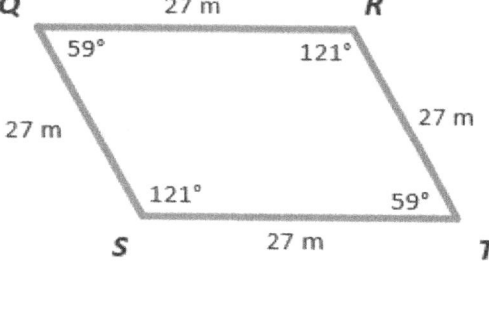
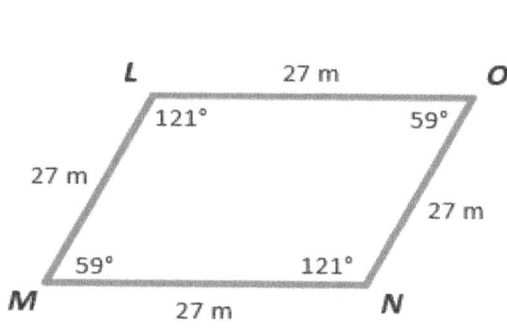

(8.G.A.2)

GEOMETRY

5. Figure A is shown on the graph.

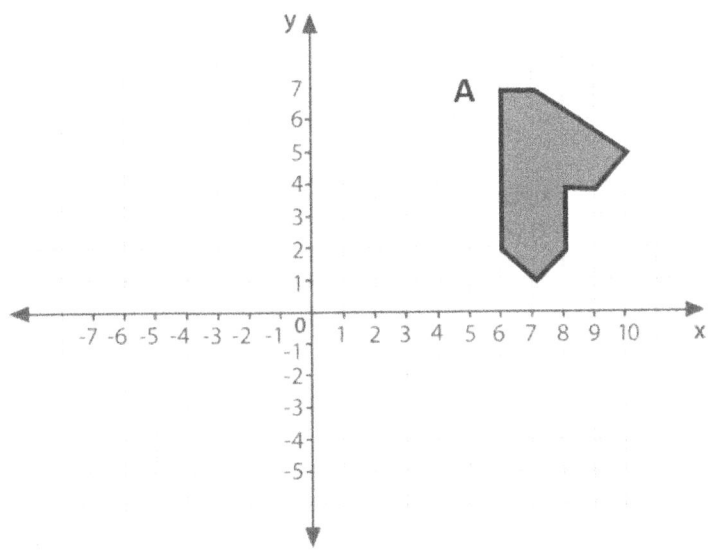

Figure B is created by rotating Figure A 180 degrees about the origin.

Which ordered pairs represent the vertices of Figure B'?

_____

8.G.A.2

6. These figures are congruent. What is m ∠ K? _____

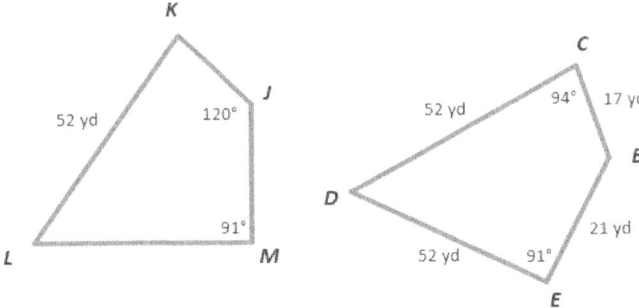

8.G.A.2

GEOMETRY

7. **True or False:** A reflection flips a figure across a line or point to create a mirror image.

   A. True   **B.** False

   (8.G.A.3)

8. Figure A is reflected across the y – axis and then reflected across the x – axis to create Figure A'.

   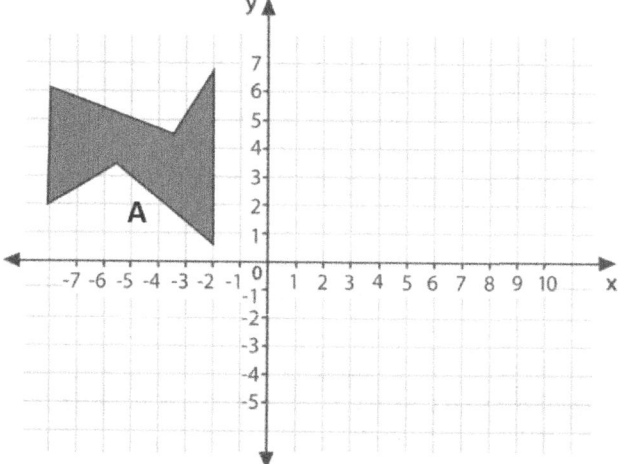

   Draw Figure A' on the coordinate grid.

   (8.G.A.3)

9. These two figures are similar and oriented the same way. What is the degree measure of the angle marked with the "?" ?

   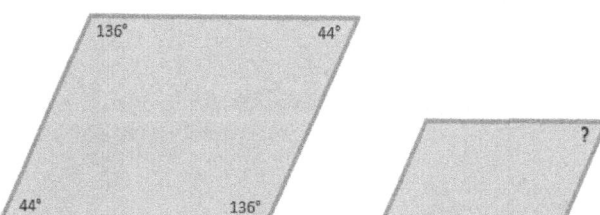

   (8.G.A.4)

GEOMETRY

10. Triangle DEF is dilated by a scale factor of 3 and rotated about a point to create Triangle D'E'F'. How would you compare the angle measures side lengths of Triangle DEF to Triangle D'E'F'?

_____

(8.G.A.4)

11. The figure below contains horizontal and vertical lines. Brandi determines that Angle A is congruent to Angle D.

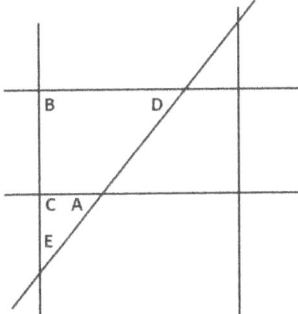

Do you agree with Brandi? Explain why.

_____

_____

_____

(8.G.A.5)

12. Which postulate explains the congruency of these triangles?

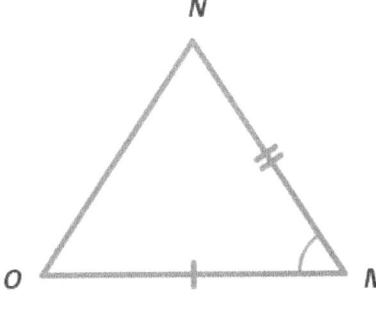 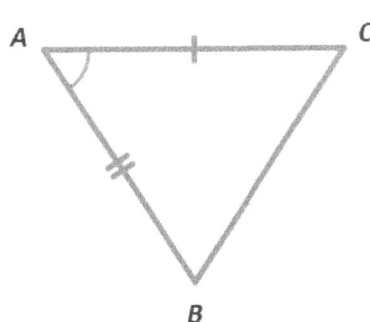

_____

(8.G.A.5)

GEOMETRY

EXTRA PRACTICE

13. If the lengths of the legs of a right triangle are 10 centimeters and 15 centimeters, what is the length of the hypotenuse?

   A. $6\sqrt{3}$ cm   B. 18 cm   C. 19 cm   D. $5\sqrt{13}$ cm

   (8.G.B.6)

14. If the lengths of the legs of a right triangle are 13 centimeters and 15 centimeters, what is the length of the hypotenuse?

   A. 20 cm   B. 21 cm   C. $9\sqrt{6}$ cm   D. $\sqrt{394}$ cm

   (8.G.B.6)

15. Martin's ladder is 13 feet long. If he places the bottom of the ladder 5 ft from a wall, how far from the ground surface does the ladder touch the wall?

   _____ ft

   (8.G.B.7)

16. Kimi takes a sheet of paper and cuts from one corner to the opposite corner, making two triangles.

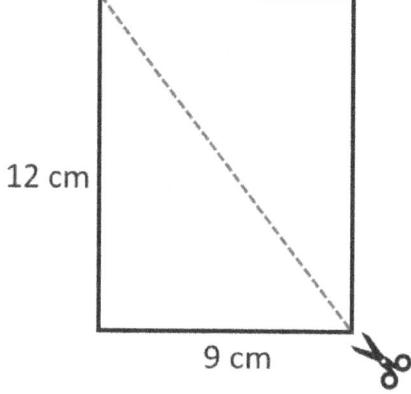

12 cm

9 cm

What is the length of the diagonal cut that Kimi made?

_____ cm

(8.G.B.7)

GEOMETRY

17. What is the approximate distance, to the nearest tenth of a unit, between the points $(-2, 5)$ and $(8, -5)$, without using a graph?

_____

(8.G.B.8)

18. What is the approximate distance, to the nearest tenth of a unit, between the points $(-1, -3)$ and $(7, -5)$, without using a graph?

_____

(8.G.B.8)

19. True or False: The approximate volume of a cylinder with a height of 10 yd and a radius of 7 yds is 2546 yd^3.

A. True   **B.** False

(8.G.C.9)

20. True or False: The approximate volume of a cone with a radius of 4 in and a height of 12 in is 216 in^3.

A. True   **B.** False

(8.G.C.9)

STATISTICS AND PROBABILITY

APPLICATION OF SCATTERPLOTS	**137**
APPLICATION OF LINEAR MODELS	**147**
APPLICATION OF BIVARIATE DATA	**154**
CHAPTER REVIEW	**166**
EXTRA PRACTICE	**173**

STATISTICS AND PROBABILITY

APPLICATION OF SCATTERPLOTS

1. Which correlation does this scatter plot show?

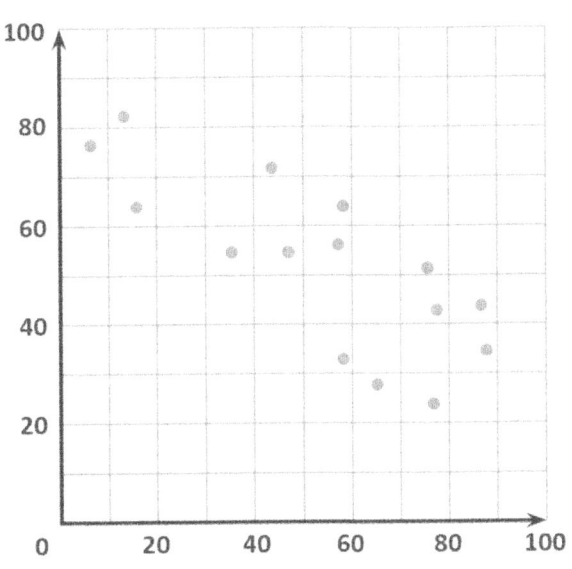

   A. Positive correlation
   B. Negative correlation
   C. No correlation
   D. Discontinuous correlation

   8.SP.A.1

2. Which correlation does this scatter plot show?

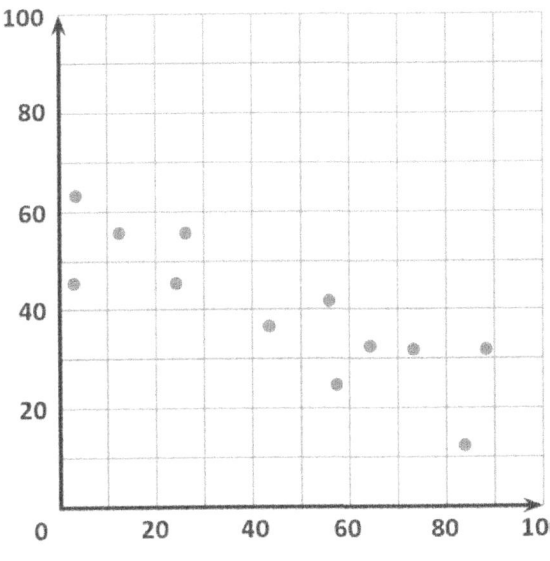

   A. Positive
   B. Negative
   C. No correlation
   D. Discontinuous

   8.SP.A.1

STATISTICS AND PROBABILITY

APPLICATION OF SCATTERPLOTS

3. Which correlation does this scatter plot show?

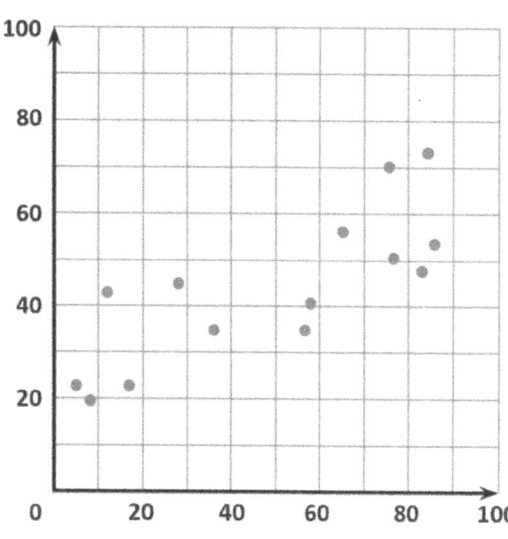

A. Positive
B. Negative
C. No correlation
D. Discontinuous

8.SP.A.1

4. Which correlation does this scatter plot show?

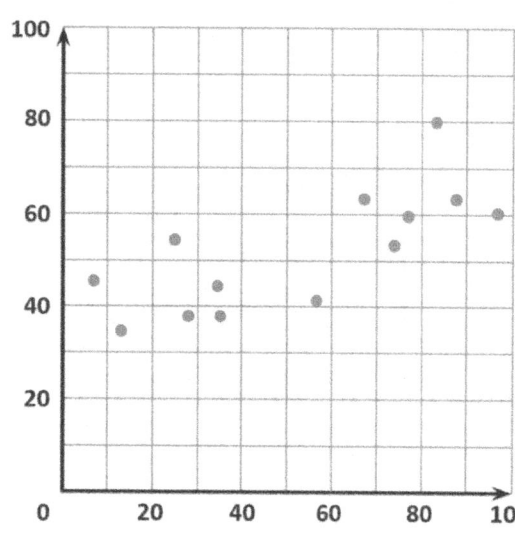

A. Positive
B. Negative
C. No correlation
D. Discontinuous

8.SP.A.1

STATISTICS AND PROBABILITY

5. Which correlation does this scatter plot show?

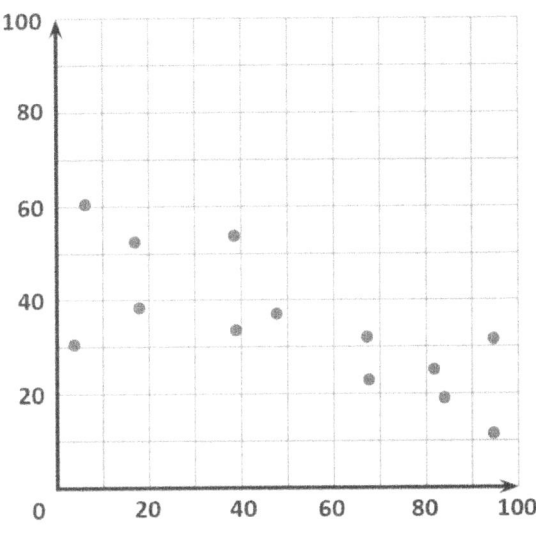

A. Positive
B. Negative
C. No correlation
D. Discontinuous

6. Which correlation does this scatter plot show?

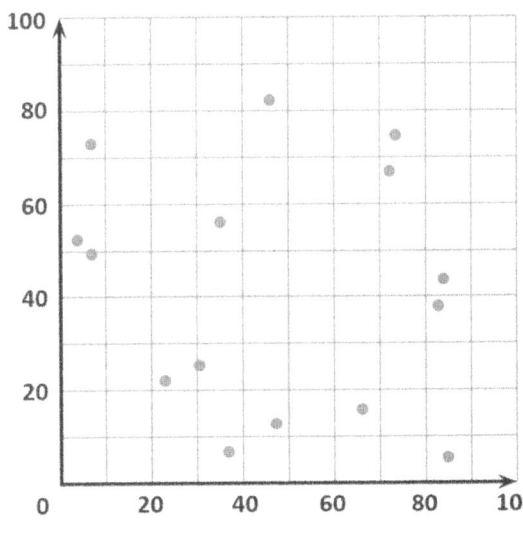

A. Positive
B. Negative
C. No correlation
D. Discontinuous

STATISTICS AND PROBABILITY

APPLICATION OF SCATTERPLOTS

7. Which trend does this scatter plot show?

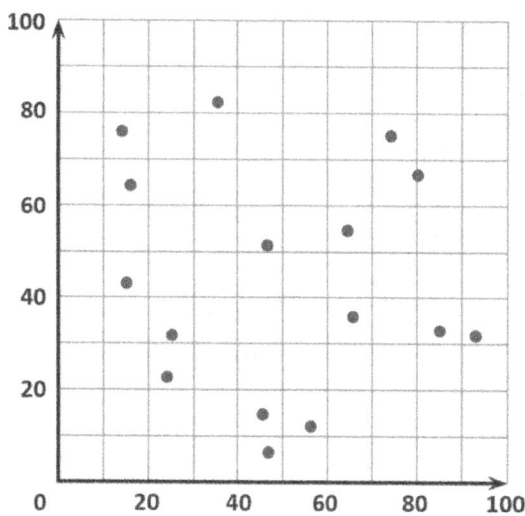

- **A.** Positive trend
- **B.** Negative trend
- **C.** No trend
- **D.** Discontinuous trend

8.SP.A.1

8. In which scatterplot does Point A appear to be an outlier?

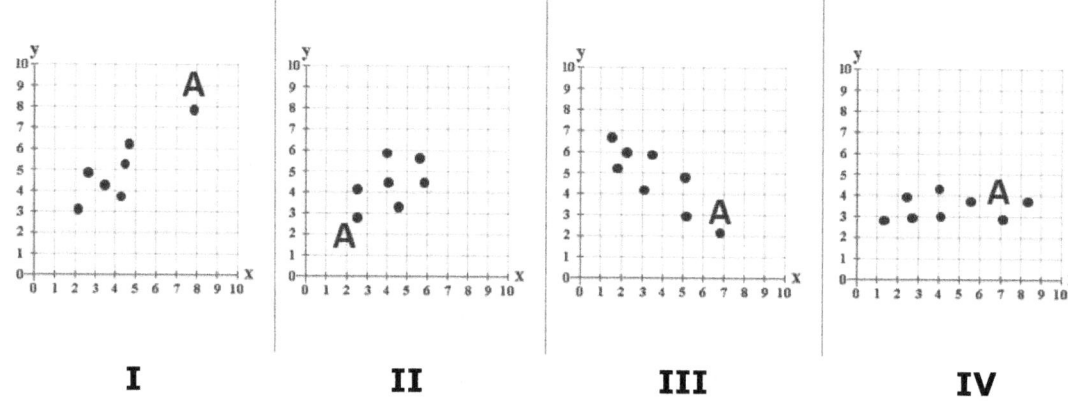

I   II   III   IV

- **A.** Graph I
- **B.** Graph II
- **C.** Graph III
- **D.** Graph IV

8.SP.A.1

STATISTICS AND PROBABILITY

9. In which scatterplot does Point A appear to be an outlier?

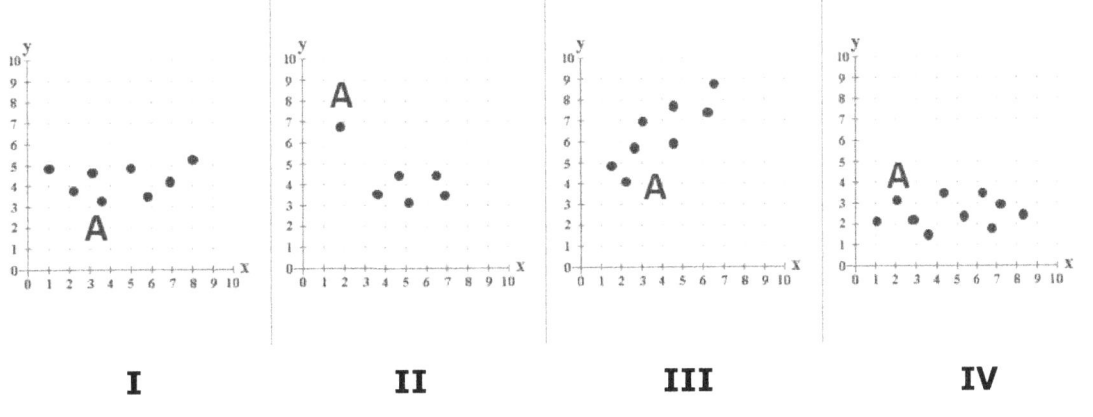

I II III IV

A. Graph I   B. Graph II   C. Graph III   D. Graph IV

10. In which scatterplot does Point A appear to be an outlier?

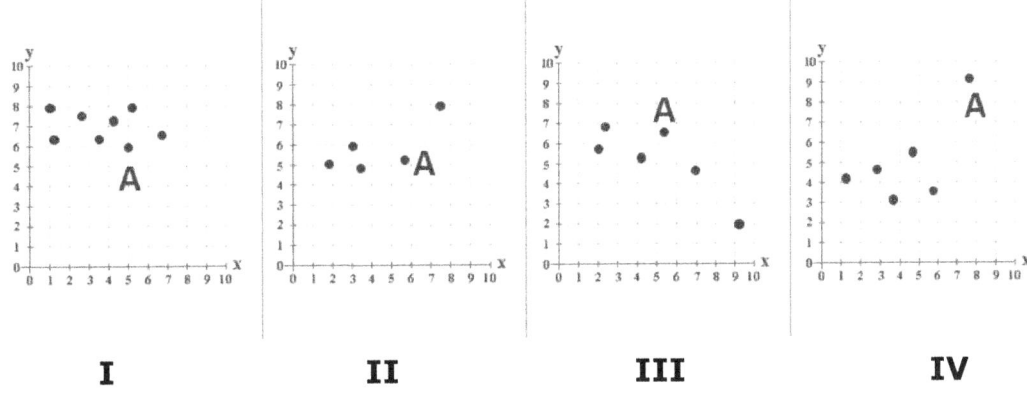

I II III IV

A. Graph I   B. Graph II   C. Graph III   D. Graph IV

APPLICATION OF SCATTERPLOTS

STATISTICS AND PROBABILITY

11. What is the equation of the trend line in the scatter plot?

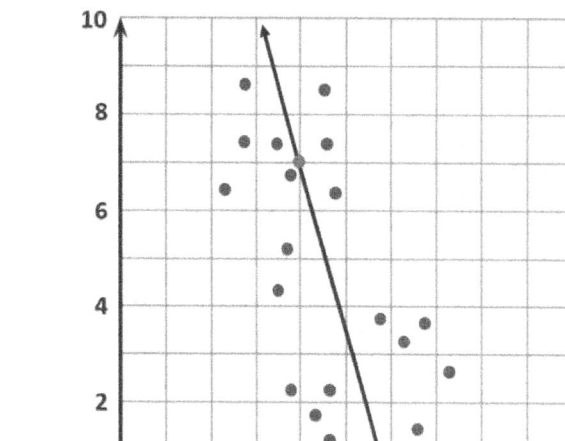

A. $y = -\frac{7}{2}x + 21$
B. $y = \frac{7}{2}x + 21$
C. $y = -\frac{7}{2} + 11$
D. $y = -\frac{7}{2} + 21$

12. What is the equation of the trend line in the scatter plot?

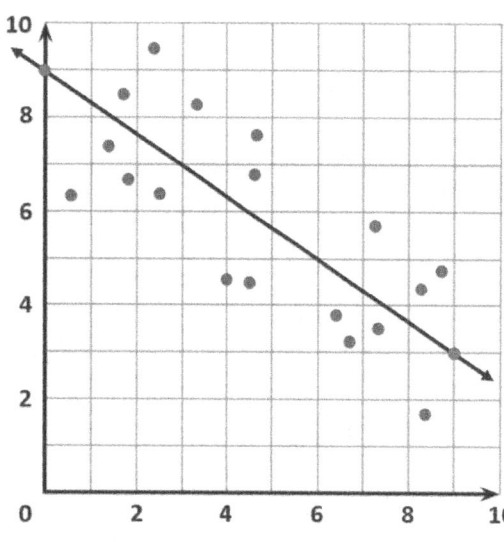

A. $y = \frac{2}{3}x + 9$
B. $y = -\frac{2}{3}x + 3$
C. $y = -\frac{2}{3}x + 9$
D. $y = \frac{2}{3}x + 3$

APPLICATION OF SCATTERPLOTS

STATISTICS AND PROBABILITY

13. What is the equation of the trend line in the scatter plot?

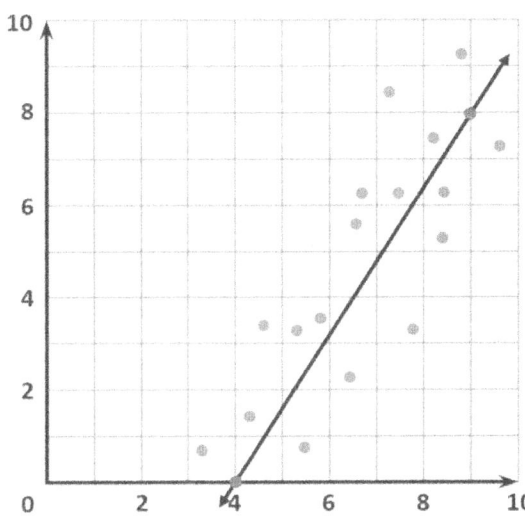

A. $y = -\frac{8}{5}x + \frac{32}{5}$

B. $y = -\frac{8}{5}x - \frac{32}{5}$

C. $y = \frac{8}{5}x + \frac{32}{5}$

D. $y = \frac{8}{5}x - \frac{32}{5}$

14. What is the equation of the trend line in the scatter plot?

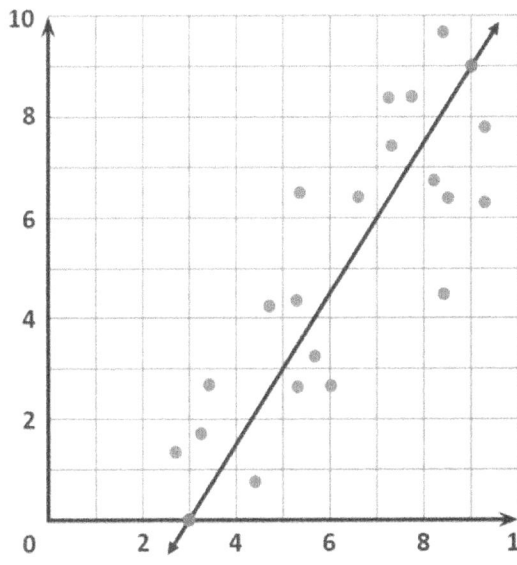

A. $y = \frac{3}{2}x + \frac{9}{2}$

B. $y = \frac{3}{2}x - \frac{9}{2}$

C. $y = -\frac{3}{2}x - \frac{9}{2}$

D. $y = -\frac{3}{2}x + \frac{9}{2}$

APPLICATION OF SCATTERPLOTS

STATISTICS AND PROBABILITY

APPLICATION OF SCATTERPLOTS

15. The data points on a scatterplot shows a strong positive linear correlation. Line *m* is the line of best fit. Which graph represents this situation?

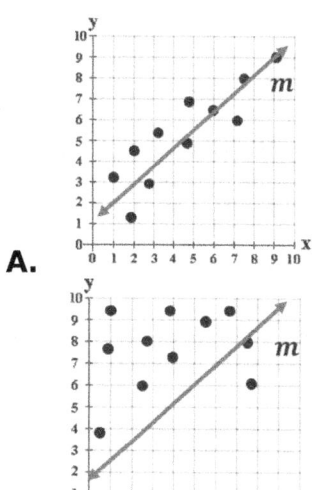
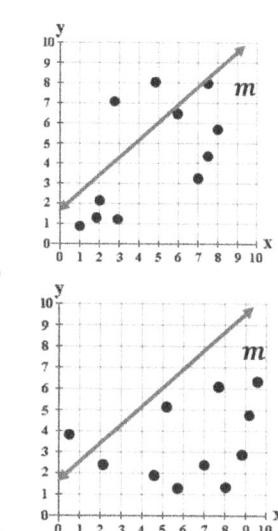

A.   B.   C.   D.

(8.SP.A.2)

16. The data points on a scatterplot shows a weak positive linear correlation. Line *p* is the line of best fit. Which graph represents this situation?

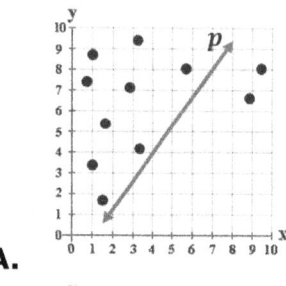
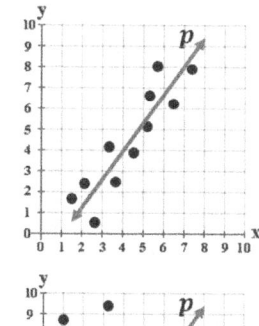
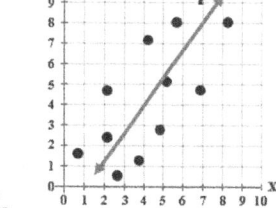
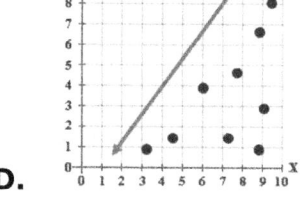

A.   B.   C.   D.

(8.SP.A.2)

STATISTICS AND PROBABILITY

17. Which relationship could be modeled by line of best fit shown on this graph?

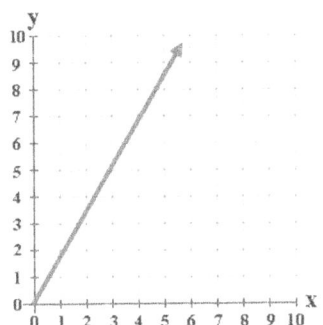

A. The relationship between the amount of weight y a person loses on a diet over x weeks.

B. The relationship between the distance traveled in miles y by a car waiting at a stop sign for x seconds.

C. The relationship between the cost of candy y and the amount x of candy purchased.

D. The relationship between the height y of a burning candle over time x.

(8.SP.A.2)

18. Linda creates a scatterplot and determines these two possible lines of best fit.

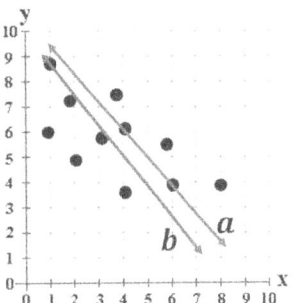

Which line of best fit is the most accurate based on the vertical distance between each data point and the line? Explain your reasoning.

_____

_____

_____

_____

_____

_____

(8.SP.A.2)

APPLICATION OF SCATTERPLOTS

STATISTICS AND PROBABILITY

APPLICATION OF SCATTERPLOTS

19. Draylon creates a scatterplot and determines these two possible lines of best fit.

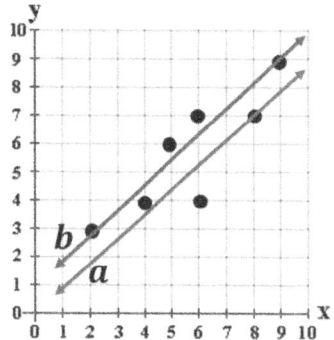

Which line of best fit is the most accurate? Explain your reasoning.

_____
_____
_____
_____
_____

(8.SP.A.2)

20. Kenneth creates a scatterplot and determines these two possible lines of best fit.

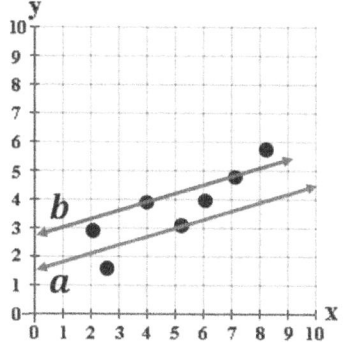

Which line of best fit is the most accurate? Explain your reasoning.

_____
_____
_____
_____
_____

(8.SP.A.2)

UNIT 2: APPLICATION OF LINEAR MODELS

STATISTICS AND PROBABILITY

1. This graph shows how the time, in seconds, required to ring up a customer, at a cash register, is related to the number of items the customer purchases. How long does it take to ring up an item? Round to the nearest whole number.

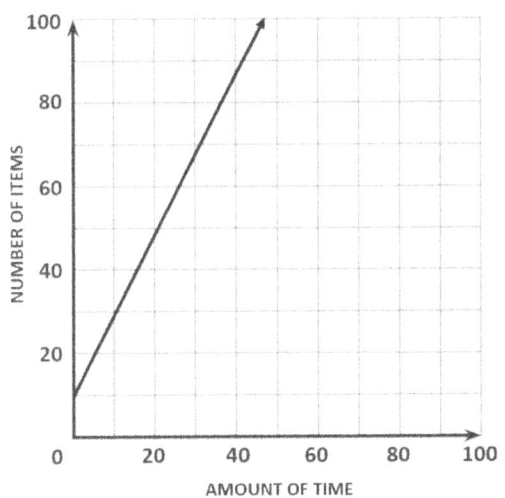

A. 4 seconds per item

B. 2 seconds per item

C. 3 seconds per item

D. 1 second per item

8.SP.A.3

2. This graph shows how the amount of jam, in liters, Pam makes is related to the number of days she spends making the jam. What is the rate of change in the amount of Jam Pam makes per day? Round to the nearest whole number.

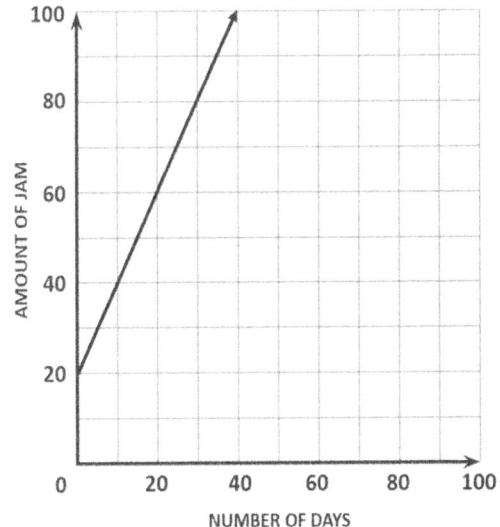

A. 1

B. 4

C. 3

D. 2

8.SP.A.3

APPLICATION OF LINEAR MODELS

STATISTICS AND PROBABILITY

3. This graph shows how the total cost, in dollars, of a members-only speaking series is related to the number of events attended. What is the rate of change? Round to the nearest whole number.

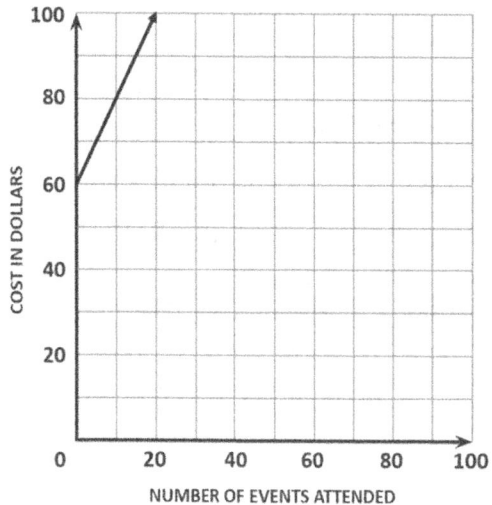

A. 4 dollars per event

B. 3 dollars per event

C. 2 dollars per event

D. 1 dollar per event

4. This graph shows how the total cost, in dollars, of a member visiting an art museum is related to the number of visits. What is the rate of change? Round to the nearest whole number.

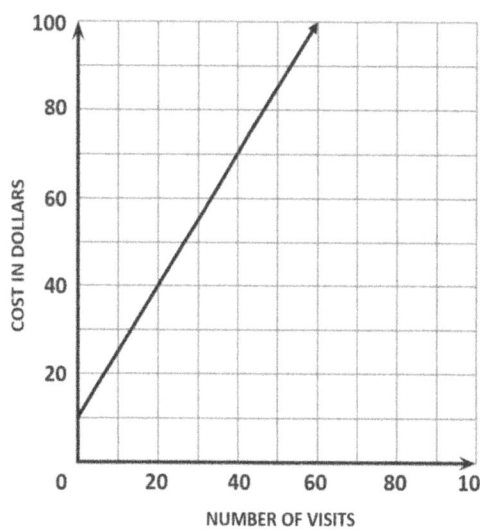

A. 4 dollars per visit

B. 1 dollar per visit

C. 3 dollars per visit

D. 2 dollars per visit

STATISTICS AND PROBABILITY

5. This graph shows how the total number of novels Marlon has in his collection is related to the amount of money, in dollars, he spends on additional novels. What is the rate of change? Round to the nearest whole number.

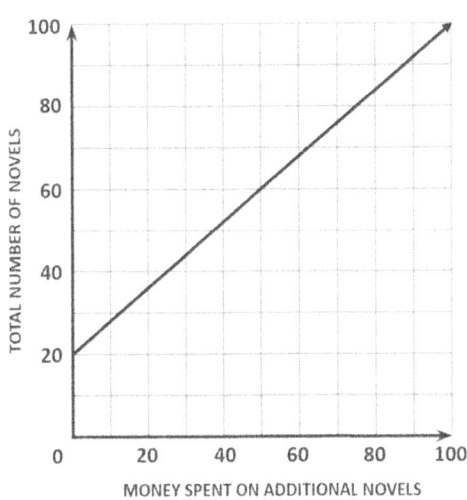

A. 4 dollars per novel
B. 1 dollar per novel
C. 3 dollars per novel
D. 2 dollars per novel

(8.SP.A.3)

6. This graph shows how the total number of hair bands Fredda owns is related to the amount of money, in dollars, she spends on additional hair bands. What is the rate of change? Round to the nearest whole number.

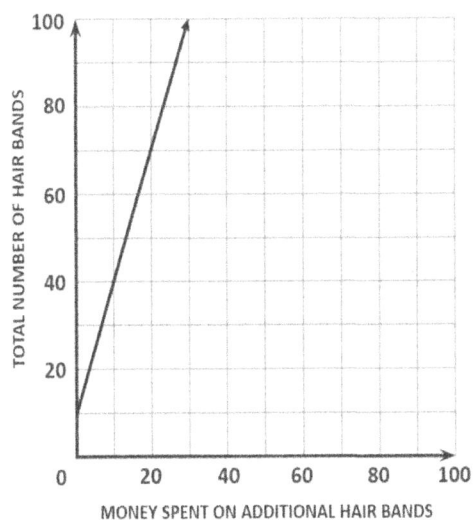

A. 4 dollars per hair band
B. 1 dollar per hair band
C. 3 dollars per hair band
D. 2 dollars per hair band

(8.SP.A.3)

APPLICATION OF LINEAR MODELS

STATISTICS AND PROBABILITY

APPLICATION OF LINEAR MODELS

7. The equation below is used to fit a data set representing the value of a car y after x years.

$$y = 28{,}000 - 1{,}300x$$

What does the slope of the graph of this equation represent?

  A. The original cost of the car.
  B. The value of the car after 1 year.
  C. The amount of interest paid on the car.
  D. The depreciation in the value of the car each year.

8. This graph shows the relationship between the amount of hot chocolate sold and the temperature on a given day.

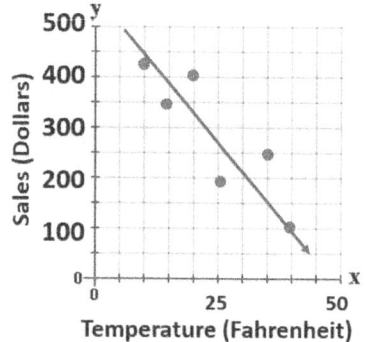

In this situation, what does the slope of the line of best fit represent?

  A. The amount of money earned altogether.
  B. How the average amount of money earned changes based on the outside temperature.
  C. The difference between the highest and lowest temperatures.
  D. The average amount of money earned.

STATISTICS AND PROBABILITY

9. This equation was used to fit a data set representing the total monthly cost y of a phone plan, based on the number of minutes used m.

$$y = 25 + 0.50m$$

What does the slope of the graph of this equation represent?

A. The cost after speaking for 25 minutes.
B. The monthly fee
C. The cost per plan
D. The cost per minute

APPLICATION OF LINEAR MODELS

10. A mobile phone company determines this equation represents the number of hours y of battery life remaining after x hours of use.

$$y = 100 - 4.25x$$

Based on this equation, what is the best prediction of the percent of power remaining after 13 hours?

_____

11. Sarah determines this equation represents the number of hours y of battery life remaining in her phone, after x hours of use.

$$y = 75 - 10.85x$$

What does the y-intercept of this equation represent?

_____

STATISTICS AND PROBABILITY

12. The computers in the library are charging on the power station. This equation is used to fit the data which represents the total percent y of battery power of the computers after x minutes.

$$y = 35 + 9x$$

What does the y-intercept of the equation represent?

_____

13. True or False: Isaac cycles 19 kilometers during each trip to work. The equation that shows the relationship between the number of trips to work (x) and the total distance cycled (y) is $y = 19/x$.

A. True   **B.** False

14. During each week of piano lessons, Maggie learns to play an average of 15 new pieces. What equation shows the relationship between the weeks of lessons (x) and the total number of pieces learned (y)?

_____

15. A receptionist named Brett spends 8 minutes routing each incoming phone call. What equation shows the relationship between the phone calls routed (x) and the minutes (y) Brett is on the phone routing calls?

_____

_____

_____

STATISTICS AND PROBABILITY

APPLICATION OF LINEAR MODELS

16. Camille's graduation picnic costs $1.75 for each attendee. What equation shows the relationship between the attendees (x) and the cost (y)?

_____

(8.SP.A.3)

17. Jacob reads 12 books each month as part of his book club. What equation shows the relationship between the months (x) and the total books Jacob reads (y)?

_____

(8.SP.A.3)

18. Rosa's wedding reception costs $200 for each guest she invites. What equation shows the relationship between the number of guests (x) and the cost (y) of the reception?

_____

(8.SP.A.3)

19. Sancho can grow 14 flowers with every seed packet. What equation shows the relationship between the number of seed packets (x) and the total number of flowers (y) Sancho can grow?

_____

(8.SP.A.3)

20. Leo reads 6 books each month as part of his book club. What equation that the relationship between the months (x) and the total books Leo reads (y).

_____

(8.SP.A.3)

UNIT 3: APPLICATION OF BIVARIATE DATA

STATISTICS AND PROBABILITY

APPLICATION OF BIVARIATE DATA

1. Mr. Benson wonders if boys and girls like different ice cream flavors. He collects data on three flavors: chocolate, strawberry, and vanilla. The results are as follows:

    - Of the 24 students who prefer chocolate ice cream, 17 are boys.
    - Of the 39 students who prefer strawberry ice cream, 18 are girls.
    - Of the 40 students who prefer vanilla, 21 are girls.

    Which statement correctly describes the results of Mr. Benson's survey?

    A. About 17% of the students surveyed prefer chocolate ice cream.
    B. About 18% of those surveyed were boys who prefer strawberry ice cream.
    C. About 7% of those surveyed were girls who prefer chocolate ice cream.
    D. About 39% of the girls surveyed prefer vanilla ice cream.

    (8.SP.A.4)

2. Henri wants to know whether most baseball players are left-handed, right-handed, or able to use both hands to throw a pitch. He collects data on pitchers from 3 baseball teams: The Angels, Red Sox and Rangers. The results are as follows:

    - Of the 12 pitchers on the Angels, 5 are left-handed and 4 are right-handed.
    - Of the 12 pitchers on the Red Sox, 6 are right-handed and 2 can use both hands.
    - Of the 13 pitchers on the Rangers, 3 can use both hands, and 5 are left-handed.

    Which statement correctly describes the results of Henri's survey?

    A. About 35% of the right-handed pitchers play for the Rangers.
    B. About 11% of the players surveyed are left-handed pitchers for the Red Sox.
    C. About 8% of the pitchers can play with both hands
    D. About 50% of the players surveyed are right-handed pitchers for the Angels.

    (8.SP.A.4)

STATISTICS AND PROBABILITY

3. Rumi wants to know whether most baseball players are left-handed, right-handed, or able to use both hands to hit the ball.

She collects data on hitters from 3 baseball teams: The Astros, Cubs and Twins. The results are as follows:

- Of the 25 players on the Astros, 9 are right-handed and 8 can use both hands.
- Of the 25 players on the Cubs, 12 are right-handed and 7 are left-handed.
- Of the 25 players on the Twins, 10 are left-handed and 14 are right-handed.

Which statement correctly describes the results of Rumi's survey?

A. About 47% of the players surveyed are right-handed hitters.

B. About 33% of the Cubs players surveyed are left-handed hitters.

C. About 8% of the Twins players are right handed hitters.

D. About 18% of the Astros players are left-handed or right-handed hitters.

8.SP.A.4

APPLICATION OF BIVARIATE DATA

4. This data table shows the national results of the 2012 Presidential Election.

	Men	Women
Obama	25,748,473	40,167,325
Romney	34,379,444	26,554,060
Other Candidates	764,218	1,154,577

What percentage of the voters were men that voted for Obama?

8.SP.A.4

STATISTICS AND PROBABILITY

5. This data table shows the national results of the 2012 Presidential Election.

	Men	Women
Obama	25,748,473	40,167,325
Romney	34,379,444	26,554,060
Other Candidates	764,218	1,154,577

What is the relative frequency of voters, as a percent, that are women and voted for Romney?

6. This data table shows the national results of the 2012 Presidential Election.

	Men	Women
Obama	25,748,473	40,167,325
Romney	34,379,444	26,554,060
Other Candidates	764,218	1,154,577

What is the relative frequency of voters, as a decimal rounded to 2 places, that are men and voted for Romney or other candidates?

STATISTICS AND PROBABILITY

7. Tiana conducts a survey to determine the average income of the residents in her city. This table shows her results.

		Amount Earned			
		Less than $30,000	At least $30,000 and less than $50,000	At least $50,000 and less than $75,000	Greater than $75,000
Age	18-24	250	500	422	184
	25-34	345	546	678	781
	35-55	578	879	1,045	947
	60 and older	402	300	1,045	987

What is the approximate relative frequency, as a decimal rounded to the nearest hundredth, of the residents between the ages of 35 and 55 who earn at least $50,000 and less than $75,000?

8.SP.A.4

8. Fred conducts a survey to determine the average income of the residents in his city. This table shows his results.

		Amount Earned			
		Less than $30,000	At least $30,000 and less than $50,000	At least $50,000 and less than $75,000	Greater than $75,000
Age	18-24	250	500	422	184
	25-34	345	546	678	781
	35-55	578	879	1,045	947
	60 and older	402	300	1,045	987

What is the approximate relative frequency, as a decimal rounded to the nearest hundredth, of the residents of the city who are between the ages of 25 and 34 and earn at least $30,000 and less than $50,000?

8.SP.A.4

APPLICATION OF BIVARIATE DATA

STATISTICS AND PROBABILITY

9. David surveys residents in his city for an academic report. This table shows the results of his survey.

	HS Graduate	Bachelor's Degree	Master's Degree
Took an AP class	11,056	13,498	9,416
Did not take an AP class	16,988	28,496	22,350

What is the relative frequency, as a two-digit decimal, of residents of the city who have a bachelor's degree and have taken an AP course?

_____

(8.SP.A.4)

10. Conover surveys residents in his city for an academic report. This table shows the frequencies he determined.

	HS Graduate	Bachelor's Degree	Master's Degree
Took an AP class	15,521	11,015	10,789
Did not take an AP class	19,648	15,495	8,748

What is the relative frequency, as a decimal rounded to the nearest 10 digits, of residents in the city who have a bachelor's degree who did not take an AP course?

_____

(8.SP.A.4)

APPLICATION OF BIVARIATE DATA

STATISTICS AND PROBABILITY

11. This relative frequency table reflects the number of people who prefer different pets.

		Men	Women
Pet	Dogs	0.36	0.20
	Cats	0.10	0.26
	Birds	0.02	0.06

What does the relative frequency of 0.26 represent?

_____

(8.SP.A.4)

12. This relative frequency table reflects the number of people who prefer different colors.

		Men	Women
Colors	Red	0.29	0.24
	Blue	0.17	0.21
	Yellow	0.05	0.04

What does the relative frequency of (0.29 + 0.17 + 0.05) represent?

_____

(8.SP.A.4)

13. This relative frequency table reflects the income of 300 people.

		Men	Women
Income	Under $20,000	0.29	0.24
	$20,000 to $39,999	0.17	0.21
	$40,000 or greater	0.05	0.04

What is the relative frequency of the individuals who are men and earn between $20,000 and $39,999?

_____

(8.SP.A.4)

APPLICATION OF BIVARIATE DATA

STATISTICS AND PROBABILITY

14. This relative frequency table reflects the mascots of 32 football teams.

		Division	
		AFC	NFC
Mascot	Animal	0.22	0.25
	Non-animal	?	0.25

What is the relative frequency of the teams that are in the AFC and have a mascot that is not an animal?

(8.SP.A.4)

15. This relative frequency table reflects the mascots of 44 hockey teams.

		Division	
		American League	Natinal League
Mascot	Animal	?	0.16
	Non-animal	0.25	0.32

What is the relative frequency of the teams that are in the American League teams and have an animal mascot?

(8.SP.A.4)

STATISTICS AND PROBABILITY

16. Simon conducts a survey to determine how many people are using social media. Use the data from this survey to create a frequency table in the space below:

- Of the 82 people surveyed between the ages of 18 and 21, 78 people use social media.
- Of the 98 people surveyed between the ages of 22 and 34, 3 do not use social media.
- Of the 103 people surveyed that are 35 and older, 21 do not use social media.

APPLICATION OF BIVARIATE DATA

(8.SP.A.4)

STATISTICS AND PROBABILITY

APPLICATION OF BIVARIATE DATA

17. Dennis conducts a survey to determine whether people prefer bananas, oranges or apples best. Use the data from this survey to create a frequency table in the space below:

- Of the 56 people surveyed under the age of 18, 21 people prefer apples, and 17 people prefer oranges.
- Of the 45 people surveyed between the ages of 18 and 34, 17 prefer bananas and 20 prefer oranges.
- Of the 72 people surveyed that are 35 and older, 19 prefer bananas, and 35 prefer apples.

(8.SP.A.4)

STATISTICS AND PROBABILITY

18. Phillip conducts a survey to determine which power 78 friends best prefer in superheroes. Use the data from his survey to create a relative frequency table in the space below. Round each relative frequency to the nearest 2 decimal places.

- 12 girls and 9 boys vote for invisibility.
- 2 girls and 14 boys vote for superhuman strength.
- 15 girls and 5 boys vote for telepathy.
- 11 girls and 10 boys vote for flying.

APPLICATION OF BIVARIATE DATA

(8.SP.A.4)

STATISTICS AND PROBABILITY

19. Maeve conducts a survey to determine whether people prefer smartphones, tablets, or laptops. Use the data from her survey to create a relative frequency table in the space below:

- Of the people under the age of 15 surveyed: 14 people prefer smartphones, 12 prefer tablets, and 8 prefer laptops.
- Of the people between the ages of 15 and 20 surveyed: 17 people prefer smartphones, 20 prefer tablets, and 18 prefer laptops.
- Of the people over the age of 20: 13 people prefer smartphones, 20 prefer tablets, and 23 prefer laptops

(8.SP.A.4)

STATISTICS AND PROBABILITY

20. This frequency table shows the food preferences of a group of students.

	Pizza	Tacos	Hamburgers
Girls	8	6	5
Boys	9	7	8

What is the difference between the relative frequency of students who are girls and like pizza and the relative frequency of girls who like pizza?

(8.SP.A.4)

APPLICATION OF BIVARIATE DATA

CHAPTER REVIEW

STATISTICS AND PROBABILITY

1. **True or False:** A scatter plot shows a negative correlation if *y* tends to increase as *x* increases.

   A. True   B. False

2. **True or False:** A scatter plot shows a positive correlation if *y* tends to decrease as *x* increases.

   A. True   B. False

3. **True or False:** A scatter plot shows no correlation if there is no obvious pattern.

   A. True   B. False

4. **True or False:** An outlier is an extreme point in a data set that is separated from all other points in the data set.

   A. True   B. False

5. **True or False:** There is no specific formula defining outliers.

   A. True   B. False

6. In which scatterplot does Point B appear to be an outlier?

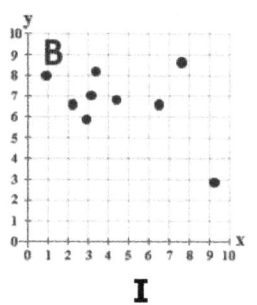
I

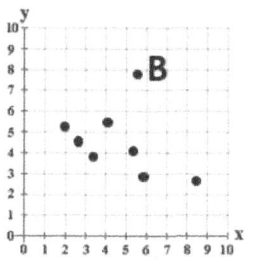
II

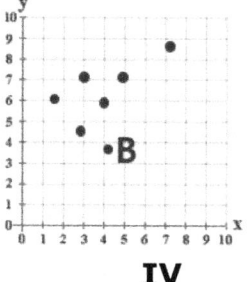
III   IV

A. Graph I   B. Graph II   C. Graph III   D. Graph IV

STATISTICS AND PROBABILITY

7. **True or False:** A trend line roughly describes the relationship between two variables in a set of data.

   A. True
   B. False

8. The data points on a scatterplot shows a strong linear correlation. Line n is the line of best fit. Which graph represents this situation?

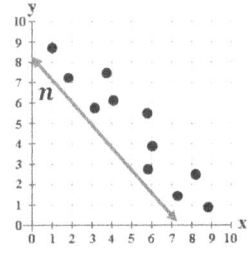
A.

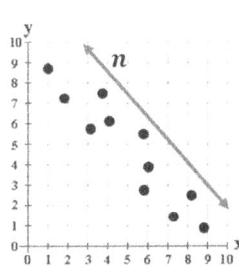
B.

C.

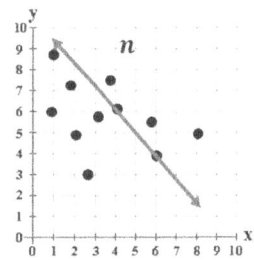
D.

9. What is the equation of the trend line in the of the scatter plot?

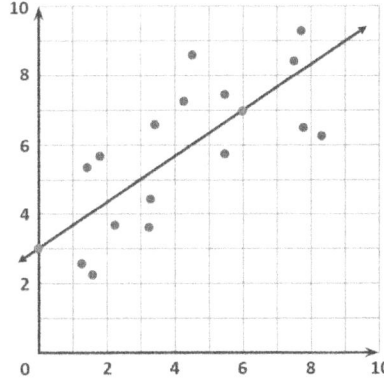

_____

_____

_____

STATISTICS AND PROBABILITY

10. What is the equation of the trend line in the of the scatter plot?

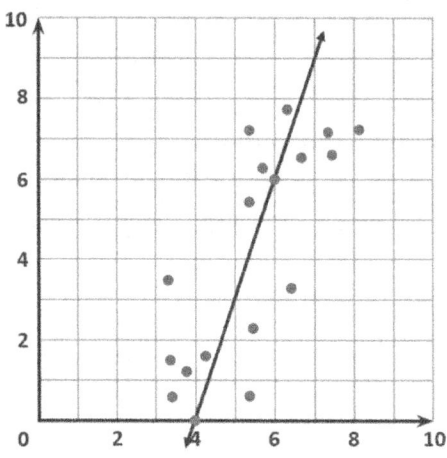

11. What is the equation of the trend line in the of the scatter plot?

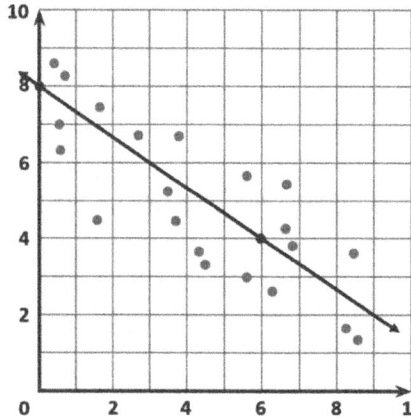

STATISTICS AND PROBABILITY

12. What is the equation of the trend line in the of the scatter plot?

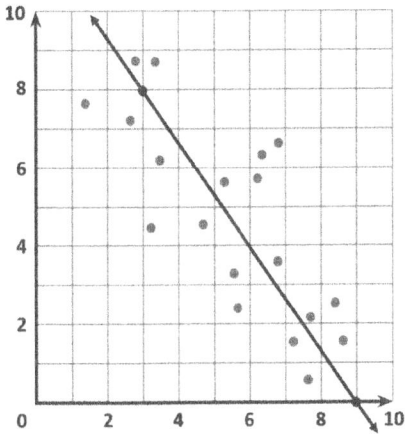

(8.SP.A.2)

13. This graph shows how the distance Garrett cycles depends on the number of trips he takes to work. What is the rate of change? Round to the nearest whole number.

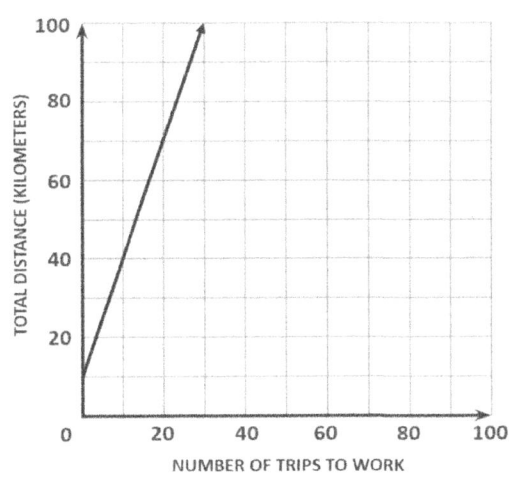

A. 1 kilometer per trip
B. 2 kilometers per trip
C. 3 kilometers per trip
D. 4 kilometers per trip

(8.SP.A.3)

STATISTICS AND PROBABILITY

14. This graph shows how the total pages of notes in Darnel's notebook depends on the number of hours he spends in class. What is the rate of change? Round to the nearest whole number.

A. 2 pages per class
B. 1 page per class
C. 3 pages per class
D. 4 pages per class

8.SP.A.3

15. This graph shows how the total amount of paper Susan's office recycles depends on the number of weeks since they started the new recycling plan. What is the rate of change? Round to the nearest whole number.

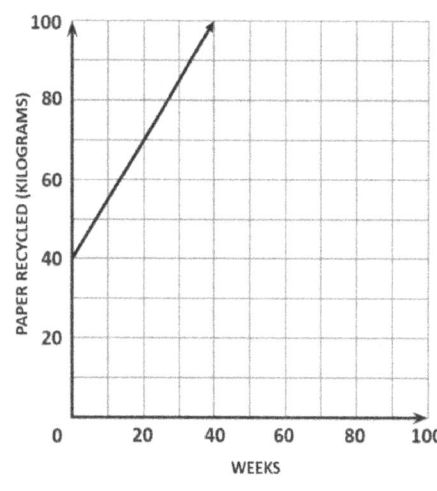

A. 1 kg per week
B. 2 kg per week
C. 3 kg per week
D. 4 kg per week

8.SP.A.3

STATISTICS AND PROBABILITY

16. This table shows bivariate measurement data for the height of a plant, in cm, over a period of 9 weeks.

Time (weeks)	1	2	4	7	9
Height (cm)	8	11	14	22	27

Explain what the slope of the line of best fit could represent in this situation.

_____

_____

8.SP.A.3

17. The data in this table shows the results of a survey. What is the relative frequency of males who had a negative opinion about the topic? Round your answer to the nearest two decimal places.

Gender	Positive Opinion	Negative Opinion	Neutral Opinion
Female	21	5	8
Male	12	25	2

_____

8.SP.A.4

18. The data in this table shows the results of a survey. What is the relative frequency of the participants who have a college degree and earn an income over $25,000? Round your answer to the nearest two decimal places.

	Income Below $25,000	Income Above $25,000
Have a College Degree	11	48
Do not a College Degree	29	17

_____

8.SP.A.4

STATISTICS AND PROBABILITY

19. How many participants in the survey shown below, do not have a college degree, but make more than $25,000?

	Income Below $25,000	Income Above $25,000
Have a College Degree	11	48
Do not a College Degree	29	17

(8.SP.A.4)

20. How many more participants, in the survey below, who do not have a college degree, and have an income that is below $25,000, than those who do not have a college degree, but have an income above $25,000?

	Income Below $25,000	Income Above $25,000
Have a College Degree	11	48
Do not a College Degree	29	17

(8.SP.A.4)

EXTRA PRACTICE

STATISTICS AND PROBABILITY

1. **True or False:** To choose the correct scatter corelation, omit the outlier.

   A. True   B. False

2. **True or False:** Just one outlier can have a drastic effect on the correlation or the least squares regression line.

   A. True   B. False

3. In the following scatter plot with the best fit line is graphed. What is a good estimate of the y-value if the x-value was 40?

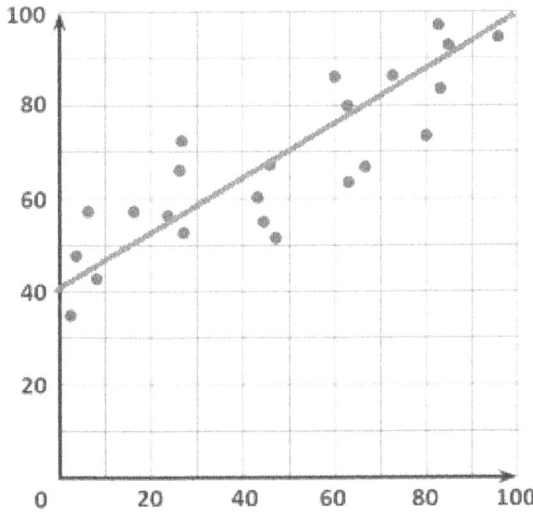

_____

STATISTICS AND PROBABILITY

4. **True or False:** In the scatter plot below, if the x-value was 60, the y-value be can easily be predicted.

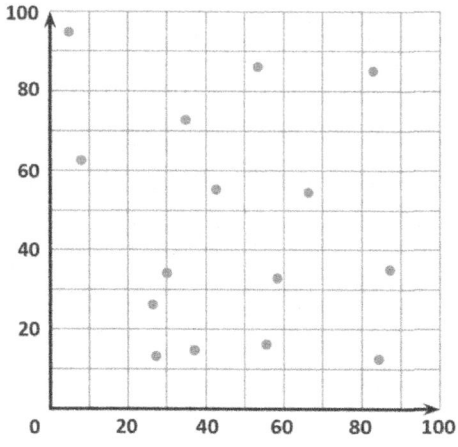

    A. True   **B.** False

5. In the scatter plot below, if the x-value was 20, what would the y-value be?

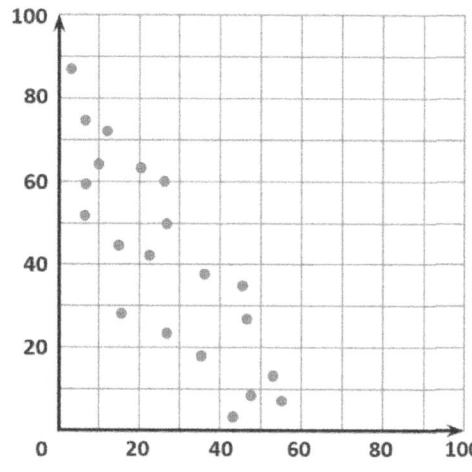

STATISTICS AND PROBABILITY

6. In the scatter plot below, if the y-value was 60, what would the x-value be?

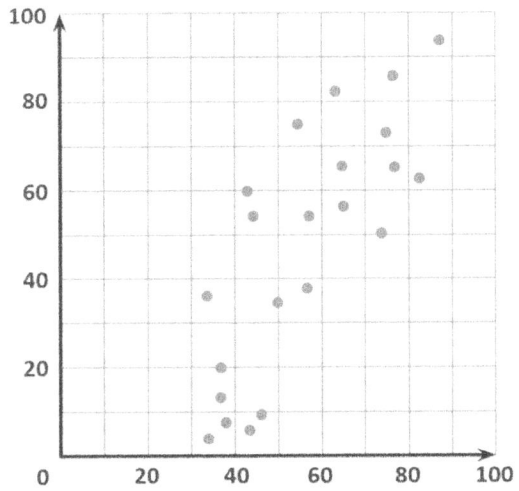

8.SP.A.1

7. What is the equation of the trend line in the of the scatter plot?

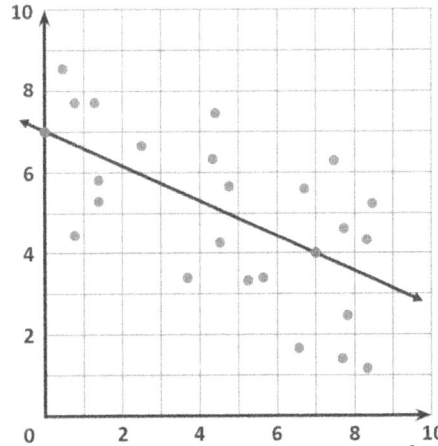

8.SP.A.2

STATISTICS AND PROBABILITY

8. What is the equation of the trend line in the of the scatter plot?

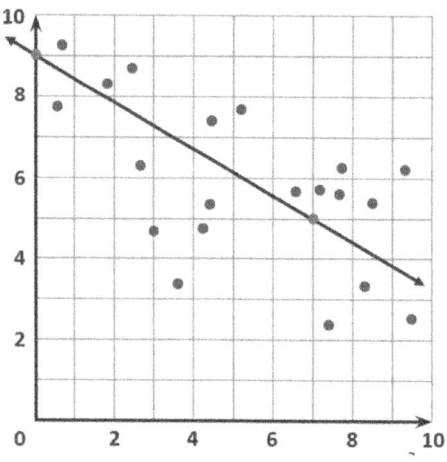

9. What is the equation of the trend line in the of the scatter plot?

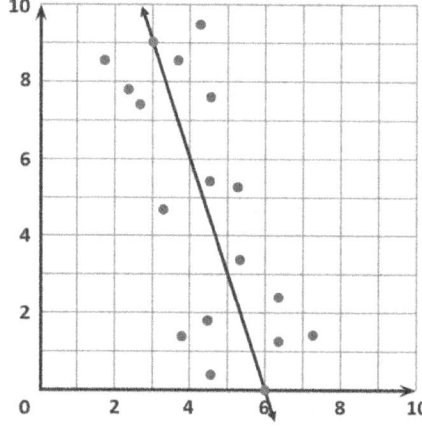

STATISTICS AND PROBABILITY

10. What is the equation of the trend line in the of the scatter plot?

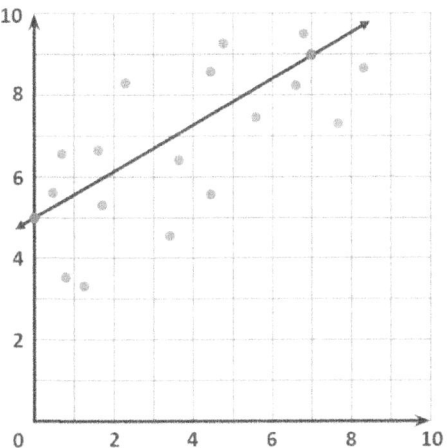

(8.SP.A.2)

11. What is the equation of the trend line in the of the scatter plot?

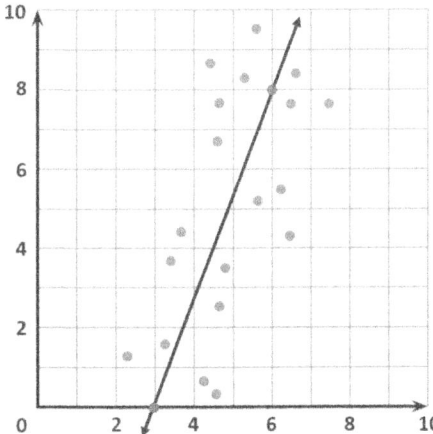

(8.SP.A.2)

STATISTICS AND PROBABILITY

12. Create a scatter plot and determine the line of best fit for the data points in this table.

Food	Total Fat (g)	Total Calories
Hamburger	9	260
Pizza	11	305
Chicken Nuggets	12	400
Turkey Sandwich	8	405
Fries	15	460
Tacos	13	410

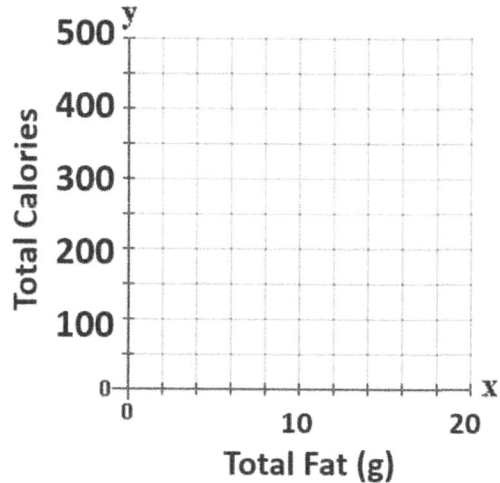

13. Roger learns 27 new appetizer recipes during each week of culinary school.

True or False: The equation that shows the relationship between the number of weeks (x) and the number of appetizer recipes (y) is $y = 27x$.

A. True

B. False

NAME: _____ DATE: _____

STATISTICS AND PROBABILITY

EXTRA PRACTICE

14. Hannah buys 104 postcards during each day of vacation.

True or False: The equation that shows the relationship between the days of vacation (x) and the number of postcards bought (y) is $y = 104 - x$.

A. True   B. False

(8.SP.A.3)

15. Eric's birthday party costs $2 for every guest he invites. What equation shows the relationship between the guests (x) and the cost (y)?

_____

(8.SP.A.3)

16. This table shows bivariate measurement data for annual income and the years of education for a group of people.

Education (years)	Annual Income (dollars)
10	40,000
12	35,000
13	67,000
14	78,000
16	127,000

Explain what the slope of the line of best fit could represent in this situation.

_____

_____

_____

(8.SP.A.3)

STATISTICS AND PROBABILITY

17. How many people prefer oranges?

Age	Prefer Oranges	Prefer Apples
Under 18	29	44
18 to 30	13	25
Over 30	36	20

(8.SP.A.4)

18. How many students, who listened to music as they studied, made below a 90 on the assessment?

	Made a 90 or above on assesment	Made below a 90 on assesment
Student listened to music as they studied	9	43
Student did not listen to music as they studied	48	7

(8.SP.A.4)

19. How many students do not prefer homework?

	Prefer Homework	Prefer Classwork
Male	2	7
Female	4	9

(8.SP.A.4)

STATISTICS AND PROBABILITY

20. How many pencils are Yellow?

Color	Pen	Pencil
Yellow	1	3
Red	5	8
Green	3	4

8.SP.A.4

COMPREHENSIVE ASSESSMENTS

prepaze   www.prepaze.com

ASSESSMENT ①

COMPREHENSIVE ASSESSMENTS

1. Which square root is an irrational number?

    A. $\sqrt{144}$ B. $\sqrt{17}$ C. $\sqrt{49}$ D. $\sqrt{625}$

2. Which letter represents the square root of 111 on this number line?

    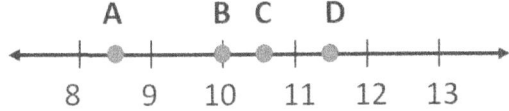

    A. A B. B C. C D. D

3. Find the value of y in the ordered pair $(-1, y)$ given the equation
    $$y = \frac{1}{2}x - 2.$$

    A. $-\frac{1}{2}$ B. $-2\frac{1}{2}$ C. -3 D. -1

4. Which situation best describes the graph below?

    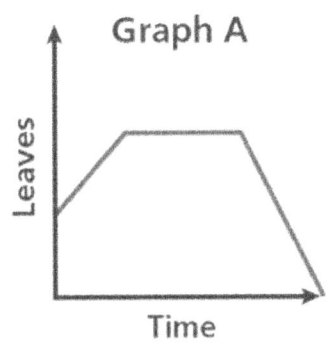

    Graph A

    A. Leaves grow on a tree in the spring, stay on a tree all summer and then fall off rapidly in the fall.

    B. Leaves begin to fall slowly at the beginning of the fall, and then fall off rapidly at the end of the season.

    C. Leaves grow on a tree in the spring and do not fall off the tree at all.

    D. The amount of leaves on this tree does not change throughout the year.

COMPREHENSIVE ASSESSMENTS

ASSESSMENT 1

5. Which situation below best represents the equation: $f(m) = 15 + 9m$?

   A. The membership of a gym costs $15 per month plus $9 initial fee
   B. The membership of a gym costs $9 per month plus $15 initial fee
   C. The membership of a gym costs $24 per month
   D. The membership of a gym costs $15 per month for adults and $9 per month for minors

   (8.F.A.2)

6. Which function is equivalent to $y = \frac{3}{5}x + 2$?

   A. $10y = 6x + 20$
   B. $6x - 10 = 20$
   C. $6x - 10y = 20$
   D. $20 - 10y = 6x$

   (8.F.A.3)

7. Students are presented with the following graph:

   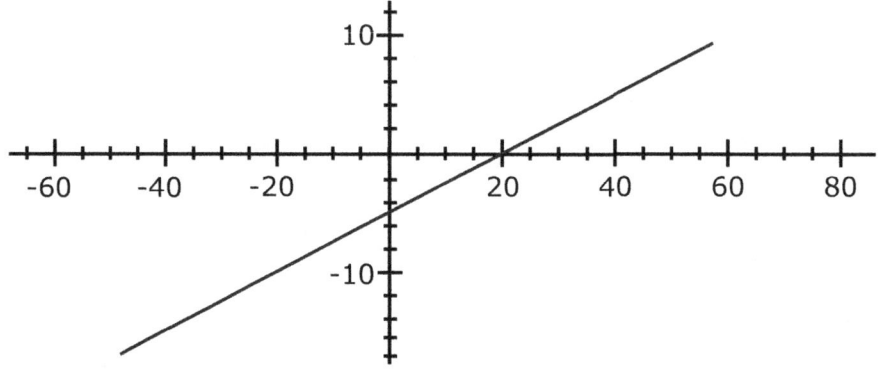

   Which student draws the correct conclusion?

   A. John says this graph is decreasing because it starts low and goes higher.
   B. Kaitlyn says this graph is nonlinear because it is in the negative y.
   C. Akbar says this graph is increasing because as the x-value increases, the y-value also increases.
   D. Edward says this graph is linear because it is a function.

   (8.F.B.4)

COMPREHENSIVE ASSESSMENTS

8. Students are presented with the following algebraic statement: $y = -6x - 6$. Which student draws the correct conclusion?

   A. John says this graph is increasing because its slope is negative.
   B. Kaitlyn says this graph is decreasing because its slope is negative.
   C. Akbar says this graph is decreasing because its y-intercept is negative.
   D. Edward says this graph is increasing because its slope is positive.

   8.F.B.4

9. Sam drew the following graph. Which function did he draw?

   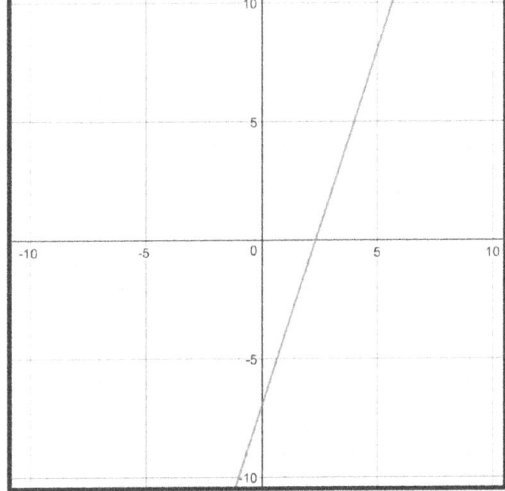

   A. $y = -3x - 7$ B. $y = 3x - 7$ C. $y = -3x + 7$ D. $y = 3x + 7$

   8.F.B.5

10. Each variable in this expression is a real integer, but not 0. Which expression is equivalent to $\dfrac{b^a}{b^{-3a}}$?

    A. b^a B. b^{3a} C. b^{4a} D. $\dfrac{1}{b^{4a}}$

    8.EE.A.1

ASSESSMENT 1

COMPREHENSIVE ASSESSMENTS

ASSESSMENT 1

11. What is the value of this expression?

$$4^2 \times 4^4$$

A. 4,096   B. 5.286   C. 4.565   D. 6.900

(8.EE.A.1)

12. The cubed root of a number n is one less than 4. What is the value of the number n?

A. 3   B. 16   C. 27   D. 64

(8.EE.A.2)

13. Find the value of $(\sqrt[3]{-8})^2$.

A. 2   B. 4   C. 8   D. 16

(8.EE.A.2)

14. Which number is 100 times larger than 7×10^7?

A. 7×10^{10} B. 7×10^5 C. 7×10^9 D. 7×10^{100}

(8.EE.A.3)

15. Write an expression in scientific notation to represent the number 100 times smaller than three thousandths.

_____

(8.EE.A.3)

16. The population of Florida in 1950 was 2.82×10^6. In 2016, the population of Florida was estimated to be 2.061×10^7. How much larger is the population of Florida in 2016 than in 1950?

A. 7.59×10^3 B. 7.59×10^6 C. 1.779×10^7 D. 1.779×10^6

(8.EE.A.4)

COMPREHENSIVE ASSESSMENTS

17. The population of Oklahoma was 3.923×10^6 and Oklahoma has 5 members in the House of Representatives. How many people does each member represent?

A. 78,460 B. 200,000 C. 784,600 D. 7,846,000

(8.EE.A.4)

18. Which equation has a slope smaller than the function represented in this table?

x	1	2	3
y	3	6	9

A. $y = 4x$ B. $y = 50x$ C. $y = 10x$ D. $y = 3x$

(8.EE.B.5)

19. Vincent plans to use 2 similar triangles to determine the slope of this line.

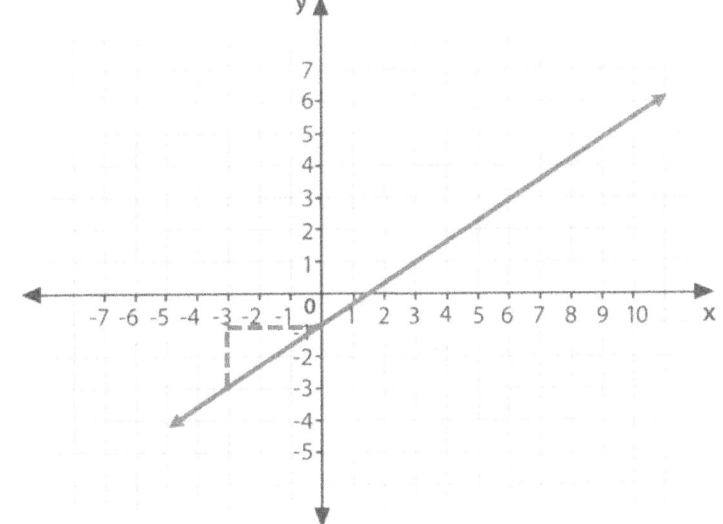

If the first ordered pair in the second triangle is (9, 5), what could the second ordered pair be?

A. $(-5, -4)$

B. $(11, 6)$

C. $(-1, 0)$

D. $(3, 1)$

(8.EE.B.6)

ASSESSMENT 1

COMPREHENSIVE ASSESSMENTS

ASSESSMENT 1

20. Solve for g.

$$3g + 2 = 4g - 1$$

A. $g = 2$ **B.** $g = -2$ **C.** $g = 3$ **D.** $g = -3$

(8.EE.C.7)

21. Melissa keeps a jar for change. The jar currently has 59 coins, which includes q quarters and n nickels. The total money in the jar is $10.75. Which system of equations represents this situation?

A. $q + n = 59$; $q + n = 10.75$

B. $q + n = 59$; $.25q + .05n = 10.75$

C. $q - n = 59$; $.25q + .5n = 10.75$

D. $q + n = 59 (.3)$; $.25q + n = 10.75$

(8.EE.C.8)

22. Sara is taking a 50 question test and she answered all the questions. She earned 2 points for each question she answered correctly, and she lost 1 point for each question she answered incorrectly. Her final test score was 94 points.

Which system of equations describe the relationship between the number of questions he answered correctly (x) and the number of questions he answered incorrectly (y)?

A. $x + 2y = 50$; $x + y = 94$

B. $2y + x = 50$; $x + y = 94$

C. $2y + 2x = 102$; $2y = 50$

D. $x + y = 50$; $2x - y = 94$

(8.EE.C.8)

COMPREHENSIVE ASSESSMENTS

23. Figure A is reflected across the x-axis and then across the y-axis to create Figure B.

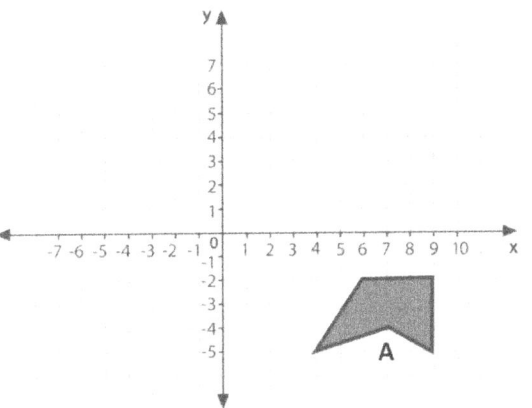

Draw Figure B on the coordinate grid.

8.G.A.1

24. Rectangle ABCD is rotated clockwise around Point B.

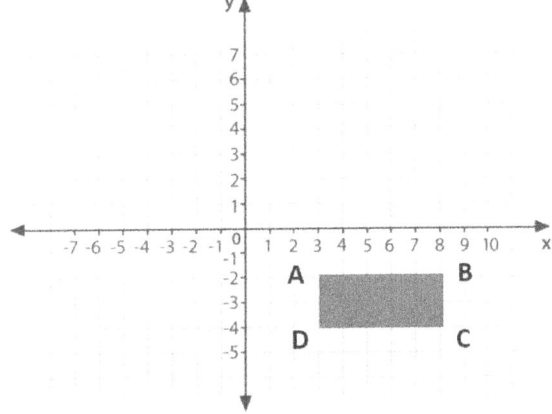

How would you describe the new image, Rectangle A'B'C'D'?

_____

_____

_____

8.G.A.1

COMPREHENSIVE ASSESSMENTS

25. Triangles ABC and JKL are shown on the graph.

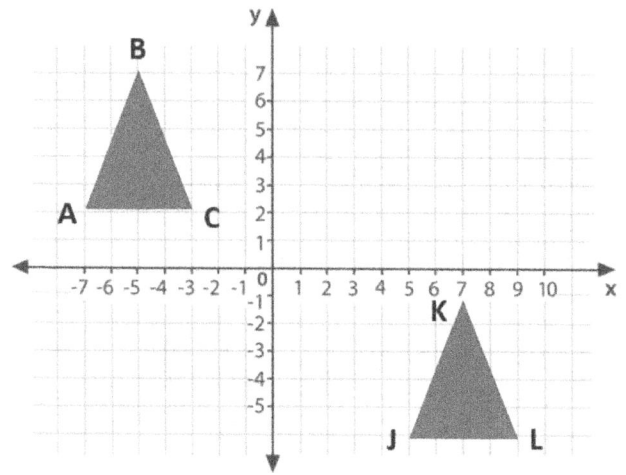

Which sequence of transformations of Triangle ABC shows that it is congruent to Triangle JKL?

A. A translation of Triangle ABC down 1 unit and to the right 7 units.
B. A translation of Triangle ABC up 8 units and to the left 12 units.
C. A translation of Triangle ABC to the right 16 units and down 13 units.
D. A translation of Triangle ABC down 8 units and to the right 12 units.

8.G.A.2

26. Jimmy draws Triangle DEF on a coordinate grid. Point D is located at (1, 3), Point E is located at (3, 7) and Point F is located at (6, 8).

Triangle DEF is translated 3 units down and 5 units to the left to create Triangle PQR.

What are the coordinates of Triangle PQR?

8.G.A.2

COMPREHENSIVE ASSESSMENTS

27. Point R is reflected over the x-axis. What are the coordinates of the resulting Point R'?

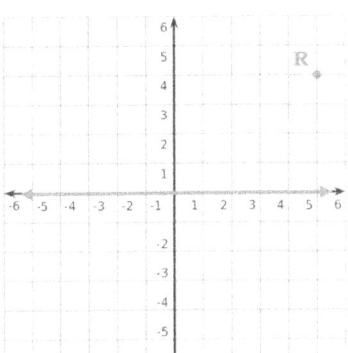

A. $(5, -5)$
B. $(5, -4)$
C. $(-4, 5)$
D. $(-5, -4)$

8.G.A.3

28. Point Z is reflected across the y-axis. What are the coordinates of the resulting Point Z'?

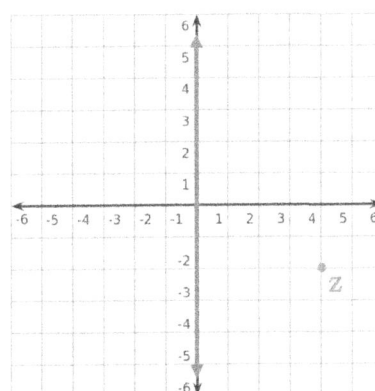

A. $(-4, 2)$
B. $(4, -2)$
C. $(-4, -2)$
D. $(4, 2)$

8.G.A.3

29. Triangle ABC is dilated by a scale factor of $\frac{5}{2}$ to create Triangle A'B'C'. How would you compare the lengths the sides of Triangle ABC to Triangle A'B'C'?

_____

_____

_____

8.G.A.4

COMPREHENSIVE ASSESSMENTS

ASSESSMENT 1

30. Two transformations are performed on Rectangle ABCD. One vertex is on the origin and does not move. Point A is located at $(-4, -8)$. The first transformation is a reflection across the x-axis. The second transformation will create a similar image and reduce the side lengths of the rectangle to $\frac{1}{4}$ the original size.

What are the coordinates for A'?

_____

(8.G.A.4)

31. Margaret arranges three copies of the same triangle, so the angles connect to form a straight line. Which set of angles could represent the measures of the three angles inside the original triangle?

A. 75°, 41°, 64°
B. 105°, 90°, 84°
C. 125°, 125°, 60°
D. 98°, 145°, 78°

(8.G.A.5)

32. The figure below contains horizontal and vertical lines. What conclusion about corresponding angles you make from this diagram? Explain your reasoning.

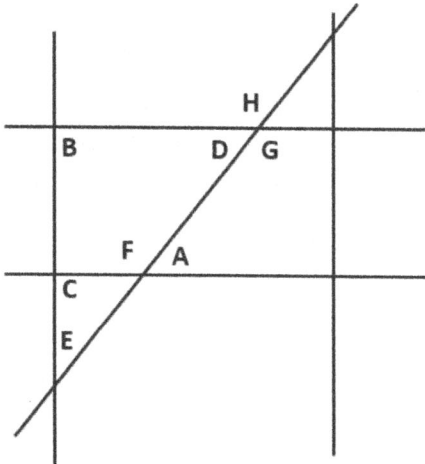

_____
_____
_____
_____
_____

(8.G.A.5)

COMPREHENSIVE ASSESSMENTS

33. If the lengths of the legs of a right triangle are 13 centimeters and 25 centimeters, what is the length of the hypotenuse?

    A. $\sqrt{794}$ cm   **B.** $3\sqrt{74}$ cm   **C.** 25 cm   **D.** 17 cm

34. If the lengths of the legs of a right triangle are 7 centimeters and 8 centimeters, what is the length of the hypotenuse?

    A. 10 cm   **B.** $\sqrt{113}$ cm   **C.** 9 cm   **D.** $6\sqrt{6}$ cm

35. Karin is playing hide-and-seek with Chad and Suzie. Chad is hiding 12 meters south of Karin, and Suzie is hiding east of Chad. If Karin is 20 meters from Suzie, how far apart are Chad and Suzie?

_____ m

36. Shannon takes a rectangular piece of fabric and makes a diagonal cut from one corner to the opposite corner. The cut she makes is 5 inches long and the width of the fabric is 4 inches. What is the fabric length?

_____ in

37. What is the distance between the points (2, 11) and (4, 6), without using a graph? Round your answer to the nearest tenth.

_____

38. What is the distance between the points (8, −5) and (9, −11), without using a graph? Round your answer to the nearest tenth.

_____

ASSESSMENT 1

COMPREHENSIVE ASSESSMENTS

ASSESSMENT 1

39. **True or False:** The approximate volume of a cylinder with a diameter 8 mm and a height of 12 mm is 603 mm^3.

   A. True

   B. False

   (8.G.C.9)

40. In the following scatter plot, if the x value was 50, what would the y-value be?

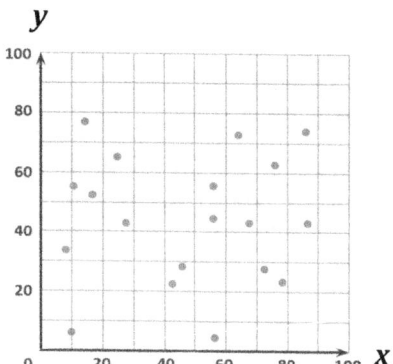

   _____

   (8.SP.A.1)

41. In which scatterplot does Point B appear to be an outlier?

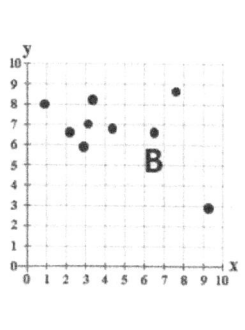 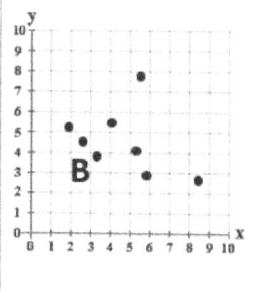 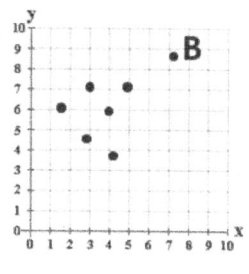

   I   II   III   IV

   A. Graph I
   B. Graph II
   C. Graph III
   D. Graph IV

   (8.SP.A.1)

COMPREHENSIVE ASSESSMENTS

42. What is the equation of the trend line in the of the scatterplot?

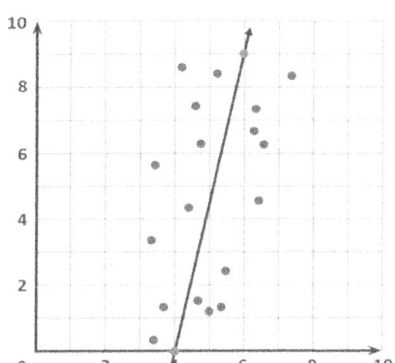

_____

_____

_____

8.SP.A.2

43. Amber creates a scatterplot and determines these two possible lines of best fit.

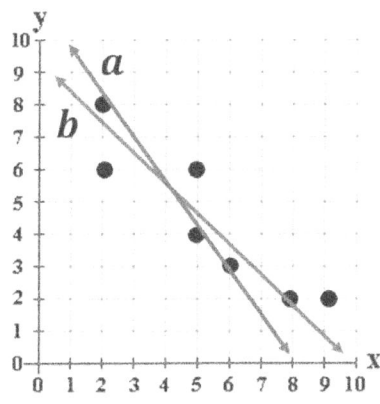

Which line of best fit is the most accurate based on the horizontal distance between each data point and the line? Explain your thinking.

_____

_____

_____

8.SP.A.2

COMPREHENSIVE ASSESSMENTS

ASSESSMENT 1

44. This equation represents the line of best fit for data comparing students' scores on a final exam y to scores on a midterm exam x.

$$y = 54.1 + 0.45x$$

This table shows the data used to determine the line of best fit.

x	35	42	45	50	51	65	60	60	70	85	88
y	65	66	67	78	80	86	90	94	95	82	87

Is it reasonable to interpret the y-intercept of this equation? Explain your reasoning.

8.SP.A.3

45. According to the data in this table, how many students use a pen?

	Male	Female
Use Pen	2	6
Use Pencil	3	4

8.SP.A.4

ASSESSMENT

COMPREHENSIVE ASSESSMENTS

ASSESSMENT 2

1. What fraction is equivalent to $0.\overline{55}$?

   A. $\frac{5}{9}$ B. $\frac{55}{100}$ C. $\frac{5}{10}$ D. $\frac{55}{9}$

   (8.NS.A.1)

2. Which expression has a value between 9 and 10?

   A. π B. π^3 C. 3π D. $\frac{1}{3}\pi$

   (8.NS.A.2)

3. Find the value of x in the ordered pair $(x, 4)$ given the equation $y = x - 5$.

   A. -1 B. -9 C. 9 D. 1

   (8.F.A.1)

4. Which of ordered pairs satisfies the function in the table?

x	1	2	3
y	1	8	27

   A. (2, 4) B. (5, 25) C. (4, 64) D. (64, 4)

   (8.F.A.2)

5. Jose has two car washes by his house. Carwash 1 charges $0.75 per minute and Carwash 2 charges $1.50 for three minutes and then an additional 1.50 per minute after that. Which carwash does this graph represent?

   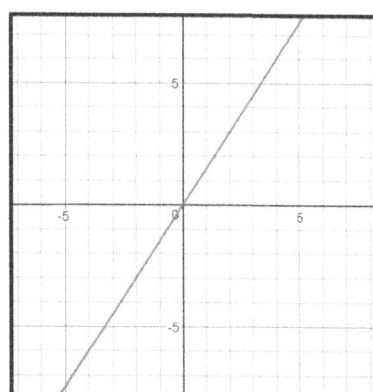

   A. Carwash 1

   B. Carwash 2

   C. Both car washes can be represented by this graph.

   D. Neither carwash is represented by this graph.

   (8.F.A.2)

COMPREHENSIVE ASSESSMENTS

6. Which function is not equivalent to this equation?

$$y = \frac{3}{4}x - 6$$

  A. $8y = 6x - 48$ B. $4y - 3x = -24$

  C. $4y - 3x = 24$ D. $6y = \frac{9}{2}x - 36$

7. Students are presented with the following table. Which student draws the correct conclusion?

x	−5	0	5
y	15	−3	−15

  A. John says the initial value of this function is −3.
  B. Kaitlyn says the initial value of this function is 15.
  C. Akbar says the initial value of this function is 3.
  D. Edward says the initial value of this function is −15.

8. Which equation matches this graph?

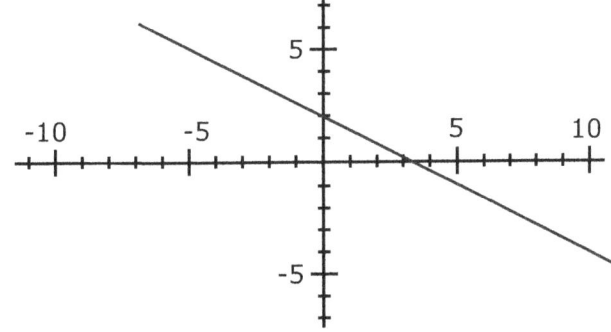

  A. $y = 2x + \frac{3}{5}$ B. $y = \frac{3}{5}x + 2$

  C. $y = -\frac{3}{5}x + 2$ D. $y = \frac{3}{5}x - 2$

COMPREHENSIVE ASSESSMENTS

ASSESSMENT 2

9. Which of the following statements are true about vertical lines?

   A. Vertical lines have undefined slopes.

   B. Vertical lines can be used to test whether a line is a function.

   C. Vertical lines are perpendicular to horizontal lines.

   D. All these statements above are true.

   (8.F.B.5)

10. The area of a circle is found with the formula $A = \pi r^2$, where r is the radius. Suppose the radius of a circle is a^{-3}, which of the following is the area of the circle?

   A. πa^6 **B.** πa^5 **C.** $\dfrac{\pi}{a^6}$ **D.** $\dfrac{\pi}{a^5}$

   (8.EE.A.1)

11. Simplify the expression $\left(\dfrac{a}{a^7}\right)^{-3}$.

   A. a^{21} **B.** a^{20} **C.** $\dfrac{1}{a^{20}}$ **D.** a^{18}

   (8.EE.A.1)

12. Find the value of $\sqrt[3]{27}$.

   A. 3   **B.** -3 **C.** 9   **D.** -9

   (8.EE.A.2)

13. Which response represents all real solutions to the equation $\frac{1}{4}x^2 = 9$?

   A. 3   **B.** ± 3 **C.** 16   **D.** ± 6

   (8.EE.A.2)

COMPREHENSIVE ASSESSMENTS

14. Which expression represents a number 10 times smaller than eight hundred million?

A. $\dfrac{(8 \times 10^8)}{10^1}$

B. $\dfrac{(8 \times 10^{10})}{10^2}$

C. $\dfrac{(8 \times 10^9)}{10^1}$

D. $\dfrac{(8 \times 10^8)}{10^0}$

8.EE.A.3

15. What expression, as a product in scientific notation, represents the number six hundredths times 50.

_____

8.EE.A.3

16. Solve for x.

$$(3.567 \times 10^{-8}) - (5.982 \times 10^{-7}) = x$$

A. $x = 2.415 \times 10^{-7}$

B. $x = 2.968 \times 10^{-7}$

C. $x = 2.415 \times 10^{-8}$

D. $x = 2.9688 \times 10^{-8}$

8.EE.A.4

17. Solve for x.

$$(7.23 \times 10^{-5}) - x = 2.465 \times 10^{-4}$$

A. $x = -1.742 \times 10^{-4}$

B. $x = 4.765 \times 10^{-4}$

C. $x = 6.9835 \times 10^{-4}$

D. $x = 4.765 \times 10^{-5}$

8.EE.A.4

18. Which value is missing from this table?

x	3	7	11
y	2.25	?	8.25

A. 5.25   B. 2.75   C. 4.25   D. 0.75

8.EE.B.5

ASSESSMENT 2

COMPREHENSIVE ASSESSMENTS

19. Write an equation to represent the line shown on this graph.

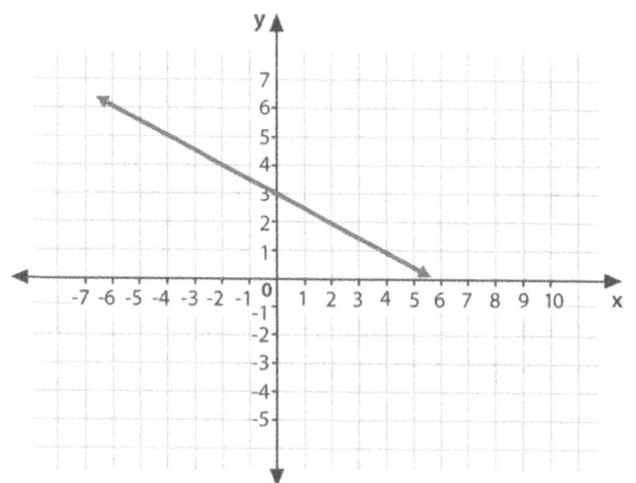

_____

(8.EE.B.6)

20. What is the value of x if $3(x-4) = 2(x+1)$?

    A. $x = -14$ **B.** $x = 14$ **C.** $x = -12$ **D.** $x = 12$

(8.EE.C.7)

21. Which equation has no solution?

    A. $2x + 5 = 3x - 2$ **B.** $2x + 7 = x - 9$

    C. $3 - x = x + 8$ **D.** $2x + 5 = 2x - 3$

(8.EE.C.7)

22. At the concession stand, two hot dogs and two sodas cost $5. Three hot dogs and one soda cost $5.50. How much does a soda cost?

_____

(8.EE.C.8)

COMPREHENSIVE ASSESSMENTS

23. Figure AFBCDE is transformed to create Figure RSTVWZ.

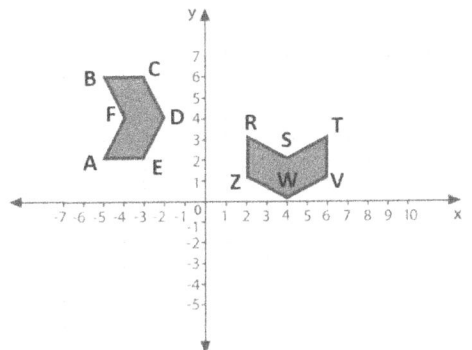

Which angle is congruent to Angle C? _____

Which angle is congruent to Angle B? _____

8.G.A.1

24. Figure A is reflected across the x-axis and then translated 10 units to the right to create Figure B.

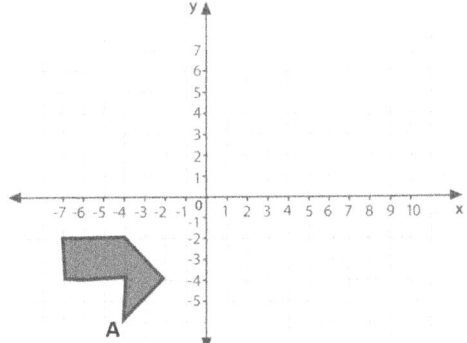

Draw Figure B on the coordinate grid.

8.G.A.1

COMPREHENSIVE ASSESSMENTS

25. Quadrilaterals ABCD and JKLM are shown on this graph.

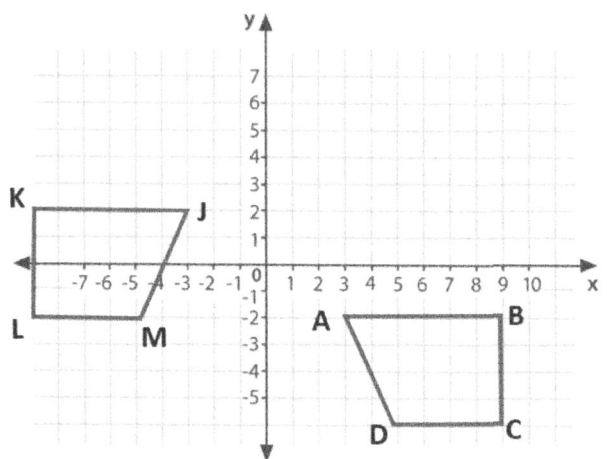

Which sequence of transformations of Quadrilateral ABCD shows that it is congruent to Quadrilateral JKLM?

A. A reflection across the y-axis and a translation 4 units down.

B. A reflection across the x-axis and a rotation of 360 degrees.

C. A reflection across the y-axis and a translation 4 units up.

D. A reflection across the x-axis and a rotation of 90 degrees.

8.G.A.2

26. Heather draws Triangle RST on a coordinate grid. Point R is located at (0, 0), Point S is located at (5, −5) and Point T is located at (−5, 5).

Triangle RST is reflected across the x-axis and translated 1 unit to the right to create Triangle R'S'T'.

What are the coordinates of Triangle R'S'T'?

8.G.A.2

COMPREHENSIVE ASSESSMENTS

27. Point T is reflected over the x-axis. What are the coordinates of the resulting point, T'?

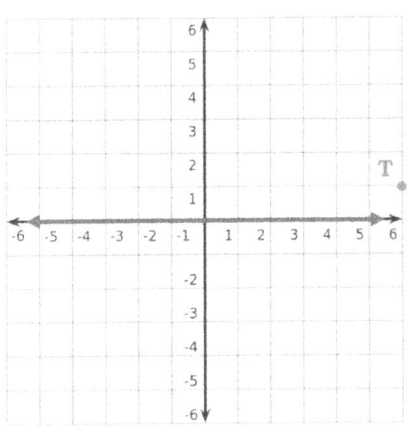

A. $(6, -1)$ B. $(-1, 6)$ C. $(6, 1)$ D. $(-6, 1)$

8.G.A.3

28. Point T is reflected over the y-axis. What are the coordinates of the resulting point, T'?

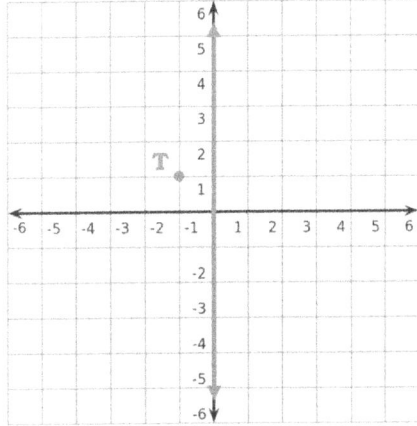

8.G.A.3

COMPREHENSIVE ASSESSMENTS

29. A transformation is performed on Triangle XYZ to create Triangle X'Y'Z'. Point X is located at (3,0). The transformation will create a similar image and enlarge the side lengths of the triangle to 4 times the original size. One vertex is at the origin and does not move.

What are the coordinates of X'?

_____

30. A transformation is performed on Triangle XYZ to form Triangle X'Y'Z'. Point X is located at $(-\frac{3}{2}, \frac{5}{2})$. The transformation will create a similar image and enlarge the side lengths of the triangle to 2 times the original size. One vertex is at the origin and does not move.

What are the coordinates of X'?

_____

31. The figure below contains horizontal and vertical lines. What conclusion about vertical angles can be made from this diagram? Explain your reasoning.

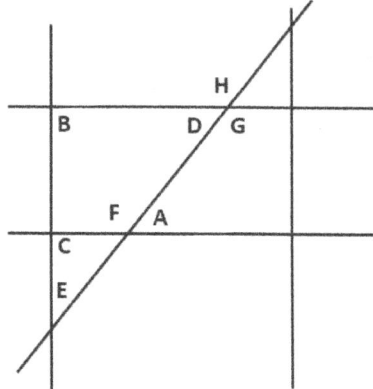

COMPREHENSIVE ASSESSMENTS

32. Lines *l* and *m* are parallel. Angle 2 has a measure of 74 degrees. What is the measure of Angles 8?

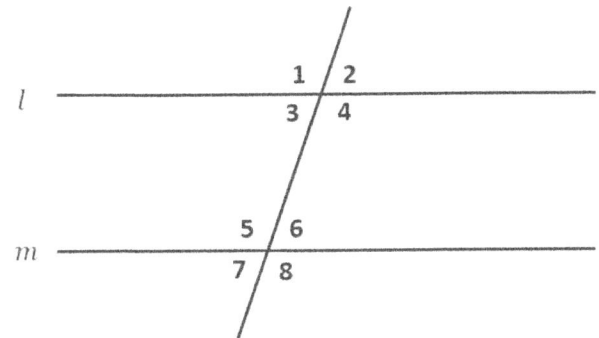

_____ degrees

33. If the lengths of the legs of a right triangle are 12 centimeters and 16 centimeters, what is the length of the hypotenuse?

A. $6\sqrt{5}$ cm   B. 21 cm   C. 20 cm   D. $15\sqrt{5}$ cm

34. If the lengths of the legs of a right triangle are 13 centimeters and 18 centimeters, what is the length of the hypotenuse?

A. $\sqrt{493}$ cm   B. $12\sqrt{2}$ cm   C. 19 cm   D. 20 cm

35. The floor of a rectangular storage unit is 6 meters long and 8 meters wide. What is the distance between two opposite corners of the floor?

_____ m

COMPREHENSIVE ASSESSMENTS

ASSESSMENT 2

36. Two window washers, Whitney and Tessa, lean a ladder against the side of a building so Whitney can wash a window while Tessa holds the ladder. The top of the ladder reaches the window, 17 feet off the ground. The base of the ladder is 8 feet away from the building.

How long is the ladder? Round your answer to the nearest tenth of a foot.

_____ ft

(8.G.B.7)

37. What is the distance between the points (2, 2) and (6, 8), without without using a graph? Round your answer to the nearest tenth.

_____

_____

_____

(8.G.B.8)

38. What is the distance between the points (−2, 4) and (−2, −2), without without using a graph?

_____

_____

_____

(8.G.B.8)

39. True or False: The volume of a cone with a diameter of 3 ft and a height of 10 ft is about 24 ft^3.

A. True   **B.** False

(8.G.C.9)

COMPREHENSIVE ASSESSMENTS

40. What type of correlation is in this scatterplot?

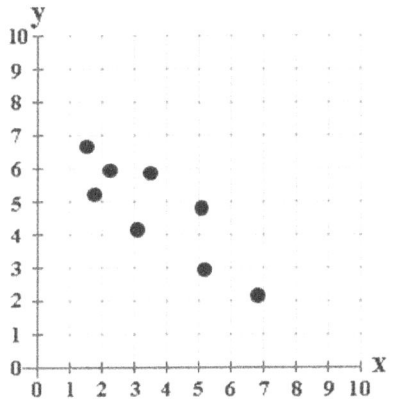

41. What type of correlation is in this scatterplot?

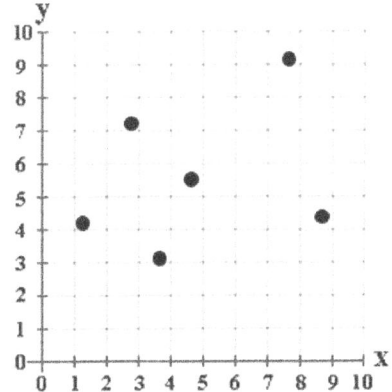

COMPREHENSIVE ASSESSMENTS

42. What is the equation of the trend line in the scatter plot below?

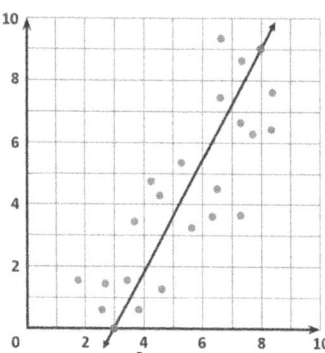

8.SP.A.2

43. Alicia draws this line of best fit to represent the relationship between the data points. Do you agree with Alicia's line? Explain why.

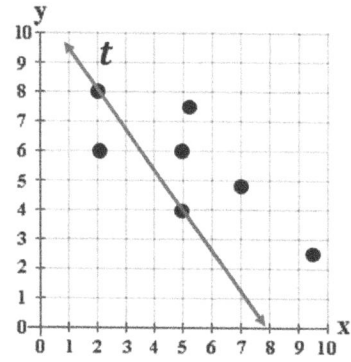

_____

_____

_____

8.SP.A.2

COMPREHENSIVE ASSESSMENTS

44. This equation represents the line of best fit for data comparing the percent of children y who are obese to the percentage of children x who exercise 5 days each week.

$$y = -0.49x + 37.2$$

This table shows the data used to determine the line of best fit.

x	35	38	41	44	46	46	50	57	58	60	68
y	20	19	17	16	15	15	13	10	9	8	4

Is it reasonable to use the y-intercept of this equation to interpret the situation? Explain your reasoning.

8.SP.A.3

45. How many people who participated in the survey in the table below have a Facebook Account?

Age	Have a Facebook Account	Do not have a Facebook Account
18 to 21	78	4
22 and over	70	67

8.SP.A.4

ANSWERS AND EXPLANATIONS

The Number System
Understanding Irrational Numbers 216
Approximation of
Irrational Numbers 217
Chapter Review 218
Extra Practice 220

Functions
Evaluate and Compare Functions 221
Understanding Linear and
Non-Linear Functions 222
Use Functions to Model
Relationships 224
Chapter Review 225
Extra Practice 226

Expressions and Equations
Radical and Integer Exponents 227
Proportional Relationships
and Linear Equations 228
Solving Linear Equations 230
Chapter Review 231
Extra Practice 232

Geometry
Congruence and Similarity 234
Pythagorean Theorem Application 235
Volume of 3-Dimensional Shapes 236
Chapter Review 237
Extra Practice 239

Statistics and Probability
Application of Scatterplots 240
Application of Linear Models 242
Application of Bivariate Data 243
Chapter Review 245
Extra Practice 246

Assessment 1 247

Assessment 2 250

ANSWERS and EXPLANATIONS

THE NUMBER SYSTEM
UNIT 1 – UNDERSTANDING IRRATIONAL NUMBERS

1 Answer: D
Explanation: The value of the square root is a non-repeating, non-terminating decimal, and cannot be written as a fraction, so it is Irrational.

2 Answer: D
Explanation: The exact value of π cannot be written as a fraction, so it is Irrational.

3 Answer: C
Explanation: The number can be $3.\overline{14}$ written as $\frac{103}{33}$, a fraction, so it is Rational.

4 Answer: C
Explanation: The number can be $-0.\overline{151}$ written as $-\frac{151}{999}$ a fraction, so it is Rational.

5 Answer: D
Explanation: The fraction $\frac{2\sqrt{2}}{2}$ contains an irrational part $\sqrt{2}$. Thus, it is Irrational.

6 Answer: B
Explanation: Divide the numerator by the denominator to convert the fraction to a decimal.

7 Answer: A
Explanation: Divide the numerator by the denominator to convert the fraction to a decimal.

8 Answer: C
Explanation: Divide the numerator by the denominator to convert the fraction to a decimal.

9 Answer: A
Explanation: Divide the numerator by the denominator to convert the fraction to a decimal. Dividing by 9's always gives a repeating decimal.

10 Answer: C
Explanation: The original fraction simplifies to $\frac{1}{2}$, so the decimal value is 0.5.

11 Answer: D
Explanation: Divide the numerator by the denominator to convert the fraction to a decimal. Dividing by 9's always gives a repeating decimal.

12 Answer: D
Explanation: Divide the numerator by the denominator to convert the fraction to a decimal.

13 Answer: A
Explanation: The original fraction simplifies to $\frac{1}{8}$, which is 0.125 when dividing the numerator by the denominator.

14 Answer: C
Explanation: Divide the numerator by the denominator to convert the fraction to a decimal. In the answer, only 6 repeats.

15 Answer: D
Explanation: Divide the numerator by the denominator to convert the fraction to a decimal. Dividing by 9's always gives a repeating decimal.

16 Answer: A
Explanation: Separate the decimal into a whole number part and a decimal part. A repeating decimal is a fraction with one 9 in the denominator for each digit that repeats.

17 Answer: B
Explanation: A repeating decimal is a fraction with one 9 in the denominator for each digit that repeats. Then simplify the resulting fraction.

18 Answer: D
Explanation: The value of 3.14 is commonly used for π. Select the choice that is closest to that decimal.

ANSWERS and EXPLANATIONS

19 Answer: A

Explanation: A repeating decimal is a fraction with one 9 in the denominator for each digit that repeats. The given decimal has 2 digits that repeat.

20 Answer: B

Explanation: A repeating decimal is a fraction with one 9 in the denominator for each digit that repeats. The given decimal has 3 digits that repeat. Then simplify the resulting fraction.

THE NUMBER SYSTEM
UNIT 2 - APPROXIMATION OF IRRATIONAL NUMBERS

1 Answer: A

Explanation: The square root of 5 is approximately 2.236068, and lies between the square root of 4 (which is 2) and the square root of 9 (which is 3).

2 Answer: A

Explanation: To find the square root of a number that is not a perfect square, first determine which two perfect squares the number falls between.

3 Answer: C

Explanation: Seven squared is 49. Eight squared is 64. The number inside the square root must be between these two values. The number 56 is between these values.

4 Answer: B

Explanation: The first step to find $\sqrt{86}$ is to identify the perfect squares that 86 is between. The number 86 is between 81 and 100.

5 Answer: D

Explanation: When evaluating each expression, $\sqrt{79}$ plus the value of x gives the largest number.

6 Answer: C

Explanation: Square each choice. The square of 9.8 is 96.04 which is closest to 96.

7 Answer: B

Explanation: Multiply 8 by itself and the answer is 64, which is the closest choice to 67.

8 Answer: B

Explanation: Perfect square roots are rational numbers but square roots of numbers that are not perfect squares are irrational.

9 Answer: C

Explanation: The square root of 39 is between the square root of 36 and the square root of 49; 39 is much closer to 36 than 49 and so the square root of 36 is going to provide a closer estimate than the the square root of 49.

10 Answer: C

Explanation: Calculate or estimate the value of each choice. The square root of 17 is greater than 4. The number π is estimated as 3.14, and multiplying by a fraction greater than one increases that value. The square root of 11 is between 3 and 4, so calculate its value, which is approximately 3.3166, making π the smallest value.

11 Answer: B

Explanation: The square root of $\sqrt{7}$ is between $\sqrt{4}$ which is 2 and $\sqrt{9}$ which is 3. The value of $\sqrt{7}$ is close to 2.6.

12 Answer: C

Explanation: The square root of $\sqrt{5}$ is between $\sqrt{4}$ which is 2 and $\sqrt{9}$ which is 3. The value of $\sqrt{5}$ is close to 2.2.

13 Answer: A

Explanation: Since two of the choices are between 1 and 2, calculate each value. Point A is approximately in the middle between 1 and 2. The closest approximation of $\sqrt{2}$ is 1.4.

ANSWERS and EXPLANATIONS

14 Answer: D
Explanation: Point F is slightly less than 2. Two choices are clearly not the answer. calculate the square root of the others. The closest approximation of $\sqrt{3}$ is 1.73.

15 Answer: B
Explanation: The $\sqrt{32}$ is less than $\sqrt{36}$ which is 6 and more than $\sqrt{25}$ which is 5. Thus, the answer must be Point F. The approximate value of $\sqrt{32}$ is 5.7.

16 Answer: D
Explanation: The $\sqrt{56}$ is less than $\sqrt{64}$ which is 8 and more than $\sqrt{49}$ which is 7. Thus, the answer must be Point H. An approximation for $\sqrt{52}$ is 7.2.

17 Answer: C
Explanation: The $\sqrt{76}$ is less than $\sqrt{81}$ which is 9 and more than $\sqrt{64}$ which is 8. An approximation for $\sqrt{76}$ is 8.7.

18 Answer: A
Explanation: The $\sqrt{96}$ is less than $\sqrt{100}$ which is 10 and more than $\sqrt{81}$ which is 9. Thus, the answer must be Point G. Point G best represents $\sqrt{96}$. It is between 9 and 10.

19 Answer: B
Explanation: When estimating a square root, it is helpful to see what perfect square the square root is closest to. In this case, the closest perfect square to $\sqrt{23}$ is $\sqrt{25}$.

20 Answer: C
Explanation: When estimating a square root, it is helpful to see what perfect square the square root is closest to. In this case, the closest perfect square to $\sqrt{45}$ is $\sqrt{49}$.

THE NUMBER SYSTEM CHAPTER REVIEW

1 Answer: D
Explanation: Step 1: Rewrite as $x = 0.\overline{13}$ and $100x = 13.\overline{13}$.
Step 2: Subtract $x = 0.\overline{13}$ from $100x = 13.\overline{13}$.
Step 3: $99x = 13$
Step 4: $x = \frac{13}{99}$

2 Answer: A
Explanation:
Step 1: Rewrite as $10x = 4.\overline{5}$ and $100x = 45.\overline{5}$.
Step 2: Subtract $10x = 4.\overline{5}$ from $100x = 45.\overline{5}$.
Step 3: $90x = 41$
Step 4: $x = \frac{41}{90}$

3 Answer: D
Explanation: The square root of 2 is an irrational number and cannot be expressed as a fraction.

4 Answer: D
Explanation: The expression $2\sqrt{3} + 1$ contains an irrational number ($\sqrt{3}$) and cannot be expressed as a fraction.

5 Answer: C
Explanation:
Step 1: Rewrite as $10x = 1.\overline{23}$ and $1000x = 123.\overline{23}$.
Step 2: Subtract $10x = 1.\overline{23}$ from $1000x = 123.\overline{23}$.
Step 3: $990x = 122$
Step 4: $x = \frac{122}{990}$
Step 5: simplify the fraction

6 Answer: A
Explanation:
Step 1: Rewrite as $x = 0.\overline{1}$ and $10x = 1.\overline{1}$.
Step 2: Subtract $x = 0.\overline{1}$ from $10x = 1.\overline{1}$.

ANSWERS and EXPLANATIONS

Step 3: $9x = 1$
Step 4: $x = \frac{1}{9}$

7 Answer: C
Explanation:
Step 1: Rewrite as $100x = 25.\overline{7}$ and $1000x = 257.\overline{7}$.
Step 2: Subtract $100x = 25.\overline{7}$ from $1000x = 257.\overline{7}$.
Step 3: $900x = 232$
Step 4: $x = \frac{232}{900}$
Step 5: Simplify the fraction which gives $x = \frac{58}{225}$

8 Answer: B
Explanation:
Step 1: Rewrite as $x = 0.\overline{97}$ and $100x = 97.\overline{97}$.
Step 2: Subtract $x = 0.\overline{97}$ from $100x = 97.\overline{97}$.
Step 3: $99x = 97$
Step 4: $x = \frac{97}{99}$

9 Answer: C
Explanation: The value of the square root of 25 is 5.

10 Answer: B
Explanation:
Step 1: Rewrite decimal as $x = 0.\overline{567}$ and $1000x = 567.\overline{567}$.
Step 2: Subtract $x = 0.\overline{567}$ from $1000x = 567.\overline{567}$.
Step 3: $999x = 567$
Step 4: $x = \frac{567}{999}$
Step 5: Simplify the fraction which gives $x = \frac{21}{37}$

11 Answer: D
Explanation: The square root of 64 is 8 and the square root of 67 is approximately 8.2.

12 Answer: A
Explanation: The square root of 89 is approximately 9.43, $\frac{93}{10}$ is 9.3, $\frac{47}{5}$ is 9.4 and $\frac{19}{2}$ is 9.5.

13 Answer: B
Explanation: The square root of 45 is approximately 6.708, therefore, it is larger than 6.7 but smaller than 6.8.

14 Answer: A
Explanation: The square root of 3 is 1.73 and $1\frac{3}{4}$ is 1.75. The correct order, in decimal form, from greatest to least is 1.75, 1.73 and then 1.7.

15 Answer: C
Explanation: The square root of 11 is approximately 3.317 and $3\frac{7}{8}$ is 3.875.

16 Answer: B
Explanation: The square root of 24 is approximately 4.899.

17 Answer: C
Explanation: Compare 21 and 16. Although there is no need to find the square roots, the square root of 21 is approximately 4.58 and the square root of 16 is 4.

18 Answer: A
Explanation: Evaluate $\sqrt{89}$. The result is approximately 9.43.

19 Answer: D
Explanation: The square root of 40 is approximately 6.324 and the square root of 41 is approximately 6.403, which makes 6.71 the largest number.

20 Answer: C
Explanation: The square root of 62 is approximately 7.874, which makes it larger than 7.87.

ANSWERS and EXPLANATIONS

THE NUMBER SYSTEM: EXTRA PRACTICE

1 Answer: C
Explanation: All of the choices are negative numbers. The number −0.003 has the greatest value, because it is closest to 0.

2 Answer: D
Explanation: To determine the equivalent fraction for a repeating decimal, multiply both sides of the equation ($x = 0.\overline{345}$) by a power of 10 (in this case, 1,000) equal to the number of repeating digits. This gives the equation $1,000x = 345.\overline{345}$. To determine the value of x, subtract the original equation from the new equation, and solve for the variable.

3 Answer: B
Explanation: To determine the equivalent fraction for a repeating decimal, multiply both sides of the equation ($x = 1.\overline{042}$) by a power of 10 (in this case, 1,000) equal to the number of repeating digits. This gives the equation $1,000x = 1,042.\overline{042}$. To determine the value of x, subtract the original equation from the new equation, and solve for the variable.

4 Answer: 0.4375
Explanation: The numerator has a value of 4375, and the denominator has a value of 10,000. $\frac{4375}{10000}$ is equivalent to 0.4375. Alternatively, the expression 5^4 in the numerator and denominator cancel. Evaluate the remaining fraction.

5 Answer: 0.001
Explanation: The numerator has a value of 1, and the denominator has a value of 1,000. $\frac{1}{1000}$ is equivalent to 0.001.

6 Answer: 3.2 (3.2) or $(3.2)^2$
Explanation: The fraction $\frac{1}{5}$ is 0.20. Find the area of the square by multiplying the length of one side by itself.

7 Answer: B
Explanation: The square root of any number that is not a perfect square is an irrational number.

8 Answer: $\sqrt{151}$ cm
Explanation: The area (151) is not a perfect square number and has no square factors which would allow its square root to be simplified.

9 Answer: Answers will vary. An area of 4 sq. cm has rational number side lengths. An area of 5 sq. cm has irrational number side lengths.
Explanation: The square root of a number that is a perfect square is a rational number. The square root of any number that is not a perfect square is an irrational number.

10 Answer: No
Explanation: The fraction $\frac{1}{3}$ can be expressed as a percent (and decimal), and but it is a repeating decimal, so the percent also contains a repeating decimal or a fraction. The correct expression is $33.\overline{3}\%$ or $33\frac{1}{3}\%$.

11 Answer: $\sqrt{5}$
Explanation: The graph begins at $\sqrt{16}$ which is 4 and ends at $\sqrt{81}$ which is 9. The letter X is located at 5. Thus, Y is the square root of 5.

12 Answer: 4 and 5
Explanation: The graph begins at $\frac{42}{3}$ which is 14 and ends at $\frac{72}{3}$ which is 24. The letter S is located at 20. Thus, T is the square root of 20, which is approximately 4.472, or between 4 and 5.

ANSWERS and EXPLANATIONS

13 Answer: 250
Explanation: Find the cube root of each number. In decimal form, the cube root of 250 is approximately 6.29. The number 250 is the product of 125 and 2 (composite number means not prime).

14 Answer: $\sqrt{5}$
Explanation: The first clue provides the answer because only one choice is an irrational number. The square root of 5 is irrational. If the number were squared, the result is 5, which is a prime number. The square root of 5 is approximately 2.24.

15 Answer:

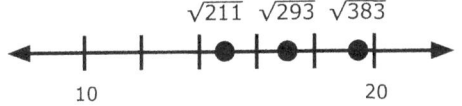

Explanation: Answers will vary. Each hash mark on the number line is counting by twos. The three points represent irrational numbers because the square root of these values cannot be expressed as a ratio.

16 Answer:

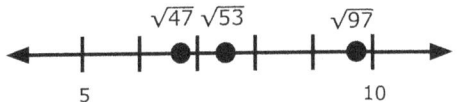

Explanation: Answers will vary. Each hash mark on the number line is counting by one. The three points represent irrational numbers because the square root of these values cannot be expressed as a ratio.

17 Answer: No
Explanation: Her formula does not include the correct value for π. The number π can be approximated as 3.14. Also, the formula for the area of a circle is $\pi \times$ (radius) $\times$ (radius). The radius of the circle is 5 inches.

18 Answer: 615 or 588 or 616
Explanation: Use the exact value of π and then round, or approximate π using 3.14. Multiply the estimate by 196 which results in 615.44 sq. cm. Round to the nearest whole number. Alternatively, approximate π using 3.

19 Answer: Yes
Explanation: Both expressions have a value of 4 π.

20 Answer: No
Explanation: Squaring a value is not the same as multiplying the value by 2. Additionally, the two expressions have different exponents of π.

FUNCTIONS
UNIT 1 - EVALUATE AND COMPARE FUNCTIONS

1 Answer: A
Explanation: A function has exactly one output for each input.

2 Answer: D
Explanation: Two identical inputs have different outputs.

3 Answer: D
Explanation: Two identical inputs have different outputs. Thus, the graph fails the vertical line test.

4 Answer: A
Explanation: A function has one output for each input. A slanted line automatically represents a function because the graph passes the vertical line test.

5 Answer: A
Explanation: There are no restrictions on the inputs of x which come from the domain.

6 Answer: B
Explanation: The inside of a square root must be greater than or equal to 0. Thus, the values that can be input for x must make the expression $2x - 5 \geq 0$.

7 Answer: C
Explanation: The given expression is a rational expression. Dividing by 0 is

undefined. If $x = 3$, the denominator is zero and the function expression is undefined.

8 Answer: D

Explanation: The given expression is a rational expression. Dividing by 0 is undefined. If $x = \frac{1}{2}$, the denominator is zero and the function expression is undefined.

9 Answer: A

Explanation: The minimum value of y is -7 and the maximum value of y is 6. The range is between these two values, inclusive.

10 Answer: B

Explanation: The domain includes the x-values, or inputs, of the graph. The inputs are between these two values, inclusive.

11 Answer: B

Explanation: Alicia charges $30 per day and Ryan charges $25 per day.

12 Answer: A

Explanation: Maria will charge $20 and Jacob will charge $25.

13 Answer: C

Explanation: The rate of change is calculated by dividing the amount of change of y by the amount of change of x: $(9 − 8)/(4 − 2) = \frac{1}{2}$, so the rate of change is $\frac{1}{2}$.

14 Answer: A

Explanation: The rate of change for Function A is $\frac{1}{2}$ and the rate of change for Function B is 3.

15 Answer: B

Explanation: The graph shows that it does not snow during the cold snap, then snow accumulating and finally a rapid drop and since the snow melted until it is gone. B best represents the graph.

16 Answer: B

Explanation: The leaves quickly drop over time due to the short windstorm and the graph shows a decline over a short time period. B is the best answer.

17 Answer: D

Explanation: The rate of change for Function G is negative because the y-values get smaller. Thus, Function G is a decreasing function. The rate of change of Function H is positive because the slope is positive. Thus, Function H is an increasing function.

18 Answer: A

Explanation: The movie club would cost $100 (25.00 + 5.00 × 15) per year. Buying movies individually would cost $112.50 (7.50 x 15).

19 Answer: D

Explanation: Function F is a cubic function and function G is quadratic function and they are both not linear because their input variable has an exponent other than 1.

20 Answer: C

Explanation: The -4 in the function is a downward shift of 4 units. The parent function is a quadratic function ($y = x^2$) which is a parabola opening upward with its vertex at the origin. The parabola is shifted 4 units down.

FUNCTIONS
UNIT 2 – UNDERSTANDING LINEAR AND NON-LINEAR FUNCTIONS

1 Answer: D

Explanation: The value of $\frac{1}{3}$ in the form $y = mx + b$ means the line has a slope of $\frac{1}{3}$. Using the ratio of the change in the domain to the change in the range, the line increases one unit vertically and three units horizontally.

2 Answer: C

Explanation: The value of 6 in the form $y = mx + b$ means the line crosses the y-axis at $y = 6$.

ANSWERS and EXPLANATIONS

3 Answer: A
Explanation: When a line has a negative slope, it decreases from left to right.

4 Answer: B
Explanation: To change the standard linear equation to the slope-intercept form, solve the standard equation for y and write it in $y = mx + b$ form.

5 Answer: D
Explanation: In $y = mx + b$ form, the -12 of the original function means the graph intersects the y-axis at the point $(0, -12)$.

6 Answer: D
Explanation: This graph is a linear function because it is a straight line segment.

7 Answer: C
Explanation: While the graph does intersect the y-axis at -7, it is not a linear function because it is the graph of a curve.

8 Answer: B
Explanation: When you graph a graph in $y = mx + b$ form, it forms a line.

9 Answer: A
Explanation: Any function that includes an exponent other than 1 is nonlinear. The graph of the given function, it is a curve, and therefore, it is a nonlinear function.

10 Answer: C
Explanation: A linear function is a line when graphed. Additionally, any function that includes only exponents of 1 is linear.

11 Answer: B
Explanation: This is a function because each given x-value has one y-value output but when plotted, these points do not form a line.

12 Answer: D
Explanation: The only function given that is a line is choice D. It is the only function that can be written in one of the linear forms.

13 Answer: D
Explanation: Horizontal lines are linear functions with no rate of change because the y-value is constant.

14 Answer: A
Explanation: Linear functions are graphed as lines.

15 Answer: C
Explanation: Vertical lines are not considered to be functions because it is impossible to calculate their slope because the x-value is constant.

16 Answer: C
Explanation: The vertical line test is used to determine whether a relation is a function. A vertical line will intersect the graph of a function at only one point and if a vertical line intersects with a graph at multiple points, the relation is not a function.

17 Answer: B
Explanation: The graph is a function because at each point, a vertical line passes through the function only once.

18 Answer: B
Explanation: A vertical line goes through the graph at multiple points. Because of this, the graph is not a function because it fails the vertical line test.

19 Answer: D
Explanation: Every vertical line passes through a point only once, so the relation is a function.

20 Answer: B
Explanation: The graph of the line decreases (negative slope) and has a positive y-intercept. Only choice B has these characteristics.

ANSWERS and EXPLANATIONS

FUNCTIONS
UNIT 3 - USE FUNCTIONS TO MODEL RELATIONSHIPS

1 Answer: A
Explanation: While a function can contain an infinite number of points and graph as a line, those don't have to be true for the relationship to be defined as a function. To be a function, each input value can have one and only one output value.

2 Answer: C
Explanation: Plot the given point to determine whether the relationship passes the vertical line test. If so, they can be represented as a function.

3 Answer: B
Explanation: The best way to create a table based on a function is to use values for x from the domain and calculate the corresponding y-values using the function's definition.

4 Answer: A
Explanation: When given a function in table form, one way is to first plot the points and then try to write the relationship based on the graph.

5 Answer: B
Explanation: There is no clear rule for creating a function from narrative form and writing the rule. The best tactic is to analyze the situation and write the rule accordingly. Then test the rule using values in the narrative.

6 Answer: B
Explanation: When given a function rule, the best way to graph is to choose a few values for x from the domain of the function and calculate their corresponding y-values.

7 Answer: D
Explanation: After you have created a table with points, you should graph them to see if you can discern a pattern to the line.

8 Answer: D
Explanation: Use the points in the table. There is no set number of points needed to graph a function. Create more points if needed.

9 Answer: A
Explanation: Given any situation, to write a function of the relationship, first determine the dependent and independent variables.

10 Answer: C
Explanation: Each value of y is 6 more than the corresponding x value. The table also shows a rate of change of 1.

11 Answer: A
Explanation: As the function's x values increase, the y values also increase because the slope of the graph is positive. The graph is that of a line, so it can also be defined as linear.

12 Answer: B
Explanation: As the function's x values increase, the y values decrease because the slope of the graph is negative. The graph is that of a line, so it can also be defined as linear.

13 Answer: C
Explanation: The slope of choice C is positive, so that function is an increasing function.

14 Answer: D
Explanation: When rearranged into slope-intercept form, the slope of choice D is negative, so that function is a decreasing function.

15 Answer: D
Explanation: A horizontal line is also called a constant function, its y-values do not increase or decrease.

16 Answer: A
Explanation: This function is a linear decreasing function because the values of y decrease from left to right.

ANSWERS and EXPLANATIONS

17 Answer: C
Explanation: The slope is negative so the function is a decreasing function.

18 Answer: B
Explanation: The slope is positive so the function is an increasing function.

19 Answer: B
Explanation: This graph is a nonlinear function and decreased on the left and increases on the right.

20 Answer: A
Explanation: The graph is that of a horizontal line and therefore neither increases or decreases.

FUNCTIONS CHAPTER REVIEW

1 Answer: A
Explanation: The outputs (y-values) are between these two values, inclusive.

2 Answer: A
Explanation: The inputs (x-values) are between these two values, inclusive.

3 Answer: B
Explanation: Substitute -3 for x to calculate the correct output.

4 Answer: D
Explanation: Substituting -2 for x results in the correct output.

5 Answer: C
Explanation: The x-value of this function is the number of pounds and the y-value is the cost. Multiply each number of pounds by 1.27.

6 Answer: B
Explanation: Check the values of x and y in the table against the graph, the values in the table in choice B match the points on the graph.

7 Answer: A
Explanation: While the car is not moving, the line representing distance remains constant. Since the line is horizontal, the car is not moving.

8 Answer: D
Explanation: Function A has a positive slope which means it is increasing and function B has a negative slope which means it is decreasing.

9 Answer: A
Explanation: When given a function in slope-intercept form, the coefficient of the x-variable is the slope or rate of change of the linear function.

10 Answer: A
Explanation: The y-intercept is the b value in the slope intercept equation ($y = mx + b$). In this situation, the y-intercept is 3.

11 Answer: B
Explanation: Laura was incorrect because when you graph this function, its shape is like a V, and it passes the vertical line test.

12 Answer: D
Explanation: Choice D is a linear function in the slope-intercept form.

13 Answer: C
Explanation: A negative slope gives you a line that decreases from left to right.

14 Answer: B
Explanation: The larger the the slope, the steeper the graph of the line will be.

15 Answer: C
Explanation: When the x-value is 0, the y-value is 10.

16 Answer: B
Explanation: When $x = 0, y = -9$ for this function.

17 Answer: B
Explanation: Choice B is a cubic functions which is not linear.

ANSWERS and EXPLANATIONS

18 Answer: B
Explanation: The function can be defined as $f(x) = x^2$. When graphed, the function is not a line. It's a curve.

19 Answer: A
Explanation: Depending on the points you choose, you may need to use more than three points for this function to clearly see the pattern created by the graph. The absolute value graph looks like a V.

20 Answer: C
Explanation: Select x-and y-values to see the pattern or relationship. The graph given matches the function $y = x^2$.

FUNCTIONS EXTRA PRACTICE

1 Answer: B
Explanation: Substitute -3 for x in the function and simplify the expression.

2 Answer: C
Explanation: Substituting the value in for x results in a negative inside the radical. Negative numbers are not in the domain of the square root function.

3 Answer: D
Explanation: Correctly substituting the values in results in a true statement if the point is a solution. Only choice D shows a correct true statement.

4 Answer: A
Explanation: $y = -2(2) + 7$
$y = -4 + 7$
$y = 3$

5 Answer: A
Explanation: Both the variables and the operation match the description of the function.

6 Answer: A
Explanation: Carwash 1 will cost Jose $6 (0.75 x 8) and Carwash 2 will cost Jose $9 (1.50 + 5 × 1.50) for 8 minutes of use, which means Carwash A is a better deal.

7 Answer: C
Explanation: The cost of rental is an initial $149 plus $29.99 times the number of days they need to rent the truck.

8 Answer: D
Explanation: $9y - 3x = 54$ is the standard form representation of the given linear function. Solving for y reveals the same slope as in the given equation.

9 Answer: B
Explanation: Choice B represents a vertical line, so it is linear but not a function.

10 Answer: A
Explanation: Choice A is not a linear function because i contains an exponent other than 1 on a variable.

11 Answer: C
Explanation: The vertical line test is used to determine whether a graph is a function.

12 Answer: B
Explanation: The slope-intercept form provides the y-intercept (a place to start) and the slope (a direction to go) when graphing a line. It is considered a graphing-ready equation.

13 Answer: D
Explanation: The initial value of the function is 29.99 plus 14 times the number of dvds purchased.

14 Answer: B
Explanation: The relationship between x and y is that y is 5 times x.

15 Answer: A
Explanation: To find the slope from a graph, select two points where the values are integers, such as $(-2, -2)$ and $(0, 10)$ and calculate the slope using those two points. This graph represents a line with a slope of 6.

ANSWERS and EXPLANATIONS

16 Answer: A
Explanation: The rate of change is the slope. This function is expressed in slope intercept form ($y = mx + b$), and the value of m, or the coefficient of x, is -7.

17 Answer: D
Explanation: The slope-intercept form provides the y-intercept (a place to start) and the slope (a direction to go) when graphing a line. It is considered a graphing-ready equation.

18 Answer: D
Explanation: The y-intercept of the nonlinear function is 8. This is the value of y in the graph when $x = 0$.

19 Answer: A
Explanation: The slope of the equation is positive, so the graph is increasing.

20 Answer: A
Explanation: The y-intercept of the function should be at the point $(0, -2)$.

EXPRESSIONS AND EQUATIONS
UNIT 1 - RADICAL AND INTEGER EXPONENTS

1 Answer: B
Explanation: When multiplying same bases with exponents, the rule is add the exponents. Filling 4^6 into the blank gives $4^2 \times 4^6 = 4^8$, since $2 + 6 = 8$, the answer is 4^6.

2 Answer: A
Explanation: When multiplying same bases with exponents, the rule is add the exponents. The area is length times width, so add 4 and 7. Do not multiply the bases.

3 Answer: C
Explanation: Substituting any integer for x will yield a positive number. Recall that 0 is neither positive nor negative.

4 Answer: D
Explanation: To simplify this expression, consider 3^3 which is equal to 27. Then consider 2^5, which is equal to 32. Finally, multiply 27 . 32 = 864.

5 Answer: B
Explanation: When you substitute the value in for x you get, $(-2)^6 = (-2)(-2)(-2)(-2)(-2)(-2) = 64$.

6 Answer: C
Explanation: The number 20 in $\sqrt{20}$ is not a perfect square, therefore, it is irrational.

7 Answer: B
Explanation: The largest value is 9.2 because $\sqrt{81} = 9$ and $\sqrt{64} = 8$.

8 Answer: A
Explanation: A rational number can be written as a fraction. $\sqrt{49} = 7$, therefore, it is a rational number. Only square roots that contain a perfect square are rational numbers.

9 Answer: D
Explanation: To solve the equation, take the square root of both sides. This would give $x = 6$. However, when taking the square root to solve an equation, consider a negative value that makes the equation true. This gives $x = -6$. Therefore, the solution of the equation is $x = \pm 6$.

10 Answer: D
Explanation: First, Substitute 64 into the area formula for A. This gives $64 = x^2$. To solve, take the square root of both sides of the equation, which gives $x = \pm 8$. Since the context of the problem is a side length of a square, reject the negative solution.

11 Answer: A
Explanation: To write a number in scientific notation, the first-factor is greater than or equal to 1 and less than 10. The second-factor is a power of ten. In this problem, 7.86 is the first-factor. The decimal must move

eight places to the right to give the original number, making the second factor of 10^8.

12 Answer: B
Explanation: To write a number in scientific notation, the first-factor is greater than or equal to 1 and less than 10. The second-factor is a power of ten. In this example, 5.82 is the first-facto. The decimal must move seven places to the left to ie the original number, making the second-factor 10^{-7}.

13 Answer: C
Explanation: When she rewrote the number in scientific notation, she should have written it as 4.107×10^{10}. All significant digits must be included in the first factor.

14 Answer: B
Explanation: The number 5 times larger than 80,000 . Recognize that number in scientific notation.

15 Answer: A
Explanation: The number is very small so the second-factor exponent should be negative. Alternatively, when converting a standard number to scientific notation, if the decimal point moves to the right to create the first factor, the exponent is the negative of the number of places the decimal point is moved.

16 Answer: A
Explanation: The product rule for exponents states that when multiplying two numbers with exponents and the same base, add their exponents, but do not multiply the bases.

17 Answer: C
Explanation: The quotient rule for exponents states that when dividing two numbers with the same base, subtract the exponent in the denominator from the exponent in the numerator.

18 Answer: B
Explanation: when converting a standard number to scientific notation, if the decimal point moves to the right to create the first factor, the exponent is the negative of the number of places the decimal point is moved. In this problem, the decimal was moved 6 places to the left, and no significant digit in the first factor is changed.

19 Answer: D
Explanation: The original problem already contains the correct first factor for the scientific notation. The expression $0.1 \times 0.1 \times 0.1$ is equivalent to 10^{-3}.

20 Answer: D
Explanation: The original problem already contains the correct first factor for the scientific notation. The expression $10 \times 10 \times 10 \times 10$ is equivalent to 10^4.

EXPRESSIONS AND EQUATIONS
UNIT 2 - PROPORTIONAL RELATIONSHIPS AND LINEAR EQUATIONS

1 Answer: C
Explanation: In the form, $y = kx$, k is the slope.

2 Answer: A
Explanation: Lines in this form are referred to as direct variations. As different x values are substituted into the equation, the y values change but the k remains the same. It is called the "constant" of the variation.

3 Answer: D
Explanation: In a direct variation relationship, all of the terms are proper ways to refer to k.

4 Answer: B
Explanation: Lines in direct variation form always intersect the y-axis at (0,0) or the origin. If the intersection is elsewhere, then the relation is not a direct variation.

5 Answer: B
Explanation: Lines in direct variation form always intersect the x-axis at (0,0) or the origin.

ANSWERS and EXPLANATIONS

6 Answer: A
Explanation: When the line follows the form $y = kx$, the k-value is the slope. In the equation $y = 5x$, $k = 5$.

7 Answer: D
Explanation: When the line follows the form $y = kx$, the slope is the k-value, also called the constant of the variation. In the equation $y = \frac{1}{3}x$, $k = \frac{1}{3}$.

8 Answer: C
Explanation: Each y-value is 10 times its corresponding x-value.

9 Answer: B
Explanation: Each y-value is $\frac{1}{3}$ times its corresponding x-value. Alternatively, when x increases by 1, y increases by $\frac{1}{3}$.

10 Answer: A
Explanation: By picking two points on the line, the constant of proportionality, or the slope, can be calculated as 6.

11 Answer: C
Explanation: The graph shows 2 similar triangles. The slope is the length of the vertical leg divided by the length of the horizontal leg in each triangle.

12 Answer: B
Explanation: The graph shows 2 similar triangles. The slope is the length of the vertical leg divided by the length of the horizontal leg in each triangle. However, since the slope is negative, each ratio must include a negative sign.

13 Answer: D
Explanation: Each set of ordered pairs represents 2 points on the line which can be used to create 2 similar triangles. To calculate the slope accurately, those points should always contain integer values for both x and y.

14 Answer: A
Explanation: Each set of ordered pairs represents 2 points on the line which can be used to create 2 similar triangles. To calculate the slope accurately, those points should always contain integer values for both x and y.

15 Answer: B
Explanation: Each set of ordered pairs represents 2 points on the line which can be used to create 2 similar triangles. To calculate the slope accurately, those points should always contain integer values for both x and y.

16 Answer: D
Explanation: The line passes through the origin, meaning it will take the form of $y = kx$. The slope of the line is $\frac{1}{2}$ and the y-intercept is $(0,0)$.

17 Answer: A
Explanation: The line passes through the origin, meaning it will take the form of $y = kx$. The slope of the line is $\frac{2}{5}$ and the y-intercept is $(0,0)$.

18 Answer: $y = \frac{9}{2}x$
Explanation: The line passes through the origin, meaning it will take the form of $y = kx$. From the origin, the rise is 9 and the run is 2. The slope of the line is $\frac{9}{2}$.

19 Answer: $y = \frac{3}{7}x$
Explanation: The line passes through the origin, meaning it will take the form of $y = kx$. From the origin, the rise is 3 and the run is 7. The slope of the line is $\frac{3}{7}$.

20 Answer: B
Explanation: The line passes through $(0,2)$, which means it will take the form of $y = mx + b$. From the point $(0, 2)$, the rise is 1 and the run is 5. The slope of the line is $\frac{1}{5}$.

ANSWERS and EXPLANATIONS

EXPRESSIONS AND EQUATIONS
UNIT 3 - SOLVING LINEAR EQUATIONS

1 Answer: B
Explanation: When solving an equation, the best way to do it is to use inverse order of operations. Isolate the variable with the inverse of the operations in the equation.

2 Answer: D
Explanation: When solving an equation, perform operations to both sides to keep the equation terms equal.

3 Answer: C
Explanation: To solve $n + 7 = 17$, subtract 7 from both side resulting in $n = 10$.

4 Answer: B
Explanation: The inverse operation is the opposite operation. Addition and subtraction are inverse operations, multiplication and division are inverse operations.

5 Answer: B
Explanation: When working in inverse order of operations, add and subtract before multiplying and dividing.

6 Answer: C
Explanation: To solve for t, first subtract 4 from both sides. Then divide each side by 2. The result is $t = -6$.

7 Answer: D
Explanation: The first step to solve an equation, is simplify by combining like terms.

8 Answer: A
Explanation: Begin by multiplying both sides by 2. Then subtract 2 from both sides. Next, divide both sides by 5, resulting in $y = 4$.

9 Answer: A
Explanation: Start by subtracting 9 from both sides. Then you add 2a to both sides. After that, divide both sides by 6, resulting in $-3 = a$.

10 Answer: B
Explanation: First, distribute -4 to the terms in the parentheses on the left side of the equation. the new equation is $10m + 4m - 12 = 16$. Next, combine like terms on the left side to get the following equation: $14m - 12 = 16$. Now, add 12 to both sides. Lastly, divide both sides by 14 giving $m = 2$.

11 Answer: B
Explanation: If you are given two variables in two equations, there are many different ways to solve for the solution to both equations. This situation is called solving a system of equations in two variables.

12 Answer: C
Explanation: When graphing two equations, the point at which the graphs intersect is the solution to both equations. The values satisfy both equations.

13 Answer: A
Explanation: A system of equations can have 1 solution if the lines intersect, no solution if the lines are parallel, or infinite solutions if the lines are one and the same, but the system cannot have two solutions.

14 Answer: D
Explanation: The solution to a system of equations is usually represented by an ordered pair.

15 Answer: C
Explanation: If x is the number of nights, then both Wrenn and Lisa's total pages can be represented by y as it is dependant on x. For Wrenn, the total pages is $y = 2x + 14$ and for Lisa, the total pages is $y = 3x + 6$.

16 Answer: B
Explanation: The system has no solution because, when graphed, parallel lines do not intersect because there is no solution that makes both equations true.

ANSWERS and EXPLANATIONS

17 Answer: C
Explanation: Coinciding lines have infinitely many solutions because any point on both lines is a solution for both equations.

18 Answer: A
Explanation: The solution to the system of equations is the point of intersection for these two equations: $(-2, 3)$.

19 Answer: D
Explanation: When solving by substitution, first isolate one variable in one equation. Then, substitute the expression in that equation into the other equation for that variable to get an equation with one variable. Solve to find the solution.

20 Answer: A
Explanation: Plan A can be represented by the equation $A = 20m + 25$ and Plan B can be represented by $B = 18m + 40$.

EXPRESSIONS AND EQUATIONS CHAPTER REVIEW

1 Answer: B
Explanation: When multiplying bases that are the same, the product rule states add the exponents. The bases do not change. This gives $a^x \cdot a^y = a^{x+y}$.

2 Answer: C
Explanation: Divide the whole number constants ($\frac{24}{6} = 4$), then, using the quotient rule for exponents subtract the exponent in the denominator from the exponent in the numerator ($10 - 3 = 7$) because the bases are the same.

3 Answer: A
Explanation: Divide -18 by 3 for the constant part. Subtract the exponent in the denominator from the exponent in the numerator because the bases are the same ($-1 - 5 = -6$). Then using the negative exponent rule, $a^{-1} = \frac{1}{a}$, the base and exponent move to the denominator of the fraction and the exponent becomes positive.

4 Answer: A
Explanation: The cube root of 64 is 4 because $4 \cdot 4 \cdot 4 = 64$.

5 Answer: C
Explanation: The radical $\sqrt[3]{16}$ irrational because 16 is not a perfect cube.

6 Answer: C
Explanation: First, substitute 125 into the formula for V. This gives $125 = s^3$. To find s, take the cube root of both sides. This gives $\sqrt[3]{125} = s$ or $s = 5$.

7 Answer: A
Explanation: For the first-factor, all significant digits are included in a decimal that is greater than or equal to 1 and less than 10 and for the second-factor, the decimal point is moved 7 places to the left, so the exponent of 10 is 7.

8 Answer: B
Explanation: The first-factor is written as 1 and the second-factor represents the decimal being moved to the right 12 places so the exponent of 10 is -12.

9 Answer: D
Explanation: In scientific notation, the first-factor base contains the significant digits of the standard notation number as a number greater than or equal to 1 and less than 10, and the second-factor base is 10 to the power equal to the number of places the decimal point is moved to the left.

10 Answer: A
Explanation: Divide 1.03×10^7 by 3.451×10^6. The result is approximately 0.298×10^1. This can be rewritten as 3 times larger.

ANSWERS and EXPLANATIONS

11 Answer: B
Explanation: First, rewrite 1.975×10^7 as 19.75×10^6. Then, add the first factors together and the second factors together. The answer is 28.69×10^6, which becomes 2.869×10^7.

12 Answer: C
Explanation: Multiply 7.17×10^5 by 10, which adds 1 to the exponent making the second factor 10^6.

13 Answer: A
Explanation: The rise over run in this graph is $\frac{10}{2}$ or 5.

14 Answer: D
Explanation: The relation in the table can be represented by the equation $y = 3x$. The only choice with a higher slope than 3 is D.

15 Answer: B
Explanation: The ratio of the vertical side to the horizontal side for both triangles and the slope of the line is $\frac{5}{3}$.

16 Answer: A
Explanation: The line passes through (0, −4), which means in the form $y = mx + b$, the slope of the line is −1 and the y-intercept is −4.

17 Answer: C
Explanation: To remove the fractions, multiply each term by 8, the least common denominator of the fractions. The result is $6 + y = 48$.

18 Answer: D
Explanation: To remove the decimals, multiply each term by 10, which results in $15 = 12y − 57$.

19 Answer: A
Explanation: Alice's amount is represented by the expression $4w + 9$. Elias's amount is represented by the expression $w + 18$. Set the expressions equal to each other and solve for w.

20 Answer: C
Explanation: Using the variable j to represent each job, solve the equation: $25j + 1.75j = 1750$. Solving for j, gives 65.42, so they must do at least 66 jobs to break even.

EXPRESSIONS AND EQUATIONS: EXTRA PRACTICE

1 Answer: B
Explanation: Substitute the dimensions into the volume formula: $V = (x^2)(2x)(6x)$. Multiply the like-bases by adding the exponents. The volume is $V = 12x^4$.

2 Answer: A
Explanation: Substitute the expression y^4 into the area formula for r: $A = \pi(y^4)^2$. Raise the exponential expression to the power by multiplying the exponents. The area expression is $A = \pi y^8$.

3 Answer: B
Explanation: Square the term inside the second parentheses changing the expression to $(2x^5 y^{-2})(9x^2 y^6)$. Next, multiply the constants and add the exponents with like-bases. The result is $18x^7 y^4$.

4 Answer: D
Explanation: The correct answer must be a perfect square that gives an even number as a square root. Take the square root of 16, which is 4. Now, divide 4 by 2 to get 2. Since this is a positive integer, 16 is the correct answer.

5 Answer: A
Explanation: Since the number multiplied by 2 gives 10, the cube root has to be 5. The cube root of 125 is 5. When you double 5, you get 10. Therefore, 125 is the answer.

6 Answer: C
Explanation: Substitute 144 for A in the formula, giving. $144 = s^2$. To solve for , take the square root of both sides: $s = \pm 12$. Delete the negative solution, since it does not fit

ANSWERS and EXPLANATIONS

with the situation. The length of the square is 12 inches.

7 Answer: B
Explanation: Moving the decimal to the right means the number is multiplied to become larger to form the first factor. Only a negative exponent will make a number smaller when transformed from scientific notation back into standard notation.

8 Answer: C
Explanation: When rewriting numbers in scientific notation, a very large number has a positive exponent in the second factor, and a very small number has a negative exponent in the second factor.

9 Answer: D
Explanation: The first-factor is 1.56 and 10^7 indicates that the decimal point is moved to the left 7 places.

10 Answer: C
Explanation: Rewrite 1.2852×10^7 as 128.52×10^5 and then divide 128.52 by 7.14. The 10^5 terms cancel each other so the answer is 18.

11 Answer: D
Explanation: Rewrite 39,580,000 as 395.8×10^5. Add this number to 5.85×10^5 by combining the constant terms (two coefficients) resulting in 401.65×10^5, which is rewritten as 4.0165×10^7.

12 Answer: A
Explanation: Between 1950 and 2016, the population increased approximately three fold which means it tripled. One way to find this is to change the scientific notation into standard form (1,428,000) and then divide by the 1950 population.

13 Answer:

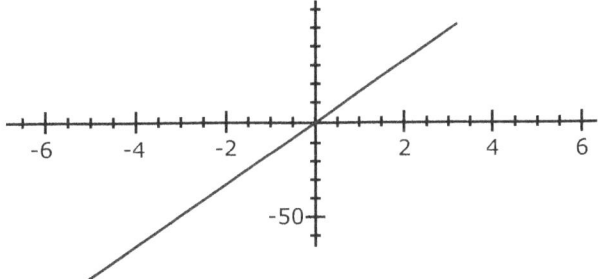

Explanation: Start with a point at the origin and go up 12 (make each line represent 2) and to the right 1 (which would be ½ block). Place the second point at (1,12) draw the line through the two points.

14 Answer:

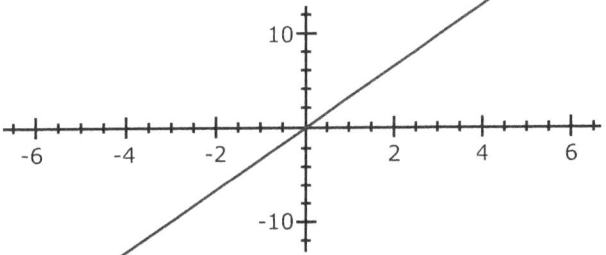

Explanation: Start with a point at the origin and go up 7 units and to the right 2 units. Place the second point at (2,7) draw the line through the two points.

15 Answer: No. The line has a slope of 0.
Explanation: The line has a slope of 0. There is no rise, only a run, to use to draw triangles.

16 Answer: $y = -\frac{4}{9}x + 7$
Explanation: The line passes through (0,7), which means in the form of $y = mx + b$, $b = 7$. The slope of the line, using squares on the graph, is $-\frac{4}{9}$.

ANSWERS and EXPLANATIONS

17 Answer: $36.95
Explanation: Substitute 36 for s in: $9.95 + 0.75s = c$. Calculate the value.

18 Answer: $6.50
Explanation: To get the cost of 1 soda, set up the following equation:
$2(12) + 2(7.5) + 2s = 42 + 10$. Solve for s; $s = 7.5$.

19 Answer: 62
Explanation: The cupcakes sales is represented by the system of equations: $l + s = 105$ and $1.25l + 0.75s = 109.75$. Solve the first equation for s: $s = 105 - l$. Substitute this equation into the other equation and get $1.25l + 0.75(1 - 5 - l) = 109.75$ Solve for l value. They sold 62 large cupcakes.

20 Answer: 90
Explanation: The farm animals is represented by the system of equations: $c + s = 270$ and $s = 2c$. Solving for c using substitution gives 90 cows.

GEOMETRY
UNIT 1 - CONGRUENCE AND SIMILARITY

1 Answer: C
Explanation: Figure A is translated along the x-axis in a positive direction, then translated along the y-axis in a negative direction, and then rotated clockwise.

2 Answer: B
Explanation: Note that Figure B is a "flip" of Figure A. Thus, Figure A is reflected across the horizontal line, $y = 5$ to create Figure B.

3 Answer: D
Explanation: Because the square is reflected across the x-axis, the y-coordinates become opposites, and the x-coordinates remain the same.

4 Answer: B
Explanation: Because the rectangle is reflected across the y-axis and then translated up 8 units, the new rectangle will be in the first quadrant, and the y-coordinate of each vertex increase by 8.

5 Answer: A
Explanation: Note from the graph that Triangle K is 8 units higher and 10 units to the right of Triangle J.

6 Answer: B
Explanation: The x-coordinates are the same, but the y-coordinates become opposites. Each angle should correspond as well: Angle R with Angle W, Angle S with Angle X, Angle T with Angle Y, and Angle V with Angle Z.

7 Answer: $(-4, -6)$, $(-10, -8)$, $(-10, -6)$
Explanation: Rotating the shape 180 degrees about the origin transforms each vertex from (x, y) to $(-x, -y)$. Translating the shape 1 unit down will decrease the y-coordinate by 1.

8 Answer: $(7, -3)$, $(6, -6)$, $(2, -6)$, $(3, -3)$
Explanation: A reflection across the y-axis transforms each vertex from
(x, y) to $(-x, y)$. The reflection across the x-axis translates each translated vertex from $(-x, y)$ to $(-x, -y)$.

9 Answer: B
Explanation: A translation slides a figure to a different location. Moving 2 units to the right, the x-coordinate increases by 2. The y-coordinate remains the same.

10 Answer: A
Explanation: A translation slides a figure to a different location. Moving 4 units to the right, the x-coordinate increases by 4. The y-coordinate remains the same.

11 Answer: B
Explanation: A translation slides a figure to a different location. Moving the point up 1 unit, adds 1 to the y-coordinate. The x-coordinate remains the same.

ANSWERS and EXPLANATIONS

12 Answer: (−1, 0)
Explanation: A translation slides a figure to a different location. Moving 1 unit to the right, the *x*-coordinate increases by 1. The *y*-coordinate remains the same.

13 Answer: D
Explanation: In the dilation, every coordinate of the original triangle is multiplied by the scale factor (2). Then, translating the shape up 3 units increases the *y*-coordinates by 3.

14 Answer: B
Explanation: In the dilation, every coordinate of the original triangle is multiplied by the scale factor (3). Then, reflecting across the *y*-axis changes the sign of the *x*-coordinate.

15 Answer: C
Explanation: In the dilation, every coordinate of the original quadrilateral has been multiplied by the scale factor ($\frac{1}{5}$).

16 Answer: (−12, 10), (−6, 10), (−4, −10), (−14, −10)
Explanation: In the dilation, every coordinate of the original triangle is multiplied by the scale factor (2).

17 Answer: B
Explanation: The Triangle Sum Theorem states that the interior angles of a triangle have a sum of 180 degrees. The diagram shows how 3 angles are combined to add up to 180 degrees.

18 Answer: B
Explanation: Triangle ABC and BDE are similar triangles that share with two congruent angles formed by the parallel horizontal lines. This makes the two triangles similar triangles using the AA Similarity rule.

19 Answer: 102 degrees
Explanation: Angle B is a vertical angle to Angle A. Angle A is supplementary to the 78 degree angle and has a measure of 102 degrees.

20 Answer: Angle 3 = 89 degrees
Angle 5 = 91 degrees
Explanation: Angle 3 and Angle 6 are alternate interior angles so they have the same measure. Angle 3 is a same side interior angle with Angle 5 so they are supplementary, which means their measures have a sum of 180 degrees.

GEOMETRY
UNIT 2 - PYTHAGOREAN THEOREM APPLICATION

1 Answer: A
Explanation: Use the equation $a^2 + b^2 = c^2$ to find the hypotenuse: $8^2 + 9^2 = \sqrt{145}^2$.

2 Answer: C
Explanation: Use the equation $a^2 + b^2 = c^2$ to find the hypotenuse: $11^2 + 13^2 = \sqrt{290}^2$.

3 Answer: B
Explanation: Use the equation $a^2 + b^2 = c^2$ to find the hypotenuse: $14^2 + 16^2 = (2\sqrt{113})^2$.

4 Answer: B
Explanation: Use the equation $a^2 + b^2 = c^2$ to find the hypotenuse: $8^2 + 15^2 = 17^2$.

5 Answer: True
Explanation: Using the converse of the Pythagorean theorem, the triangle is a right triangle because $a^2 + b^2 = c^2$; $5^2 + 12^2 = 13^2$

6 Answer: True
Explanation: Using the converse of the Pythagorean theorem, the triangle is a right triangle because $a^2 + b^2 = c^2$; $3^2 + 4^2 = 5^2$

7 Answer: False
Explanation: Using the converse of the Pythagorean theorem, the triangle isn't a right triangle because $a^2 + b^2 \neq c^2$; $3^2 + 6^2 = \sqrt{45}^2$ not 7^2.

ANSWERS and EXPLANATIONS

8 Answer: B
Explanation: To find the length of one of the legs, use the modified Pythagorean theorem equation $c^2 - b^2 = a^2$; $17^2 - 8^2 = 15^2$.

9 Answer: A
Explanation: To find the length of one of the legs, use the modified Pythagorean theorem equation $c^2 - b^2 = a^2$; $15^2 - 9^2 = 12^2$.

10 Answer: D
Explanation: To find the length of one of the legs, use the modified Pythagorean theorem equation $c^2 - b^2 = a^2$;
$20^2 - 12^2 = 16^2$

11 Answer: C
Explanation: To find the length of one of the legs, use the modified Pythagorean theorem equation $c^2 - b^2 = a^2$; $13^2 - 12^2 = 5^2$.

12 Answer: 10 km
Explanation: To find the hypotenuse, use the Pythagorean theorem equation
$a^2 + b^2 = c^2$; $6^2 + 8^2 = 10^2$.

13 Answer: 15 mi
Explanation: To find the hypotenuse, use the Pythagorean theorem equation
$a^2 + b^2 = c^2$; $9^2 + 12^2 = 15^2$.

14 Answer: 20 cm
Explanation: To find the hypotenuse, use the Pythagorean theorem equation
$a^2 + b^2 = c^2$; $12^2 + 16^2 = 20^2$.

15 Answer: B
Explanation: Given two points on a coordinate system, imagine a right triangle and calculate the distance using the Pythagorean Theorem.

16 Answer: C
Explanation: Given two points on a coordinate system, imagine a right triangle and calculate the distance using the Pythagorean Theorem.

17 Answer: B
Explanation: Given two points on a coordinate system, imagine a right triangle and calculate the distance using the Pythagorean Theorem.

18 Answer: A
Explanation: Given two points on a coordinate system, imagine a right triangle and calculate the distance using the Pythagorean Theorem.

19 Answer: 8
Explanation: The distance formula is an algebraic expression used to determine the distance between two points with the coordinates (x_1, y_1) and (x_2, y_2).

$d = \sqrt{(x_2 - x_1)^2 + (y_2 - y_1)^2}$

$\sqrt{(64 + 0)}$

20 Answer: 6
Explanation: The distance formula is an algebraic expression used to determine the distance between two points with the coordinates (x_1, y_1) and (x_2, y_2).

$d = \sqrt{(x_2 - x_1)^2 + (y_2 - y_1)^2}$

$\sqrt{(36 + 0)}$

GEOMETRY
UNIT 3 - VOLUME OF 3-DIMENSIONAL SHAPES

1 Answer: B
Explanation: The formula for the volume of a cylinder is $\pi r^2 h$. This formula translates to the area of the base times the height.

2 Answer: C
Explanation: The formula for the volume of a cone is $\frac{1}{3}\pi r^2 h$. This formula translates to one-third times the area of the base times the height.

ANSWERS and EXPLANATIONS

3 Answer: B
Explanation: The formula for the volume of a sphere is $\frac{4}{3}\pi r^3$.

4 Answer: A
Explanation: Enter the given values into the formula for the volume of a cone: $\frac{1}{3}\pi r^2 h$.

5 Answer: B
Explanation: Enter the given values into the formula for the volume of a sphere: $\frac{4}{3}\pi r^3$.

6 Answer: A
Explanation: Enter the given values into the formula for the volume of a sphere: $s = \frac{4}{3}\pi r^3$.

7 Answer: D
Explanation: Enter the given values into the formula for the volume of a cylinder: $\pi r^2 h$.

8 Answer: C
Explanation: Enter the given values into the formula for the volume of a cylinder: $\pi r^2 h$.

9 Answer: C
Explanation: Enter the given values into the formula for the volume of a cylinder: $\pi r^2 h$.

10 Answer: 301
Explanation: Enter the given values into the formula for the volume of a cylinder: $\pi r^2 h$.

11 Answer: 314
Explanation: Enter the given values into the formula for the volume of a cone: $\frac{1}{3}\pi r^2 h$.

12 Answer: 2093
Explanation: Enter the given values into the formula for the volume of a cone: $\frac{1}{3}\pi r^2 h$.

13 Answer: 198
Explanation: Enter the given values into the volume formula for a cylinder. Multiply the area of the base by the height of the cylinder.

14 Answer: 85
Explanation: Enter the given dimensions into the volume formula of a cone: $\frac{1}{3}\pi r^2 h$.

15 Answer: 4186.7
Explanation: Enter the radius into the formula for the volume of a sphere: $\frac{4}{3}\pi r^3$.

16 Answer: 65.4
Explanation: Calculate the volume using $\frac{4}{3} \times 3.14 \times 2.5^3$.

17 Answer: 2950
Explanation: $\frac{1}{3} \times 3.14 \times (11.9)^2 \times 19.9$.

18 Answer: 1360
Explanation: $\frac{1}{3} \times 3.14 \times (9.6)^2 \times 14.1$.

19 Answer: A
Explanation: The formula for the volume of a cylinder is $\pi r^2 h$.

20 Answer: B
Explanation: The formula for the volume of a cylinder is $\pi r^2 h$. The approximate volume is 2543 cubic yards.

GEOMETRY
CHAPTER REVIEW

1 Answer: D
Explanation: Figure A is rotated counterclockwise, then translated 2 units to the right along the *x*-axis.

2 Answer: B
Explanation: A translation slides the figure to a different location. The figure in the second graph was rotated 90 degrees clockwise and then translated to the right.

ANSWERS and EXPLANATIONS

3 Answer: B
Explanation: A translation slides the figure to a different location; in this case up 2 units. The coordinates of Point S' coordinates are (1, 2).

4 Answer: C
Explanation: The two quadrilaterals are congruent, which means corresponding parts (sides and angles) are congruent. Side YV corresponds to side MN. Therefore, the length of side YV is 40 inches.

5 Answer: B
Explanation: The two triangles are congruent, which means corresponding parts (sides and angles) are congruent. Side NO corresponds to side DB. Therefore, the length of side DB is 82 mm.

6 Answer: A
Explanation: A reflection across the y-axis transforms each vertex from (x, y) to $(-x, y)$. The reflection across the x-axis means the x-coordinates remains the same but the sign of the y-coordinates Change. The congruence must match the vertices in the order from ABCD to JKLM.

7 Answer: (2, −4)
Explanation: Moving the point right 6 units and adds 6 to the x-coordinate.

8 Answer: (6, 0)
Explanation: Moving the point up 4 units and adds 4 to the y-coordinate.

9 Answer: A
Explanation: One figure is a square and the other figure is a rectangle.

10 Answer: They are $\frac{2}{3}$ of the lengths in Triangle A'B'C'
Explanation: Answers may vary. Multiplying each coordinate by a scale factor of $\frac{3}{2}$ is equivalent to multiplying each coordinate by 1.5. Thus, the side lengths in Triangle ABC are $\frac{2}{3}$ of the lengths in Triangle A'B'C'.

11 Answer: D
Explanation: By the triangle sum theorem, the measures of the three angles add up to 180 degrees. The sum of the measures of the interior angles of a triangle is 180 degrees.

12 Answer: B
Explanation: Angle EGF and DGE are complementary angles. If angle EGF has a measure of 30 degrees, angle DGE has a measure of 60 degrees. Angle AGB is a vertical angle with angle DGE so the two angles are congruent.

13 Answer: C
Explanation: Use the Pythagorean theorem equation $a^2 + b^2 = c^2$ to find the hypotenuse: $9^2 + 12^2 = 15^2$.

14 Answer: D
Explanation: Use the Pythagorean theorem equation $a^2 + b^2 = c^2$ to find the hypotenuse: $6^2 + 15^2 = (3\sqrt{29})^2$.

15 Answer: 48
Explanation: First, find the hypotenuse using $a^2 + b^2 = c^2$. Then, add the hypotenuse and the legs together, which is $16 + 12 + 20 = 48$.

16 Answer: 12
Explanation: First, find the hypotenuse using $a^2 + b^2 = c^2$. Then, add the hypotenuse and the legs together, which is $3 + 4 + 5 = 12$.

17 Answer: D
Explanation: Given two points on a coordinate system, imagine a right triangle and calculate the distance using the Pythagorean Theorem.

18 Answer: D
Explanation: Given two points on a coordinate system, imagine a right triangle and calculate the distance using the Pythagorean Theorem.

19 Answer: A
Explanation: Enter the given dimensions into the formula for the volume of a cylinder: $\pi r^2 h$.

ANSWERS and EXPLANATIONS

20 Answer: B
Explanation: The radius was not squared. Enter the given dimensions into the formula for the formula for the volume of a con: $\frac{1}{3}\pi r^2 h$.

GEOMETRY EXTRA PRACTICE

1 Answer: A
Explanation: 180° is half of a full turn. A full turn is 360°.

2 Answer: D
Explanation: Positive angles are measured counterclockwise and negative angles are measured clockwise.

3 Answer: B
Explanation: When a point is reflected over the *y*-axis, the *x*-coordinate changes sign.

4 Answer: Answers may vary
  MLON
  OLMN
  MNOL
  ONML

Explanation: A congruence statement says that two polygons are congruent. The vertices of one figure in the statement must match corresponding vertices in the other figure. Because the figure is a rhombus, the answers can vary

5 Answer: $(-7,-7), (-7,-1), (-6,-2), (-8,-2), (-8,-4), (-9,-4), (-10,-5), (-6,-7)$

Explanation: Rotating the shape 180 degrees about the origin transforms each vertex from (x,y) to $(-x,-y)$.

6 Answer: 94 degrees
Explanation: The two figures are congruent. Therefore, the lengths of their corresponding sides are equal and the measures of their corresponding angles are equal.

7 Answer: A
Explanation: A reflection flips a figure over a line or point to create a mirror image.

8 Answer:

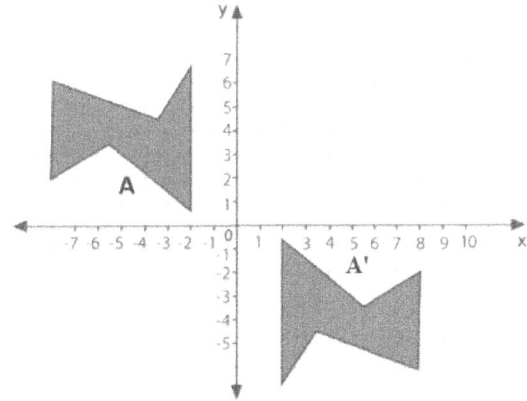

Explanation: The figure is reflected across the vertical axis and then the horizontal axis.

9 Answer: 44
Explanation: The corresponding angles of similar shapes have the same measure.

10 Answer: The angle measures remain the same, and the side lengths of Triangle D'E'F' is 2 times larger than the side lengths of DEF.
Explanation: Every coordinate of the original triangle has been multiplied by the scale factor (2).

11 Answer: Yes. The angles are corresponding angles.
Explanation: In the figure, the two horizontal lines are parallel. Angle A and Angle D are corresponding angles, so they are congruent. Alternatively, Triangle AEC and DEB are right triangles which share the common angle E. The two triangles are similar triangles, and Angle A is congruent to Angle D.

12 Answer: SAS
Explanation: Two corresponding sides and the angle between them are marked as congruent.

ANSWERS and EXPLANATIONS

13 Answer: D
Explanation: Use the Pythagorean theorem equation $a^2 + b^2 = c^2$ to find the hypotenuse: $10^2 + 15^2 = (5\sqrt{13})^2$.

14 Answer: D
Explanation: Use the Pythagorean theorem equation $a^2 + b^2 = c^2$ to find the hypotenuse: $13^2 + 15^2 = \sqrt{394}^2$.

15 Answer: 12
Explanation: The wall and the ladder make a right angle triangle. The length of the triangle 13 ft is the hypotenuse of the triangle. The ladder is 5 ft away from the wall. Using Pythagorean theorem, find the other side of the triangle.
$a^2 + b^2 = c^2$.
$a^2 + 5^2 = 13^2$.
$a^2 = 169 - 25 = 144$.
$a = \sqrt{144} = 12$ ft.

16 Answer: 15
Explanation: Find the hypotenuse using $a^2 + b^2 = c^2$: $12^2 + 9^2 = 15^2$.

17 Answer: 14.1
Explanation: The distance formula is an algebraic expression used to determine the distance between two points with the coordinates (x_1, y_1) and (x_2, y_2).

$d = \sqrt{(x_2 - x_1)^2 + (y_2 - y_1)^2}$

$\sqrt{(100 + 100)} \sim 14.1$

18 Answer: 8.2
Explanation: The distance formula is an algebraic expression used to determine the distance between two points with the coordinates (x_1, y_1) and (x_2, y_2).

$d = \sqrt{(x_2 - x_1)^2 + (y_2 - y_1)^2}$

$\sqrt{(64 + 4)} \sim 8.2$

19 Answer: B
Explanation: The problem used 9 as the radius. Enter the given dimensions into the formula for the volume of a cylinder: $\pi r^2 h$.

20 Answer: B
Explanation: Enter the given dimensions into the formula for the volume of a cone: $\frac{1}{3}\pi r^2 h$. The correct volume is 200.96 cubic inches.

STATISTICS AND PROBABILITY
UNIT 1 - APPLICATION OF SCATTERPLOTS

1 Answer: B
Explanation: A scatter plot shows a negative correlation if y tends to decrease as x increases.

2 Answer: B
Explanation: A scatter plot shows a negative correlation if y tends to decrease as x increases.

3 Answer: A
Explanation: A scatter plot shows a positive correlation if y tends to decrease as x increases.

4 Answer: A
Explanation: A scatter plot shows a positive correlation if y tends to increase as x increases.

5 Answer: B
Explanation: A scatter plot shows a negative correlation if y tends to decrease as x increases.

6 Answer: C
Explanation: A scatter plot shows no correlation there is no obvious pattern of the behavior of the variables.

7 Answer: C
Explanation: A scatter plot shows no trend if there is no obvious pattern.

8 Answer: A
Explanation: Look for a point that is separated from all other points in the data set. That point could be an outlier.

ANSWERS and EXPLANATIONS

9 Answer: B
Explanation: Look for a point that is separated from all other points in the data set. That point could be an outlier.

10 Answer: D
Explanation: Look for a point that is separated from all other points in the data set. That point could be an outlier.

11 Answer: A
Explanation: Find the slope using the two given points, (6,0) and (4,7). The slope is $-\frac{7}{2}$. Then, find the y-intercept, which is 21.

12 Answer: C
Explanation: Find the slope using the two given points, (0,9) and (9,3). The slope is $-\frac{2}{3}$. Then, find the y-intercept, which is 9.

13 Answer: D
Explanation: Find the slope using the two given points, (4,0) and (9,8). The slope is $\frac{8}{5}$. Then, find the y-intercept, which is $-\frac{32}{5}$.

14 Answer: B
Explanation: Find the slope using the two given points, (3, 0) and (9, 9), which is $\frac{3}{2}$. Then, find the y-intercept, which is $-\frac{9}{2}$.

15 Answer: A
Explanation: The data shows a strong positive linear correlation because the pattern of the points is distinct and relatively close to the trend line. The line of best fit is centered inside the patter of the data points.

16 Answer: C
Explanation: The data shows a weak positive linear correlation because the pattern of the points is distinct but not all close to the trend line. The line of best fit is centered inside the patter of the data points.

17 Answer: C
Explanation: As the amount of candy increases, the cost of the candy increases as well. An line with a positive slope would be used to model this situation.

18 Answer: Line b
Explanation: The number of data points above and below line b are approximately equal. Therefore Line b is the better line of best fit. Alternatively, the tally of the approximate vertical distances can also be used. In this problem, the tallies of approximate distances are nearly the same.

X	Y	Approx. Vertical distance (a)	Approx. Vertical distance (b)
1	6	3.5	2.8
1	8.7	0.5	0
1.7	7.2	1	0.4
2	4.9	3.2	2.5
3	5.8	1.6	0.5
3.7	7.5	1	2
4	3.6	2.5	1.5
4	6.2	0	1
5.8	5.5	1.1	2.1
6	4	0	1.3
8	3.9	2.3	3
		16.7	17.1

19 Answer: Line b
Explanation: The number of data points above and below Line b are approximately the same.

20 Answer: Line b
Explanation: Neither lines are very good, but Line b passes through more data points on the scatter plot.

ANSWERS and EXPLANATIONS

STATISTICS AND PROBABILITY:
UNIT 2 - APPLICATION OF LINEAR MODELS

1 Answer: B
Explanation: The rate of change is equal to the slope. Slope equals change in y divided by the change in x: approximately $90/50 = 2$.

2 Answer: D
Explanation: The rate of change is equal to the slope. Slope equals change in y divided by the change in x: $80/40 = 2$.

3 Answer: C
Explanation: The rate of change is equal to the slope. Slope equals change in y divided by the change in x: $40/20 = 2$.

4 Answer: D
Explanation: The rate of change is equal to the slope. Slope equals change in y divided by the change in x: approximately $90/60 = 2$.

5 Answer: B
Explanation: The rate of change is equal to the slope. Slope equals change in y divided by the change in x: approximately $80/100 = 1$.

6 Answer: C
Explanation: The rate of change is equal to the slope. Slope equals change in y divided by the change in x: approximately $90/30 = 3$.

7 Answer: D
Explanation: The rate of change is equal to the slope. The slope shows the that the value of the car decreases $1,300 per year.

8 Answer: B
Explanation: As the temperature increases, the sales of hot chocolate decreases. The slope shows the rate at which the sales change.

9 Answer: D
Explanation: The slope equals change in the cost y based on the number of minutes used x.

10 Answer: 44.75
Explanation: Substitute 13 for x into the equation $y = 100 - 4.25x$

11 Answer: The hours of a fully charged battery
Explanation: The variable y represents the hours remaining. When x is zero, the phone is fully charged.

12 Answer: The computer had a 35% charge when it was put on the charging station
Explanation: The variable x is zero when the computer is placed on the charging station. The y-intercept is the amount of charge the computer had at that time.

13 Answer: B
Explanation: The equation should multiply, not divide, 19 and x.

14 Answer: $y = 15x$
Explanation: Every week, she learned 15 new pieces so multiply 15 by x.

15 Answer: $y = 8x$
Explanation: Each phone call takes 8 minutes so the equation is total minutes equals 8 multiplied by x.

16 Answer: $y = 1.75x$
Explanation: It costs $1.75 for each attendee so multiply 1.75 by x (number of attendees) to get total cost.

17 Answer: $y = 12x$
Explanation: He reads 12 books each month so multiply 12 by x (number of months) to get the number of books read.

18 Answer: $y = 200x$
Explanation: It costs $200 for each guest she invites so multiply 200 by x to get the total cost.

19 Answer: $y = 14x$
Explanation: Each seed packet can grow 14 flowers so multiply x by 14 to get the total number of flowers.

ANSWERS and EXPLANATIONS

20 Answer: $y = 6x$
Explanation: Leo reads 6 books each month so multiply 6 by x.

STATISTICS AND PROBABILITY
UNIT 3 - APPLICATION OF BIVARIATE DATA

1 Answer: C
Explanation: Mr. Benson surveyed 103 students. If the data were represented by a two-way frequency table, the cell relative frequency of the number of girls who prefer chocolate ice cream would be 7/103 or about 7% of the total population surveyed.

2 Answer: B
Explanation: Henri surveyed 37 players. If the data were represented by a two-way frequency table, the cell relative frequency of the number of left-handed Red Sox pitchers would be $\frac{4}{37}$ or 11% of the total population surveyed.

3 Answer: A
Explanation: Rumi surveyed 75 players, and 35 are right handed. If the data were represented by a two-way frequency table, the cell relative frequency of the number of right-handed hitters is $\frac{35}{75}$ or 47% of the total population surveyed.

4 Answer: 20%
Explanation: The percentage of voters who are men who voted for Obama is 25,748,473/128,768,097 or 20%.

5 Answer: 21
Explanation: The relative frequency of voters who are women who voted for Romney is 26,554,060/128,768,097 converted to a percent.

6 Answer: 0.27
Explanation: The relative frequency of voters who are men who voted for Romney or other candidates is (34,379,444 + 764,218)/128,768,097, which rounds to 0.27.

7 Answer: 0.30
Explanation: The relative frequency is the number of people matching this description out of the total number of the subgroup identified. There are 3,449 students in the "35-55" age group. The proportion representing this frequency is 1,045/3,449.

8 Answer: 0.06
Explanation: The relative frequency is the number of people matching this description out of the total number of those identified. The proportion representing this frequency is $\frac{546}{9,889}$.

9 Answer: 0.13
Explanation: The relative frequency is the number of people matching this description out of the total number of those identified. The proportion representing this frequency is $\frac{13,498}{101,804}$

10 Answer: 0.19
Explanation: The relative frequency is the number of people matching this description out of the total number of those identified. The proportion representing this frequency is $\frac{15,495}{81,216}$.

11 Answer: The fraction of the number of people surveyed who are women who prefer cats
Explanation: The relative frequency is ratio of the number of people surveyed who who prefer a given option to the total number of people surveyed.

ANSWERS and EXPLANATIONS

12 Answer: The ratio of number of men surveyed to the total number of people surveyed.

Explanation: The relative frequency is the number of people who prefer a given option as a ratio against the total number of people surveyed.

13 Answer: 0.3

Explanation: The relative frequencies add up to 100%, so the missing relative frequency is 0.30. There are 90 people in this category. $\frac{90}{300} = 0.3$

14 Answer: 0.28

Explanation: The relative frequencies add up to 100%, so the missing relative frequency is 0.28. There are 9 teams in this category. $\frac{9}{32} = 0.281$

15 Answer: 0.27

Explanation: The relative frequencies add up to 100%, so the missing relative frequency is 0.27. There are 12 teams in this category. $\frac{12}{44} = 0.27$

16 Answer:

		Use Social Media	Do Not Use Social Media
Age	18-21	78	4
	22-34	95	3
	35 and older	82	21

Explanation: The table represents the preferences of the number of people in each of the 3 categories.

17 Answer:

		Bananas	Oranges	Apples
Age	Under 18	18	17	21
	18-34	17	20	8
	35 and older	19	18	35

Explanation: The table represents the preferences of the number of people in each of the 3 categories.

18 Answer:

		Girls	Boys
Power	Invisibility	≈0.15	≈0.12
	Superhuman Strength	≈0.03	≈0.18
	Telepathy	≈0.19	≈0.06
	Flying	≈0.14	≈0.13

Explanation: The table represents the preferences of the number of people recorded as a relative frequency in each of the 4 categories.

19 Answer:

		Smartphone	Tablet	Laptop
Age	Under 15	≈0.10	≈0.08	≈0.06
	15-20	≈0.12	≈0.14	≈0.12
	Over 20	≈0.09	≈0.14	≈0.16

Explanation: The table represents the preferences of the number of people recorded as a relative frequency in each of the 3 categories.

ANSWERS and EXPLANATIONS

20 Answer: Answers will vary. 0.19 and 0.42. The totals for each value are different because they are based on different sample groups.

Explanation: The relative frequency of students who are girls who like pizza is based out of the total of 43 students surveyed. $\frac{8}{43} \approx 0.19$.
The relative frequency of girls who like pizza is based out of the total of 19 girls surveyed. $\frac{8}{19} \approx 0.42$.

STATISTICS AND PROBABILITY CHAPTER REVIEW

1 Answer: B
Explanation: A scatter plot shows a negative correlation if y tends to decrease as x increases.

2 Answer: B
Explanation: A scatter plot shows a positive correlation if y tends to increase as x increases.

3 Answer: A
Explanation: A scatter plot with no obvious pattern has no correlation because the correlation cannot be identified as positive or negative.

4 Answer: A
Explanation: An outlier is an extreme point in a data set that is separated from all other points.

5 Answer: A
Explanation: An outlier can be thought of as an outsider, but there is no specific formula that defines outliers. However, they are still important to understand when performing a statistical analysis because they affect measures of central tendency.

6 Answer: C
Explanation: Look for a point that is separated from all other points in the data set.

7 Answer: A
Explanation: The trend line is the line of best fit between the variables and is used to make approximations.

8 Answer: B
Explanation: The data shows a strong linear correlation because the data points are in a relatively tight group, and the line of best fit is centered in the data and represents all data points.

9 Answer: $y = \frac{2}{3}x + 3$
Explanation: Find the slope using the two given points, (0,3) and (6,7) The slope is $\frac{2}{3}$. Then, find the y-intercept, which is 3.

10 Answer: $y = 3x - 12$
Explanation: Find the slope using the two given points, (4,0) and (6,6). The slope is 3. Then, find the y-intercept, which is 12.

11 Answer: $y = -\frac{2}{3}x + 8$
Explanation: Find the slope using the two given points, (0,8) and (6,4). the slope is $-\frac{2}{3}$. Then, find the y-intercept, which is 8.

12 Answer: $y = -\frac{4}{3}x + 12$
Explanation: Find the slope using the two given points, (3,8) and (9,0). The slope is $-\frac{4}{3}$. Then, find the y-intercept, which is 12.

13 Answer: C
Explanation: The rate of change is equal to the slope. Slope equals change in y divided by the change in x. 90/30 = 3.

14 Answer: A
Explanation: The rate of change is equal to the slope. Slope equals change in y divided by the change in x. 70/45 = 2.

ANSWERS and EXPLANATIONS

15 Answer: B
Explanation: The rate of change is equal to the slope. Slope equals change in y divided by the change in x. $60/40 = 2$.

16 Answer: Average growth per week (approx. 2.3 cm)
Explanation: The equation of the line of best fit for this situation is $y = 2.3x + 5.6$.

17 Answer: 0.65, 64%, or $\frac{25}{39}$
Explanation: There were 39 males surveyed. Twenty-five of them had a negative opinion.

18 Answer: 0.46, $\frac{48}{105}$, or 46%
Explanation: There were 105 people surveyed. Forty-eight of them meet the criteria.

19 Answer: 17
Explanation: Look at the last column and then to the last row.

20 Answer: 12
Explanation: Go to the last row and subtract 17 from 29.

STATISTICS AND PROBABILITY EXTRA PRACTICE

1 Answer: B
Explanation: To choose the correct scatter plot correlation, find the outlier. Look for a point that is separated from all other points in the data set, but it is not necessary to remove the outlier to see the correlation.

2 Answer: A
Explanation: An outlier has a large distance from the best fit line. Just one outlier can have a drastic effect on the correlation or the least squares regression line.

3 Answer: 63, 64, 65, or 66
Explanation: Answers can vary. The equation of the line of best fit appears to be $y = \frac{3}{5}x + 40$. So, using the equation, the y-value is approximately 64.

4 Answer: B
Explanation: A scatter plot shows no trend if there is no obvious pattern so the x-value could be any number on the graph.

5 Answer: Answers will vary. Any number less than 70
Explanation: The scatter plot shows a negative correlation, but has no line of best fit. Therefore, the y-value could be any number less than 70.

6 Answer: Any number near 60
Explanation: The scatter plot shows a positive correlation, but has no trend line. Since 60 is in the center of the data set around the value of $x = 60$, the x-value can be any number around 60.

7 Answer: $y = -\frac{3}{7}x + 7$
Explanation: Find the slope using the two given points, $(7,4)$ and $(0,7)$. The slope is $-\frac{3}{7}$. Then, find the y-intercept, which is 7.

8 Answer: $y = -\frac{4}{7}x + 9$
Explanation: Find the slope using the two given points, $(0,9)$ and $(5,7)$. The slope is $-\frac{4}{7}$. Then, find the y-intercept, which is 9.

9 Answer: $y = -3x + 18$
Explanation: Find the slope using the two given points, $(3,9)$ and $(6,0)$. The slope is -3. Then, find the y-intercept, which is 18.

10 Answer: $y = \frac{4}{7}x + 5$
Explanation: Find the slope using the two given points, $(0,5)$ and $(7,9)$. The slope is $\frac{4}{7}$. Then, find the y-intercept, which is 5.

ANSWERS and EXPLANATIONS

11 Answer: $y = \frac{8}{3}x - 8$

Explanation: Find the slope using the two given points, (3,0) and (6,8). The slope is $\frac{8}{3}$. Then, find the y-intercept, which is -8.

12 Answer:

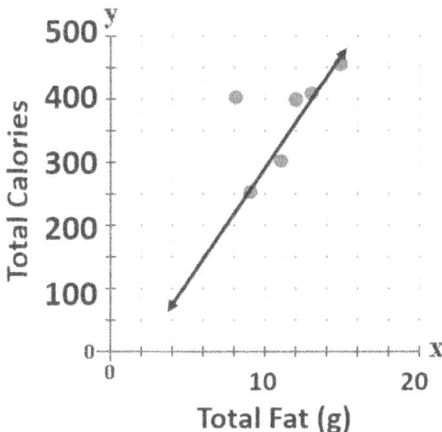

Explanation: The data has a strong linear correlation, but there appears to be an outlier. A reasonable line of best fit should be as close as possible to all the data points.

13 Answer: A

Explanation: There are 27 new recipes per week so multiply 27 by x.

14 Answer: B

Explanation: The equation should multiply 104 by x. There is no subtraction.

15 Answer: $y = 2x$

Explanation: It costs $2 for every guest he invites, so multiply 2 by x.

16 Answer: The average change in annual income per year of education (approx. 15,200)

Explanation: The equation of the line of best fit for this situation would be $y = 15,200x - 128,200$.

17 Answer: 78

Explanation: Add the numbers in the Prefer Oranges column.

18 Answer: 43

Explanation: Look at the last column in the first row of the table.

19 Answer: 6

Explanation: According to the table, 2 males and 4 females prefer homework over classwork.

20 Answer: 3

Explanation: Look at the yellow row under the pencil column.

COMPREHENSIVE ASSESSMENTS
ASSESSMENT 1

1 Answer: B

Explanation: The square root of 17 is an irrational number because 17 is not a perfect square number.

2 Answer: C

Explanation: The square root of 111 lies between the square root of 100 and the square root of 121 which means between 10 and 11.

3 Answer: B

Explanation: Substitute the value in for x and determine the value for y.

4 Answer: A

Explanation: The best description for a situation represented by this graph is a description that includes a steady increase, a constant value and then a rapid decrease at the end.

5 Answer: B

Explanation: The cost of the gym membership starts with a $15 fixed cost and then adds 9 each month as a variable cost.

ANSWERS and EXPLANATIONS

6 Answer: A
Explanation: Multiplying each term in the given equation by 10 results in the equation $10y = 6x + 20$.

7 Answer: C
Explanation: The graph is a linear, increasing function. It is increasing because the slope is positive.

8 Answer: B
Explanation: The graph is decreasing because the equation has a negative slope.

9 Answer: B
Explanation: This graph is an increasing linear function with a slope of 3 and a y-intercept at $(0, -7)$.

10 Answer: C
Explanation: When dividing like-bases, subtract the exponent in the denominator from the exponent in the numerator. Subtracting the exponents gives $a - (-3a) = 4a$ which results in a final answer of b^{4a}.

11 Answer: A
Explanation: When multiplying like-bases with exponents, add the exponents. This gives 4^6, which is $4 \cdot 4 \cdot 4 \cdot 4 \cdot 4 \cdot 4 = 4{,}096$.

12 Answer: C
Explanation: The problem says the cube root of the number is one less than 4. This means the cube root of the number is 3. The cube root of 27 is 3.

13 Answer: B
Explanation: The cube root of -8 is -2 because $-2 \cdot -2 \cdot -2 = -8$. Then, square -2 to get 4.

14 Answer: C
Explanation: The number 100 times larger than 7×10^7 is equivalent to $7 \times 10^7 (10^2)$ which is 7×10^9.

15 Answer: 3×10^{-5}
Explanation: The expression is initially written as $(3 \times 10^{-3})/10^2$. Convert the quotient to scientific notation by subtracting the exponents ($3 \times 10^{-3-2} = 3 \times 10^{-5}$). Dividing this number by 100 will allow you to find the number 100 times smaller.

16 Answer: C
Explanation: Rewrite the second figure as 20.61×10^7. Then subtract $20.61 - 2.82$. The second exponent carries along to rewrite the result as scientific notation.

17 Answer: C
Explanation: Rewrite 3.923×10^6 as $3{,}923{,}000$ and divide it by 5 = $784{,}600$.

18 Answer: D
Explanation: The relation in the table satisfies the equation $y = 3x$. The only choice with a lower slope than 3 is D.

19 Answer: D
Explanation: The point he needs to use is on the line in the graph. Only the point $(3, 1)$ is on the line.

20 Answer: C
Explanation: To solve for g, add 1 to both sides and subtract $3g$. the result is $g = 3$.

21 Answer: B
Explanation: The first equation represents the number of coins: $q + n = 59$. The second equation represent the sum of the values of the coins: $0.25q + 0.05n = 10.75$.

22 Answer: D
Explanation: The first equation can represents the sum of the correct and incorrect questions: $x + y = 50$. The second equation represent the points for correct questions and the penalty for incorrect questions: $2x - y = 94$.

ANSWERS and EXPLANATIONS

23 Answer:

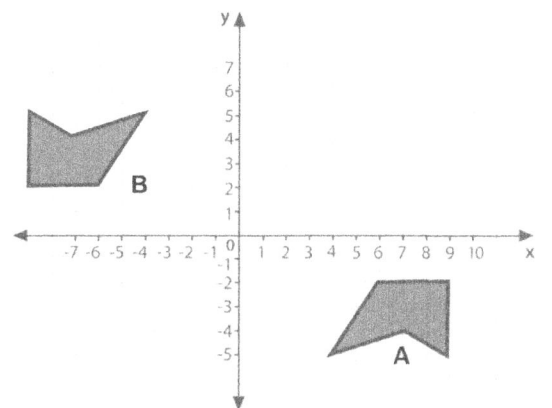

Explanation: The figure is reflected across the horizontal axis and then the vertical axis.

24 Answer: The location of Point B remains the same, Points A, C, and D are rotated into either the first or fourth quadrants.

Explanation: Rotating the rectangle around Point B in a clockwise motion means this vertex will remain in the same position.

25 Answer: D

Explanation: If Triangle ABC is translated 12 units to the right along the *x*-axis and 8 units down along the *y*-axis, it will become Triangle KKL.

26 Answer: $(-4, 0), (-2, 4), (1, 5)$

Explanation: Translating the triangle 3 units down I decreases the *y*-coordinates by 3. Translating the triangle 5 units to the left decreases the *x*-coordinates by 5.

27 Answer: B

Explanation: A reflection across the *x*-axis changes the point (x, y) to (x, −y). The *y*-coordinate changes sign.

28 Answer: C

Explanation: A reflection across the *y*-axis changes the point (x, y) to (−x, y). The *x*-coordinate changes sign.

29 Answer: The side lengths of Triangle A'B'C' are 2½ times larger than the side lengths of Triangle ABC.

Explanation: Dilating by a scale factor of $\frac{5}{2}$ multiplies the lengths of each side by by $\frac{5}{2}$.

30 Answer: $(-1, -2)$

Explanation: The scale factor is ¼, and the values in the coordinates of the vertices that are not on the origin are divided by 4. Thus, the reflected point (−4, 8) changes to (−1, 2).

31 Answer: A

Explanation: The measures of the three interior angles of a triangle add up to 180 degrees.

32 Answer: Angles F and H are corresponding angles and are congruent.

Explanation: Corresponding angles are those which occupy the same location with respect to 2 parallel lines and the transversal. Corresponding angles are congruent.

33 Answer: A

Explanation: Use the Pythagorean theorem equation $a^2 + b^2 = c^2$ to find find the hypotenuse: $25^2 + 13^2 = \sqrt{794}^2$.

34 Answer: B

Explanation: Use the Pythagorean theorem equation $a^2 + b^2 = c^2$ to find the hypotenuse: $7^2 + 8^2 = \sqrt{113}^2$.

35 Answer: 16

Explanation: Use the modified Pythagorean theorem equation. 20 meters is the hypotenuse and 12 meters is one of the legs, so $20^2 - 12^2 = 16^2$.

36 Answer: 3

Explanation: The 5 inches is the hypotenuse and 4 inches is the leg, so use the modified Pythagorean theorem equation: $5^2 - 4^2 = 3^2$.

ANSWERS and EXPLANATIONS

37 Answer: 5.4
Explanation: The distance formula is an algebraic expression used to determine the distance between two points with the coordinates (x_1, y_1) and (x_2, y_2).

$d = \sqrt{(x_2 - x_1)^2 + (y_2 - y_1)^2}$

$\sqrt{(4 + 25)} \sim 5.4$

38 Answer: 6.1
Explanation: The distance formula is an algebraic expression used to determine the distance between two points with the coordinates (x_1, y_1) and (x_2, y_2).

$d = \sqrt{(x_2 - x_1)^2 + (y_2 - y_1)^2}$

$\sqrt{(1 + 36)} \sim 6.1$

39 Answer: A
Explanation: The formula for the volume of a cylinder is $\pi r^2 h$. Substitute the dimensions into the formula for the variables.

40 Answer: It could be any number from 0 to 80
Explanation: The scatter plot shows no correlation so there is no way to estimate the value.

41 Answer: D
Explanation: Look for a point that is separated from all other points in the data set. An outlier is often called an outsider.

42 Answer: $y = \frac{9}{2}x - 18$
Explanation: Find the slope using the two given points, (4,0) and (6,8). The slope is $\frac{9}{2}$. Then, find the y-intercept, which is −18.

43 Answer: Line b
Explanation: By creating a table of values, such as the one below, it can be determined the horizontal distance is greater between the data points and Line a. Alternatively, the number of data points above line b and the number of data points below line b are either the same or almost the same, which makes line b a reasonable line of best fit.

X	Y	Approx. Horizontal distance (a)	Approx. Horizontal distance (b)
2	6	1.8	1.5
2	8	0.1	0.5
5	4	0.8	0.1
5	6	1.3	1.5
6	3	0	0.7
8	2	1.4	0
9	2	2.4	1.1
		7.8	5.4

44 Answer: Yes, the model shows that if a student scores a 54.1% on the final, their score on the mid-term exam would have been a 0%.
Explanation: The y-intercept of a bivariate data situation should be interpreted based on the variables in the situation.

45 Answer: 8
Explanation: Add the first row.

COMPREHENSIVE ASSESSMENTS
ASSESSMENT 2

1 Answer: A
Explanation: The repeating decimal can be determined by dividing 5 by 9. One digit repeats so the denominator has one 9.

2 Answer: C
Explanation: π has a value of approximately 3.14, when multiplied by 3, the value is 9.42, between 9 and 10.

ANSWERS and EXPLANATIONS

3 Answer: C
Explanation: Substitute the value in for y into the equation to find the x-value.

4 Answer: C
Explanation: The relation is $y = x^3$, when $x = 4$, $y = 64$.

5 Answer: D
Explanation: This graph represents the function $y = 1.5x$.

6 Answer: C
Explanation: The equation in choice C has a sign error for the constant term.

7 Answer: A
Explanation: When the x-value is 0, the y-value is -3. This situation is commonly called the initial value.

8 Answer: C
Explanation: The graph intersects the y-axis at (0, 2) and the slope is $-\frac{3}{5}$.

9 Answer: D
Explanation: All of these items are true about vertical lines.

10 Answer: C
Explanation: First, substitute the expression a^{-3} into the equation for r which is $A = \pi(a^{-3})^2$. Raising an exponent to a power, multiplies the exponents. This gives $A = \pi a^{-6}$. Negative exponents become positive by moving them to the other side of the fraction, resulting in π/a^6.

11 Answer: D
Explanation: First, simplify the expression inside of the parentheses by subtracting the exponents. This gives $(a^{-6})^{-3}$. Raising a power to a power, multiplies the exponents resulting in a^{18}.

12 Answer: A
Explanation: The cube root of 27 is 3 because $3 \cdot 3 \cdot 3 = 27$.

13 Answer: D
Explanation: To solve this equation, get x by itself. To do so, multiply both sides by 4.
$x^2 = 36$
Take the square root of both sides, giving solutions of $x = \pm 6$.

14 Answer: A
Explanation: Eight hundred million can be expressed as (8×10^8). Dividing this number by 10 makes the number 10 times smaller.

15 Answer: $(6 \times 10^{-2})(5 \times 10^1)$
Explanation: Six hundredths is expressed as (6×10^{-2}) and 50 is expressed as (5×10^1).

16 Answer: D
Explanation: Rewrite 5.982×10^{-7} as 0.5982×10^{-8}. Subtract the first coefficient from the second, resulting in $x = 2.9688 \times 10^{-8}$.

17 Answer: A
Explanation: This problem can be rewritten as $(7.23 \times 10^{-5}) - (2.465 \times 10^{-4}) = x$. Rewrite 7.23×10^{-5} as 0.723×10^{-4} and then subtract the first factors. The exponent remains the same at 10^{-4} resulting in -1.742×10^{-4}.

18 Answer: A
Explanation: The table illustrates the relation $y = 0.75x$. Insert the 7 value for x, and $y = 5.25$.

19 Answer: $y = -\frac{1}{2}x + 3$
Explanation: The line passes through (0,3), which means in the form $y = mx + b$. The slope of the line is $-½$ and $b = 3$.

20 Answer: B
Explanation: First distribute the values outside of parentheses. The equation becomes: $3x - 12 = 2x + 2$. Subtract $2x$ from both sides and add 12, $x = 14$.

21 Answer: D
Explanation: This equation has no solution because subtracting $2x$ from both

ANSWERS and EXPLANATIONS

sides, eliminates the variable and leaves a statement that is not true: $(5 \neq -3)$.

22 Answer: $1

Explanation: First, write 2 equations: $2h + 2s = 5$ and $3h + s = 5.5$. Solve one of the equations for h, a hot dog is worth $1.50. Substitute 1.5 for h into the first equation to find s: $s = 1$.

23 Answer: V
T

Explanation: The transformation that has taken place rotated and translated the first figure to create the second (new image). Find the angles that correspond to each other.

24 Answer:

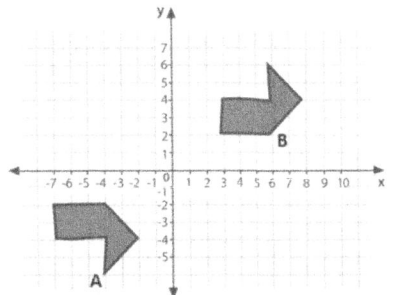

Explanation: The figure is reflected across the x-axis, and then translated 10 units to the right along the x-axis.

25 Answer: C

Explanation: Quadrilateral ABCD is reflected across the vertical axis, and then translated up 4 units.

26 Answer: (1, 0), (6, 5), (−4, −5)

Explanation: The reflection across the x-axis means the x-coordinates remain the same but the y-coordinates change sign. Translating the triangle 1 unit to the right increases the x-coordinates by 1.

27 Answer: A

Explanation: When a point is reflected over the x-axis, the y-coordinate changes sign.

28 Answer: (1,1)

Explanation: When a point is reflected over the y-axis, the x-coordinate changes sign.

29 Answer: (12, 0)

Explanation: The scale factor is 4, and since one vertex is at the origin, all coordinates are multiplied by 4 to determine the new vertices.

30 Answer: (−3, 5)

Explanation: The scale factor is 2, and each coordinate is multiplied by 2 to determine the new location.

31 Answer: Angles H and G are vertical angles and are congruent.

Explanation: Use properties of parallel lines cut by a transversal to show congruent and supplementary angles. This process will show that vertical angles, those which share opposite rays for sides, are congruent.

32 Answer: 106 degrees

Explanation: Angle 2 corresponds to Angle 6. Angle 6 is supplementary to Angle 8. Subtract 74 from 180 to determine the measure of Angle 8.

33 Answer: C

Explanation: Use the Pythagorean theorem equation $a^2 + b^2 = c^2$ to find the hypotenuse: $12^2 + 16^2 = 20^2$.

34 Answer: A

Explanation: Use the Pythagorean theorem equation $a^2 + b^2 = c^2$ to find the hypotenuse: $13^2 + 18^2 = \sqrt{493}^2$.

35 Answer: 10

Explanation: The dimensions 6 meters and 8 meters are the legs of a right triangle. Find the hypotenuse using the Pythagorean theorem equation: $6^2 + 8^2 = 10^2$.

36 Answer: 18.9

Explanation: The lengths 17feet and 8feet are the legs of a right triangle. The ladder is

ANSWERS and EXPLANATIONS

the hypotenuse. Find the hypotenuse using the Pythagorean equation: $17^2 + 8^2 = 353$, $\sqrt{353} \sim 18.9$

37   Answer: 7.2
Explanation: The distance formula is an algebraic expression used to determine the distance between two points with the coordinates (x_1, y_1) and (x_2, y_2).

$d = \sqrt{(x_2 - x_1)^2 + (y_2 - y_1)^2}$

$\sqrt{(16 + 36)} \sim 7.2$

38   Answer: 6
Explanation: The distance formula is an algebraic expression used to determine the distance between two points with the coordinates (x_1, y_1) and (x_2, y_2).

$d = \sqrt{(x_2 - x_1)^2 + (y_2 - y_1)^2}$

$\sqrt{(0 + 36)} = 6$

39   Answer: A
Explanation: The formula for the volume of a cone is $\frac{1}{3}\pi r^2 h$

40   Answer: negative
Explanation: The data points in the scatterplot decrease in a downward trend, so the data set have a negative correlation.

41   Answer: none
Explanation: The data points in the scatterplot have no pattern, so the is no correlation.

42   Answer: $y = \frac{9}{5}x - \frac{27}{5}$
Explanation: Find the slope using the two given points, $(3,0)$ and $(8,9)$. The slope is $\frac{9}{5}$. Then, find the y-intercept, which is $-\frac{27}{5}$.

43   Answer: No
Data points are mostly on one side of the line.
Explanation: Answers will vary. Most of the points in the data set are on one side of Alicia's line. The number of points on each side should be approximately equal.

44   Answer: Yes, the model shows that 37.2% of children are obese because 0% of them exercise 5 days each week.

Explanation: The y-intercept of a bivariate data situation should be interpreted based on the variables in the situation.

45   Answer: 148
Explanation: Add 78 and 70.

Made in the USA
Coppell, TX
15 May 2021